India and the United States in the 21st Century
Reinventing Partnership

Look at
Strategic
Asias

Tellis
2006
IS

Significant Issues Series
Timely books presenting current CSIS research and analysis of interest to the academic, business, government, and policy communities.
Managing Editor: Roberta L. Fauriol

About CSIS
In an era of ever-changing global opportunities and challenges, the Center for Strategic and International Studies (CSIS) provides strategic insights and practical policy solutions to decisionmakers. CSIS conducts research and analysis and develops policy initiatives that look into the future and anticipate change.

Founded by David M. Abshire and Admiral Arleigh Burke at the height of the Cold War, CSIS was dedicated to the simple but urgent goal of finding ways for America to survive as a nation and prosper as a people. Since 1962, CSIS has grown to become one of the world's preeminent public policy institutions.

Today, CSIS is a bipartisan, nonprofit organization headquartered in Washington, D.C. More than 220 full-time staff and a large network of affiliated scholars focus their expertise on defense and security; on the world's regions and the unique challenges inherent to them; and on the issues that know no boundary in an increasingly connected world.

Former U.S. senator Sam Nunn became chairman of the CSIS Board of Trustees in 1999, and John J. Hamre has led CSIS as its president and chief executive officer since 2000.

CSIS does not take specific policy positions; accordingly, all views expressed herein should be understood to be solely those of the author(s).

The CSIS Press
Center for Strategic and International Studies
1800 K Street, N.W., Washington, D.C. 20006
Tel: (202) 775-3119   Fax: (202) 775-3199
E-mail: books@csis.org   Web: www.csis.org

India and the United States in the 21st Century
Reinventing Partnership

Teresita C. Schaffer

THE CSIS PRESS

Center for Strategic
and International Studies
Washington, D.C.

Significant Issues Series, Volume 31, Number 4
© 2009 by Center for Strategic and International Studies
Washington, D.C.
Printed on recycled paper in the United States of America
Cover design by Robert L. Wiser, Silver Spring, Md.
Cover photograph: Detail of the Qtab Minar, Delhi © iStockphoto.com/brytta

13 12 11 10 09   5 4 3 2 1

ISSN 0736-7136
ISBN 978-0-89206-572-1

Library of Congress Cataloging-in-Publication Data
Schaffer, Teresita C.
  India and the United States in the 21st century : reinventing partnership / Teresita
C. Schaffer.
      p. cm. — (Significant issues series ; v. 31, no. 4)
  Includes bibliographical references and index.
  ISBN 978-0-89206-572-1 (pbk. : alk. paper) 1. United States—Foreign
relations—India. 2. India—Foreign relations—United States. I. Title. II. Series.
  JZ1480.A57I45 2009
  327.54073--dc22
                                        2009011856

CONTENTS

List of Acronyms and Abbreviations   vi

Acknowledgments   ix

1 The World from Delhi and from Washington   1

2 The Economic Engine   18

3 Energy: Where Economics Meets Strategy   44

4 Shaping a Security Relationship   65

5 Nuclear and High-Tech Cooperation: Getting Beyond the Taboos   89

6 The Neighborhood: South and Central Asia   118

7 Looking East: India and East Asia   137

8 The Middle East: Israel, the Gulf, and Iran   154

9 The Other Global Powers   172

10 Global Governance   186

11 A New Partnership, A Changing World   208

Index   226

About the Author   254

ACRONYMS AND ABBREVIATIONS

APEC	Asia Pacific Economic Cooperation
ARF	ASEAN Regional Forum
ASEAN	Association of Southeast Asian Nations
BIMST–EC	Bangladesh, India, Myanmar, Sri Lanka, Thailand–Economic Cooperation
BJP	Bharatiya Janata Party
BPCL	Bharat Petroleum Corporation
BPO	business process outsourcing
BRIC	Brazil, Russia, India, China
CNG	compressed natural gas
CST	Collective Security Treaty
DRDO	Defense Research and Development Organization
EAS	East Asian Summit
FDI	foreign direct investment
FICCI	Federation of Indian Chambers of Commerce and Industry
FMCT	Fissile Material Cutoff Treaty
GAIL	Gas Authority of India Ltd.
GCC	Gulf Cooperation Council
GSLV	Geosynchronous Satellite Launch Vehicle
GSOMIA	General Security of Military Information Agreement
IAEA	International Atomic Energy Agency
IBSA	India, Brazil, South Africa [trilateral forum]

IEA	International Energy Agency
IEF	International Energy Forum
IIT	Indian Institutes of Technology
IMF	International Monetary Fund
INCOSPAR	Indian National Committee for Space Research (renamed ISRO in 1969)
IOC	Indian Oil Corporation
IPCC	Intergovernmental Panel on Climate Change
IRS	Indian Remote Sensing satellite series
ISI	Inter-Services Intelligence
ISRO	Indian Space Research Organization
ITER	International Thermonuclear Experimental Reactor
LCA	Light Combat Aircraft program
LNG	liquid natural gas
MEA	Ministry of External Affairs, India
MRCA	Multi-Role Combat Aircraft
MTCR	Missile Technology Control Regime
NAM	Non-Aligned Movement
NASA	National Aeronautics and Space Administration
NELP	New Exploration Licensing Policy
NOAA	National Oceanic and Atmospheric Administration
NPT	Non-Proliferation Treaty
NSG	Nuclear Suppliers' Group
NSSP	Next Steps in Strategic Partnership
OECD	Organization for Economic Cooperation and Development
OIC	Organization of the Islamic Conference
ONGC	Oil and National Gas Corporation
OPEC	Organization of the Petroleum Exporting Countries
OVL	ONGC Videsh Ltd.
PACs	political action committees
PSI	Proliferation Security Initiative
PSLV	Polar Satellite Launch Vehicle
SAARC	South Asian Association for Regional Cooperation
SCO	Shanghai Cooperation Organization
SEBs	State Electricity Boards
SITE	Satellite Instructional Television Experiments
TAA	Trade Adjustment Assistance
TERI	The Energy and Resources Institute

TRIPS	Trade Restricting Intellectual Property [agreement]
UAE	United Arab Emirates
UNFCCC	United Nations Framework Convention on Climate Change
USAID	United States Agency for International Development
WTO	World Trade Organization

ACKNOWLEDGMENTS

This book has been nearly three years in the making, but in a larger sense it represents 35 years of professional involvement with India and with South Asia. I owe a huge debt to far more people than I can specifically acknowledge here.

Three institutions supported my writing and research efforts. The Center for Strategic and International Studies has been my professional home since soon after I retired from the U.S. foreign service, and John Hamre, CSIS president, has been a supportive leader and wise counselor. The Kluge Center at the Library of Congress offered me an unparalleled opportunity to concentrate on this project during its final phase by appointing me to the Henry A. Kissinger Chair in Foreign Policy and International Relations. Having the resources of the library at one's fingertips, librarians like Allen Thrasher available for consultation, and mentors like Carolyn Brown, director of the library's scholarly programs, is a bit like going to heaven for a first-time book writer. The Smith Richardson Foundation provided most of the funding for this project, a vote of confidence in me that I hope I have justified.

My colleagues in the South Asia program at CSIS put in countless hours on basic research for this book, and many more in pursuing the other projects that kept the program afloat while I was drafting. Pramit Mitra, who was my alter ego when the project started, and Vibhuti Haté, who succeeded him midway through the project, helped me think through the outline and shape the project. Vibhuti made an especially important contribution to the economic analysis in the book.

During the three years the project was under way, our program benefited hugely from the work and cheerful companionship of some of Washington's finest volunteer interns. They all left their mark on the project, and on my heart: Maimuna Ahmad, Sukanya Banerjee, Sabala Baskar, Jan Cartwright, Aneesh Deshpande, Uttara Dukkipati, Jeffrey Ellis, Suzanne Fawzi, Nicole Goertzen-Tang, Raja Karthikeya Gundu, Vikram Gupta, Britni Johnson, Divyesh Lalloobhai, Elizabeth Parker, Joshua Richards, Jonathan Robins, John Ryan, Famid Sinha, Krishna Sutaria, Kim Tran and Harris Qureshi.

Many members of the India-watchers' "biradari" helped me sharpen up my ideas, in particular Ashley Tellis, Stephen Cohen, David Good, Walter Andersen, and Robert Hathaway. Countless current and former officials of the Indian and U.S. governments took the time to talk with me and share their hopes and concerns. A long list of kind friends and colleagues in both countries went through parts of the early draft and rescued me from errors of fact or analysis. Polly Nayak went through the entire draft and spent hours, not just commenting on the text but posing searching questions I needed to reflect on in revising it. I knew she was dedicated and generous, but the help she gave me with this project is in a league by itself.

Finally, a word about my family. My husband, Howard Schaffer, introduced me to South Asia and to India in 1974. Whatever I have learned about the region I owe to him. He is my sharpest and most loving critic. He went through the entire draft with his usual eagle eye. I can never adequately express my gratitude for his support—in this project and in life. My sons, Mike and Chris, and their wives, Keltie Hawkins and Juliana Hunt, live away from Washington, so they did not have to put up with my fretting over the ups and downs of the drafting process, but their loving attention from Philadelphia and Miami lights up my life. Finally, my two grandchildren, Mike and Keltie's daughter Eleanor and Chris and Juliana's son Nicholas, were born during the time I was working on this book. They will live in the future I have tried to peer into. Some day, I hope to share with them my enthusiasm for the wider world, and for India.

To all these, and to the many others who gave me time, information, and encouragement, my deepest thanks. Whatever errors of fact or analysis remain are mine alone.

THE WORLD FROM DELHI AND FROM WASHINGTON

Independent India's fiftieth anniversary in August 1997 triggered an outpouring of India talk in the world media. Excitement and promise were the dominant themes. In the Indian press, these were mixed with nostalgia and also with a sense of a mission still unfulfilled. India had enjoyed six prosperous years, its economic policy seemed to promise more good times ahead, and the world was starting to acknowledge India as a major power. However, India's hundreds of millions of poor people still had a long way to go to share in the good times.

That August celebration is a good point of departure for a closer look at where the India-U.S. relationship is headed. In the decade after the fiftieth anniversary, the India-U.S. connection, generally troubled and lacking in substance during the Cold War years, underwent a revolution. India's more outward-oriented economy, its quest for recognition as a world power, its ambition to play a larger role in a peaceful Asia, and its imperative of security in the Indian Ocean sea-lanes set new foreign policy priorities. These included seeking a close understanding with the United States, which had become its most important external friend.

For its part, the United States came to see in India not just a fellow democracy and major aid recipient but a country with important strategic interests that paralleled its own. The eastern rim of Asia, long the focus of U.S. involvement in Asia, was beset by uncertainty, with North Korea's nuclear ambitions generating regional tensions and Japan's extended economic slump contributing to shifting economic and political patterns. The growing economic and military power of China enhanced U.S. interest in the continent's other rising power. And India's economic growth, now one of the fastest in the world, made India an interesting economic partner in its own right.

Leaders of the two major parties in both countries reshaped the relationship during their respective time in office. In India, prime ministers Atal Behari Vajpayee and Manmohan Singh participated. In the United States, the transformation began in earnest in the second administration of President Bill Clinton, flowered under President George W. Bush, and is expected to continue developing under President Barack Obama. The agreement providing for civilian nuclear cooperation between the United States and India, announced by Prime Minister Singh and President Bush, quickly became the symbol of the new partnership.

The story of how this turnaround took place has been well covered elsewhere.[1] This study aims to examine the elements of the emerging U.S.-India partnership and to assess which of these will serve as good building blocks for furthering the U.S.-India partnership, which will complicate the task of working together, and what potential building blocks are missing. Based on this analysis, it will set forth a policy agenda for both governments to maximize the potential in this new partnership.

The two countries have built much of the bilateral policy infrastructure they need to work together. Investment and trade are rising; there are regular government-to-government consultations on economics, energy, defense, terrorism, and other subjects; educational and scientific exchanges are intense. But the U.S.-India partnership still has relatively little reach beyond the bilateral. The global outlook behind it is still poorly articulated in both countries, and India and the United States have thus far done little to develop the common strands in their broader regional and global visions. The two countries appear to have different expectations about how their partnership should be reflected on the world stage. For the United States, a strategic relationship implies at least some predictable level of regional or global cooperation; for its part, India puts greater weight on the bilateral relationship. In the coming decades, as both countries grapple with problems that demand a global solution, the regional and global dimension of their ties will need to grow. The two countries need to identify which aspects

India wants to see de-hyphenation carried forward; no regression

of their respective global outlooks are in harmony, which ones need work, and which are subjects of more fundamental disagreement.

The U.S.-India partnership and the transformation that made it possible start with the new Indian foreign policy that emerged from the ashes of the Cold War. For most of India's first half-century of independence, the dispute with Pakistan arising from the partition of the subcontinent remained its most galvanizing foreign policy problem. India's other dispute, with China, led to the brief India-China war in 1962 and later crystallized into a strategic rivalry that is central for India's strategic thinkers, though it did not become an organizing principle for Indian foreign policy in the same way as the dispute with Pakistan.

Beyond these two bilateral problems, India's foreign policy was built on nonalignment and Third World solidarity. Especially under prime ministers Jawaharlal Nehru and Indira Gandhi, India had a global foreign policy in the sense that it commented on and tried to influence issues in many parts of the globe. But India's ability to shape events was limited mainly to the immediate neighborhood and to international institutions dominated by the nonaligned countries. The United States was important as a source of economic aid and scientific collaboration. Periodic efforts to deepen U.S.-India relations tried to build on the common bond of democracy, and during the India-China war the United States provided security assistance. But for much of this time, India and the United States had little to say to one another, and each country's efforts to take the moral high ground often irritated the other.

Throughout this period, the Soviet Union was India's most important extra-regional friend. It provided generous economic assistance, plentiful and inexpensive military resources, and reliable diplomatic support. The breakup of the Soviet Union in 1991 was a major blow to the architecture of India's foreign policy. At the same time, India's accelerating economic growth from 1980 onward and its gradually increasing economic opening starting in the 1990s gave new depth and texture to India's economic interests around the world, and made it a much more attractive partner for international business. An increasingly successful and prominent diaspora created dynamic new bonds for India, especially in the United States, where the Indian-American community was helping to build an information technology industry that was transforming both economies. And in May 1998, India's nuclear explosions highlighted India's military power.

INDIA'S NEW FOREIGN POLICY

Five characteristics define India's new foreign policy. First, India came to see its natural place as being one of the world's major powers, and thus it redefined its relationships with the other major powers. The rearrangement was the inevitable result of Russia's relative post-Soviet weakness. Although Russia remained a valued friend, it was no longer able to play the same role in the world that it had before. A new and vital partnership with the United States and improved relations with China emerged as the most prominent parts of India's approach to the world's great powers.

India saw the United States as the key to achieving two key strategic goals: international economic success and acceptance as one of the world's movers and shakers. The phrase "natural ally," used by both Vajpayee and Manmohan Singh, would have been unimaginable in Nehru's day. India sought a relationship with the United States that spanned the full range of subjects. The partnership started with stepped-up trade and investment. These are essentially private relationships, backed up by intense government negotiations to address long-festering disputes on such issues as trade barriers and intellectual property protection, seen by business as obstacles to expanding trade and investment. By the year 2000, security had become the most active government-to-government "account," and by 2005 the United States and India had signed a ten-year defense agreement. By 2007, India topped the list of countries sending students to the United States, with over 80,000.[2]

At the same time, India and China were also intensifying their relationship. The strategic rivalry remained, and public reminders of it occurred from time to time. At the same time, trade shot up, and the governmental dialogue on their border dispute accelerated. By the late 1990s, discussions of India's place in the world gravitated toward China, which was looked on by both policymakers and India's intellectual elites as the standard for the global role to which India aspired.

India's nuclear tests in 1998 complicated this process and led to the imposition of sanctions by the United States and other countries. But in a deeper sense they accelerated the transformation of India's relations with the major powers. With Pakistan joining the nuclear weapons club three weeks after India, the nuclear rivalry within South Asia made it essential for other world powers to deal with India and understand its strategic compulsions. The U.S.-India dialogue that followed the tests was the first serious and sustained dialogue those two countries had ever conducted on strategic questions.

A second defining characteristic was that the new Indian foreign policy was driven by economics to a much greater extent than before. During the 1990s, India's exports had expanded, it had become much more interested in attracting foreign investment, and its companies had become significant investors outside of India. National leaders in both government and business came to see foreign policy as an important means to reinforce economic success and deal with future economic challenges. In an earlier era, the economic dimension of India's foreign policy had focused to a large extent on seeking economic aid. In the 1990s, the emphasis shifted to trade, investment, and especially energy security. Protecting the Indian Ocean sea-lanes, through which some 70 percent of India's oil supplies traveled, was a new priority. Partly as a result India came to see routine U.S. operations in the Indian Ocean as nonthreatening, perhaps even beneficial to India's security interests. At the same time, the Indian navy grew in stature, in light of its role as protector of energy supplies. *joint exercises*

The third aspect of the new Indian foreign policy was greater attention to India's neighbors to the East. The "Look East" policy, as it was called, was not based on hostility toward China—it coincided, as we have seen, with a deliberate effort to improve Sino-Indian ties—but it did reflect India's desire not to have China emerge as the only major player in Asia. India's aid relationship with Japan had always been important; now trade, investment, and political and security ties were added to the mix. India's trade with Southeast Asia expanded, and regular military contacts increased. Leadership in Asia (not just South Asia) had been an important theme for India's leaders in the 1950s and 1960s. During the intervening years, India's policymakers and diplomats had paid relatively little attention to the region, and they had their work cut out for them to make India a significant player in Asia-wide deliberations. But increasingly, it was on the Asia-wide stage, not just the South Asian one, that India sought to engage.

The fourth defining element of India's transformed foreign policy, India's approach to South Asia, is familiar. Indian officials describe their foreign policy in terms of the changing priorities described

[handwritten annotation: U.S. aid to Pak that strengthens it re ct and anti-Talibanism is fine, but not aid that]

above. Nonetheless, India's dispute with Pakistan remains the single most emotive issue in its foreign policy and the one with the greatest power to command the attention of officials, politicians, and elites. Despite the United States' well-publicized efforts to develop its relations with India and with Pakistan on separate tracks—to "de-hyphenate" them—U.S. ties with Pakistan remain a very sensitive point for India. India's relations with its other South Asian neighbors continue to follow the classic big neighbor/small neighbor pattern. The "persona" India is developing in the world is of a country with global and Asia-wide interests. Whether this change in outlook will lead India to make major policy changes that will eventually resolve its troubled relationships within South Asia remains to be seen.

The final characteristic of the new Indian foreign policy is its approach to global governance. Again, this is a familiar theme to students of Indian foreign policy: Nehru saw the United Nations and related institutions as an important part of India's global stage. What has changed is that India now aspires to join the most powerful councils of the international community on the basis of its own national power and international role, and not as a moral arbiter or the representative of developing countries. The big prize, a permanent seat on the United Nations Security Council, does not seem to be close at hand. But India is an active participant in other forums and a regular invited guest at gatherings of the Group of Eight (G-8). It has positioned itself as both a donor and a recipient of economic aid. Its rapid response to the Asian tsunami of 2004/2005 demonstrated a capacity and willingness to act and to work with others in complex civil-military operations, again as a donor rather than recipient.

Behind these patterns of India's foreign policy action one can discern the outlines of a strategy. India already is by far the most powerful country in South Asia. It aims to be, and to be recognized as, a power as capable as China is of shaping events in Asia, and one of the major global powers. Its security space extends from the Himalayas and Hindu Kush across the Indian Ocean. Along most of its land borders, the most pressing threats are from nonconventional sources: immigrant flows, terrorism, subversion, and competition for water. The potential strategic threats it envisages come both from its nuclear neighbors and from the long-term potential for Chinese expansion into the Indian Ocean. But its defense against these threats relies not just on foreign

[handwritten margin notes: "strengthens P vis.a.vis India. Wants U.S. to respect its dominant regional pos.,"]

and security policy but also, and most fundamentally, on economic expansion, within India's democratic tradition.

This strategic vision is compatible with the U.S. perspective. Buried in it, however, is an element that may be trickier for the United States to deal with: India's commitment to "strategic autonomy." Since the earliest days of independence, Indian leaders have insisted on crafting a foreign policy that was clearly seen to be "made in India," and that did not involve automatic support for the policies of the world's most powerful players. In the early decades, India's leadership in the Non-Aligned Movement (NAM) gave expression to this view. Today, India's more tangible ambitions dictate a partnership with the United States, and Cold War politics no longer stand in the way. For Indian governments, however, it is still essential to show that India's policies are not being dictated by Washington. Besides the inevitable U.S.-India policy differences on specific issues, there is a persistent ambivalence in Indian policy circles about becoming too publicly associated with U.S. global policies. This theme of strategic autonomy runs through the contentious issues between the United States and India.

The concept of strategic autonomy rests on a notion of Indian exceptionalism, derived from India's ancient civilization and from its success in overcoming extraordinary diversity in language and social divisions to form a united country with a half-century of almost unbroken democratic traditions. The United States has its own brand of exceptionalism. Paradoxically, this probably makes India's more difficult to deal with. Both countries like to think of themselves as unique.

Closely related is India's vision of a multipolar world. India's current policy and its approach to the United States acknowledge that the United States is the world's only remaining superpower. This position makes the United States pivotal for all of India's major goals, from economic expansion and energy security, to recognition as one of the arbiters of Asian security, to a seat at the high table of global governance. India's preference would be to see the world evolve from its present unipolar organization to one involving five or six "poles" of power that are, if not equal, at least of the same order of magnitude, and with India as one of the poles. At the regional level, India similarly would hope to see Asia emerge as a multipolar region. This view reflects India's conviction that its economic and military strength will be taken more seriously in a world with more diffused centers of power. Beyond the implications for India's power and global recognition, the ramifications of this concept have not been thought out in much detail. India's focus has been on enhancing its own status and power, not on cutting down the larger powers.

CHANGES IN THE U.S. OUTLOOK

U.S. foreign policy goals and perceptions of the U.S. place in the world also underwent a transformation during this same period, as the United States digested the end of the Cold War and September 11. During the 1990s, the balance of U.S. foreign policy shifted somewhat from security toward economics, as policymakers sought an international "peace dividend" following the breakup of the Soviet Union. But this was accompanied, even in those early years, by a growing consciousness that the primary international danger for the United States had changed. In the more distant future lay the challenge of a rising China. But the immediate issue, as U.S. policymakers saw it, was the problem posed by smaller nonstate actors whose inherent military power was tiny in comparison with that of the United States and which lay outside the international security system built up systematically by two generations of American leaders. The United States now faced a greater short-term threat from the problems of weak states at the center of disorderly regions than from the strength of rival great powers. India has undergone a similar, but much less pronounced, shift in its threat perceptions, with the major security challenges coming both from an emerging strong power, China, and from a neighborhood full of weak states, starting with Pakistan.

The attacks of September 11 brought this shift in the U.S. threat perception to the center of U.S. foreign and security policy and magnified it. In addition, the advent of the George W. Bush administration had brought a changed philosophy to the management of U.S. international interests. The result transformed the role the United States sought to play in the world and its operating style.

U.S. foreign and security policy in this new dispensation was organized around one predominant threat, terrorism, and one principal response to it, the war on terror. This was spelled out especially clearly in the Bush administration's principal statements of international policy, notably the National Security Strategy, issued in 2002 and again in 2006. The 2006 document presented strengthening alliances, defusing regional conflicts, and the expansion of international prosperity as means to the larger end of defeating terrorism. As one would expect, the conflicts in Afghanistan and Iraq, and the complex challenges of reconstruction in both countries, were presented as the key military campaigns in the war on terrorism. The strategy placed tremendous stress on building up democracy and open societies around the world and gave a stirring argument for effective economic assistance, but this too appeared in the context of the defeat of terrorism. Terrorism also figured prominently in the discussion of cooperation with the major powers.[3]

The role the United States saw itself playing in the world was that of the sole remaining superpower. This was a familiar concept ever since the end of the Cold War. The difference, starting in 2001, lay in the Bush administration's unapologetic embrace of a hegemonic role and in its enthusiastic willingness to use the full panoply of U.S. power without necessarily having a broader multilateral structure or goal. Consistent with this approach, the Bush administration was deeply skeptical of the value of treaties, especially multilateral ones. It was far less prepared than earlier governments to accept the limitations such treaties placed on U.S. power, and correspondingly less interested in the limits they placed on other countries. The Bush administration's withdrawal from the Anti-Ballistic Missile treaty and its use of a looser, less formal bilateral framework to negotiate arms control with Russia was a case in point. The Unites States became less willing to work within international institutions. The institutional initiatives it took, such as the Proliferation Security Initiative, produced looser "non-institutions," without obligations that could constrain American power. The United States continued to emphasize the value it placed on allies and alliances, but when concrete issues arose on the international scene, it was clear that this value did not extend to making significant changes in U.S. policy or priorities on account of the sensitivities of allies.

The post-September 11 American approach continued the determination, earlier expressed in President George H.W. Bush's Defense Policy Guidance draft from 1992, that the United States would not countenance the emergence of a serious rival to U.S. power. After September 11, this determination was expressed in sharply rising defense budgets, despite the fact that the U.S. defense budget already exceeded those of the rest of the world combined. The new feature of the post-September 11 policy was the doctrine of preemption, under which the administration pledged to act to counter an imminent or gathering threat rather than to rely on deterrence as in the past. While U.S. policy had long allowed for the possibility of preemption in exceptional cases, elevating it to a principle shifted U.S. policy sharply in the direction of unilateral action, specifically including military action. Strengthening this predisposition to act alone was a conviction characteristic of Americans' view of their place in the world, going back to the early days of the Republic: the belief in the inherent goodness of the American idea and the related belief that this goodness is recognized by others as well. To this, the Bush administration added a corollary: its belief that when America was willing to lead, including through unilateral military action, others would follow.

In practice, the National Security Strategy underplays the post–September 11 strategic approach of the United States to dealing with major powers, and U.S. actions since 2001 suggest that at least in some cases traditional geopolitics are still very much alive. Russia's revival, its retreat from democracy, its willingness to use its energy resources to cow its neighbors, and its international actions that undercut U.S. interests arouse concern in Washington. China remains the principal international strategic rival, although there is broad acceptance that U.S. policy should be built on engagement rather than confrontation. U.S. concerns about Russia and China derive both from their weaknesses—the possibility of internal instability, for example—and from their economic and military power. Traditional relationships in Europe remain important, despite the strains caused by disagreements over the Iraq war. NATO, its primary mission fulfilled with the end of the Soviet Union, has become a central instrument for making Afghanistan secure and thus prosecuting one of the key campaigns in the war on terror.

The center of gravity in U.S. policy toward the Middle East has also shifted. With some notable exceptions, policy since World War II generally revolved around the Arab-Israeli conflict. During the Bush years, the Iraq war was the centerpiece. The decision to go into Iraq and the conduct of the war and its aftermath were not strictly speaking unilateral, but they clearly reflected the Bush administration's preference for having the United States do what it needed to do without being constrained by international institutions or alliances. The deeply troubled aftermath of the invasion will leave its mark on U.S. foreign policy for some time. It also has intensified doubts about the side effects of the Bush administration's more assertive U.S. policy. As the administration drew to a close, it belatedly focused its attention on the Israeli-Palestinian dispute, and the Obama administration is moving to put this conflict back at the center of Middle East policy. The ineffectiveness of the Bush policy on Israel and Palestine will be a painful legacy.

Looking ahead, Iran is seen as a looming danger. To traditional American concerns about Iranian support for terrorism and its role in Iraq one must now add the U.S. determination not to allow Iran to develop nuclear weapons. There was widespread speculation in the second Bush administration about whether Iran will become the next example of U.S. unilateral action under the doctrine of preemption, and what the consequences of such action might be.

Since September 11, U.S. foreign and security policy has continued its gradual shift away from the Eurocentric structure that followed World War II to an increased focus on Asia. The economic and security relationship with Japan remains the cornerstone of the U.S. approach to the Pacific. But the major development in Asia is the rise of Chinese power, and its significance is amplified by uncertainty in other important parts of East Asia, including Japan's long economic slump, a dangerous and volatile situation on the Korean peninsula, and both political and economic questions about Indonesia, the largest and most populous country in southeast Asia.

This is where India fits into the American strategic picture. During the Cold War and for a decade after it ended, India had relatively little strategic salience for U.S. policymakers. Turbulence in East Asia and India's emergence as a more consequential economic and military power have changed that. The United States has found it essential to broaden its network of strong friendships and strategic understandings in the area between China and the trouble spots in the Middle East. Some would go further and suggest that India's rivalry with China makes it a natural partner with the United States against the day when U.S. and Chinese interests and ambitions will clash. India has no interest in looking like an instrument of U.S. policy toward China, but the U.S. expansion of ties with India is certainly intended to strengthen U.S. relations with all the significant players in the emerging Asian balance of power. To this one must add India's vigorous democracy, a bond that all American leaders have acknowledged during India's 60 years of independence, though it has not always brought India and the United States together on foreign policy.

Neither the view that "geography is strategy" nor the idea of India as a major player in an evolving Asian power structure is spelled out in the Bush administration's National Security Strategy documents. The 2002 paper discussed India in the chapter on "other main centers of global power," concluding with the sentence: "Today we start with a view of India as a growing world power with which we have common strategic interests."[4] The 2006 document deals with India briefly as an engine of economic growth, a vibrant democracy, and a country "poised to shoulder global obligations in cooperation with the United States in a way befitting a great power."[5] A White House briefing on March 25, 2005, makes the point more forcefully, expressing the intention of the United States to "help India become a major power in the twenty-first century."[6] The notion of India as a necessary part of the Asian power balance is likely to carry over to the Obama administration and beyond.

PUBLIC ATTITUDES

The Bush foreign and security policy broke with practices built up over the preceding half-century. It was less willing to have the United States act through international institutions, more prepared to act alone, and more willing to use U.S. military force. Its most dramatic international initiative, the invasion of Iraq, became highly unpopular in the United States and the focus for partisan disagreement to a degree unusual in the modern history of U.S. foreign policy. With a new administration now in office, it is therefore reasonable to ask how strong is the staying power of the Bush administration's foreign policy paradigm.

A look at public opinion suggests that there may be important elements of continuity. A series of polls carried out for the Chicago Council on Global Affairs in the summer of 2006 suggest that while the sharp rhetoric of the Bush administration will be softened and its abrasive style and embrace of unilateralism may change, the most basic priorities that animated its strategic vision are likely to continue. For the past two decades, Americans asked to comment on the top priorities for U.S. foreign policy have consistently placed the same four issues at the top of their list: protecting U.S. jobs, preventing the spread of nuclear weapons, combating international terrorism, and securing adequate energy supplies. One marked change in the 2006 poll was the increase in the percentage of people who believed that Asia was more important to the United States than Europe: 43 percent held this view,

India does not want to be a means to an America... China; it wants to be... and end

with another 3 percent finding both areas equally important, whereas in the 2002 survey only 27 percent had felt that way.

Economic concerns ranked high across the board, more so than was apparent in the Bush strategic doctrine. A substantial majority contin- Bush ued to believe that the United States needs to remain engaged in the understood world, though an even larger majority rejected the role of "world po- because liceman," and opinion was closely divided on whether the United States ?? should make active efforts to ensure that no other country becomes a superpower. The public was skeptical about the use of troops in a number of security contingencies, but considered using troops justified in a variety of humanitarian crises and, interestingly, "to prevent Iran from acquiring nuclear weapons." Over half of those surveyed considered "environmental issues" to be an important foreign policy goal, and 70 percent believed the United States should participate in the Kyoto Protocol. Differences by political party on these issues were significant only for a handful of issues. Democrats were more concerned than Republicans about environmental issues and more disposed to use and strengthen the United Nations; Republicans were more accepting than Democrats of the Bush administration's arguments about the connection between the Iraq war and terrorism.

When it came to the U.S. partnership with India, the U.S. public by 61 to 28 percent saw India as a country that is "mostly a partner of the United States (in contrast to China, viewed by 49–41 percent as "mostly a rival"). A plurality (48 percent) believed that relations between the United States and India were "staying about the same," though twice as many saw an improvement as saw a decline (30 and 16 percent respectively). As for the warmth of the relationship, India evoked a mildly favorable response from the public in the 2006 poll. Responses to a question about the overall popularity of a number of countries placed India about in the middle, ahead of China and roughly even with Mexico and South Korea. Nearly half the respondents saw India as a responsible country (49 percent) and one that keeps its commitments (45 percent). About 40 percent of respondents believed that India would take U.S. interests into account in making foreign policy decisions. A narrow majority (53 percent) favored a permanent Indian seat on the UN Security Council, ahead of South Africa but well behind Japan and Germany.

According to the poll, the U.S. public saw India as a country whose influence and capabilities were currently modest but on the rise, and appeared to welcome this. India was looked on as exerting a "somewhat positive" influence in resolving the problems facing Asia. It was ranked behind Russia, Japan, Germany, and China, and roughly level with France, in its current influence in the world, and was expected to expand its influence, pulling nearly even with Russia, in the coming decade. The public believed India currently had a rather modest role in developing new products and technologies, comparable to South Korea, but both India and South Korea were expected to expand sharply their role in product innovation in the next ten years. India's economic influence was looked on as a positive development, but growth in its military power was seen negatively. Within the economic relationship, however, nearly half (47 percent) considered India an "unfair" trader, and outsourcing was considered "mostly a bad thing" by 76 to 21 percent.

Opinions about India varied little by demographic group. The one exception was that respondents with college or post-graduate degrees were consistently more positive in their assessments of India, with differences of 10-18 percentage points. Better-informed respondents, as identified by their ability to respond correctly to a couple of basic factual questions on international affairs, were also more likely to view India positively. This would suggest that there is popular support for the U.S.-India partnership, much of it passive and rather tepid but with stronger backing among the parts of the U.S. population that are most deeply involved in international affairs. The commitment the Clinton and Bush administrations put into the relationship, however, was at that point running ahead of public opinion.[7]

Two different surveys of Indian opinion conducted at about the same time found Indian public opinion very favorably disposed toward the United States, but still wary of being taken for granted. The most interesting results come from a sample of more than 200,000 people, distributed around the country, rural and urban, from all income groups. The United States was warmly perceived by 59 percent of those surveyed and was more warmly regarded than any of the other countries included in the question, including Japan and Russia. This pro-U.S. sentiment was observed in all income groups and in all states. Respondents also believed, however, that the United States was likely to treat India "aggressively" and, by implication, that India needed to drive a hard bargain. Interestingly, the most passionate and most uniform opinions were held by the elites included in the survey. This

[handwritten annotation: public opinion: dumb / strategic elites: smart]

group had warmer feelings toward the United States, and colder ones toward Bangladesh and Pakistan, than other groups.[8]

These survey findings are much more favorable than one might expect based on the way the proposed U.S.-India nuclear deal convulsed the Indian political scene in 2007 and 2008. The answer to this apparent puzzle lies in the way the Indian and U.S. democratic systems do and do not mesh. Elite opinion and coalition politics exert a stronger influence on Indian government decisionmaking than general public opinion. Despite the fact that both of India's major political parties have participated in expanding the relationship with the United States, opposition parties still use the United States and the accusation of giving up India's strategic autonomy as weapons for attacking the party in power. Moreover, the survey found that Indians of all income levels and regions believe their government needs to strike a tough bargain with the United States. That is just what happened with the nuclear agreement, both in the negotiations themselves and in the risk-prone process of moving the agreement through two governments and two international organizations.

This experience suggests that the United States and India should not assume that their common commitment to democracy automatically leads to a foreign policy partnership. Democracy is certainly an important bond, and one both countries take seriously when it comes to their own political systems. But the democratic link has existed throughout India's years of independence, and for nearly five decades India had far stronger relations with the nondemocratic Soviet Union than with the United States, while the United States was generally closer to an often-nondemocratic Pakistan than to India. What makes today's partnership different is that India and the United States have more tangible interests in common. This opens up for the first time the possibility that their democratic values will find expression in a foreign policy that comes together on some issues that are important for both. The democratic process is as likely to complicate the partnership as to feed it. A relatively benign public opinion may give the two governments the patience they need to make the new partnership work.

LOOKING AHEAD: DRIVERS OF INDIAN AND U.S. POLICY

Based on the broad strategic perspectives outlined here, Indian policy toward the United States will be based on four major goals:

- India's need for[continued economic growth and energy security;]

  high table

- its quest for a leading role in a nonthreatening world;

  dominant in SA

- its determination to be secure in its region, and to remain the primary arbiter of South Asian security; and

- its commitment to international freedom of action, or strategic autonomy.

At least for the next decade, the first two goals depend on a strong relationship with the United States. On the third, the United States is currently seen as a reasonably positive factor except for differences over Pakistan; and the fourth often manifests itself in opposition to the United States.

For its part, the United States will base its policy toward India on four different objectives:

- the imperative of avoiding nuclear war in South Asia;

- India's role in the larger Asian balance of power;

- India's trade and investment potential; and

- the impossibility of addressing some of tomorrow's global issues, such as climate change and international finance, without a fully engaged and participating India.

The next four chapters will examine the bilateral relationship the two countries have developed since the Cold War ended. Though much remains to be done, this is a remarkable success story, with huge gains in trade and investment, common interests but less common action on energy security, a mutually satisfying security relationship, and agreements on high-tech trade, nuclear, and space cooperation opening up areas that had been taboo for years. This bilateral assessment is followed by five chapters that examine how Indian and U.S. interests do and do not mesh on the international stage, looking in turn at South Asia, East Asia, the Middle East, relations with other global powers, and finally at how India and the United States approach problems of global governance. Here, the track record is more mixed, and the conversation between the two countries much more limited.

The final chapter will examine the likely changes in the world and the U.S. position in it in the second decade of the twenty-first century, and the "wild cards"—both potential crises and long-term trends—that will affect how these two democratic giants relate to one another. Against this background, it will return to the question with which this book began: what kind of partnership can the United States and India form, and how can they get there?

NOTES

1. See in particular Dennis Kux, *India and the United States: Estranged Democracies 1941–1991* (Washington, D.C.: National Defense University Press, 1992); and C. Raja Mohan, *Crossing the Rubicon: The Shaping of India's New Foreign Policy* (New Delhi: Viking, 2003).

2. Institute for International Education, *Open Doors 2007,* November 12, 2007, http://opendoors.iienetwork.org/?p=113743.

3. The White House, "National Security Strategy of the United States of America," U.S. Government, Washington, D.C., March 2006, http://www.whitehouse.gov/nsc/nss/2006/print/index.html.

4. The White House, "National Security Strategy of the United States of America," September 2002, http://www.whitehouse.gov/nsc/nss.pdf.

5. "National Security Strategy," 2006, 39.

6. Office of the Spokesman, U.S. Department of State, "Background Briefing by Administration Officials on U.S.–-South Asia Relations," March 25, 2005.

7. "The United States and the Rise of China and India: Results of a 2006 Multinational Survey of Public Opinion," Chicago Council on Global Affairs, Chicago, October 2006, 13-29 (also available at http://www.thechicagocouncil.org/UserFiles/File/POS_Topline%20Reports/POS%202006/2006%20Full%20POS%20Report.pdf. Material on breakdown by demographic group and historical comparisons is drawn from unpublished data from the same study, in which the author participated.

8. Devesh Kapur, "India-U.S. Relations: What Does the Indian Public Think," Center for the Advanced Study of India, University of Pennsylvania, November 5, 2007, http://casi.ssc.upenn.edu/print_pages/pdf/print_Devesh.pdf.

2

THE ECONOMIC ENGINE

In mid-2006, Prime Minister Manmohan Singh's official spokesman, veteran economic journalist Sanjaya Baru, published a collection of his columns going back a decade or so under the title *Strategic Consequences of India's Economic Performance*. His message: India's economic performance held the key to India's global profile and power, and indeed to its national security. He singled out a few factors with particular importance: the pace of economic growth; the impact of that growth on India's wealth distribution, global competitiveness, and integration into the global economy; the capacity of India's economy to support the military spending India needed as well as to sustain a rising standard of living; and the economic dimension of India's key external relationships, those with the United States and East Asia.

This analysis will be familiar to students of national power, but it had not been part of mainstream economic or security analysis in India. The spotlight Baru put on economic performance was a measure of how far India's economy had come. Perhaps more importantly, it showed that India's leaders had begun to think strategically about the country's economy.

India's economy grew relatively slowly during the first 25 years after independence, and much of that "Hindu rate of growth," as Indian cynics called it, was eaten up by an expanding population. Growth accelerated starting in the early 1980s, but it first attracted international attention and pushed its way into Indian foreign and security policy after 1991. India responded to a financial crisis in that year with policy changes that began opening one of the world's most closed economies to international trade and investment. In the process, those changes laid the foundations of the more ambitious role India sought in global affairs after the Cold War ended.

Even before India's foreign policy had adjusted to the end of the Cold War, India's economic transformation laid the groundwork for changed relations with the United States. Most of the countries that loom large in U.S. foreign policy are also major trade or investment partners of the United States. India's growth, opening market, burgeoning information technology (IT) sector, and growing outsourcing business put it on Washington's radar screen.

This chapter examines the new Indian economy, and then looks at what it means for U.S.-Indian relations. The most important elements in the economic relationship are private, including trade, investment, and the linkages created by the dynamic Indian-American community, with the excitement of information technology and the periodic controversy about outsourcing. These private linkages in turn have strengthened ties between the two governments, reinforcing the tendency toward an economically driven foreign policy in India. India and other emerging markets are likely to contribute most of the world's economic growth for several years. This will make India's economic performance even more important as a foundation for its ties with the United States.

THE NEW INDIAN ECONOMY

The global financial crisis that started in late 2008 made headlines in India as well as in the United States. The preceding two decades had shown the power of India's economic transformation. The financial crisis illustrated the vulnerability that went with it. India's stock market echoed the crash on international financial markets. The Indian authorities responded, as did their counterparts abroad, with lower interest rates and measures to inject liquidity into India's markets, and, also like their counterparts elsewhere, were criticized for inadequate action. In a gesture unimaginable during India's early years of state-dominated economic policy, the prime minister held a well-publicized high-level meeting with India's top industrialists and the nation's major business organizations to review the government's efforts to keep the economy

Figure 2.1 Indian Economic Growth, various periods 1950–2008

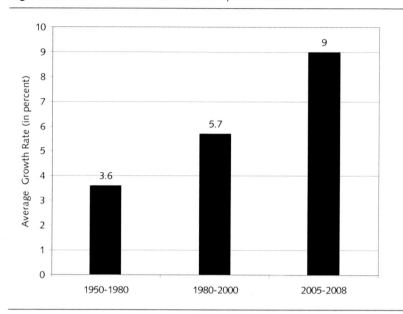

Source: Sadiq Ahmed, *India's Long-Term Growth Experience: Lessons and Prospects* (Los Angeles, Calif.: Sage Publications, 2007), 21; Ministry of Finance, Government of India, "Economic Survey of India 2007–2008," http://indiabudget.nic.in/es2007-08/chapt2008/tab13a.pdf, A-5.

humming. India's tradition of conservative financial management, and the remaining controls on capital flows, probably saved India from a much more severe impact.

India's growth record during the 20 years before the crisis had been impressive: from an average growth rate of 3.6 percent during 1950–1980, GDP growth rose to 5.7 percent in 1980–2000 and to 9 percent in 2005–2008.[1] (See figure 2.1.) The global financial crisis lowered estimates of India's growth in the coming years, but the growth that many economists now predict for India— a long-term trend of 7 percent, give or take a percentage point—is still strong by both historical and global standards.

This has led to a major increase in India's standard of living. India's per capita GDP has more than doubled since 1990. Government statistics estimate that poverty fell from 36 to 27 percent between 1994 and 2005.[2] However, even after 25 years of accelerated growth, India remains a low-income country in which about one-fourth of the population live on less than one dollar a day and more than half the population depend on a relatively sluggish agricultural sector.

Figure 2.2 Structure of the Indian Economy, 1950–1951 and 2006—2007

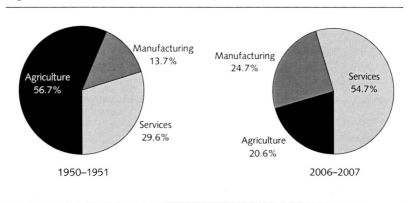

1950–1951

Agriculture
56.7%

Manufacturing
13.7%

Services
29.6%

2006–2007

Manufacturing
24.7%

Services
54.7%

Agriculture
20.6%

Note: Manufacturing is defined to include construction, electricity, gas, and water supply.
Source: Ministry of Finance, Government of India, "Economic Survey of India 2007–2008," http://indiabudget.nic.in/es2007-08/chapt2008/tab13a.pdf.

Despite the financial crisis, India's demographic profile suggests that high growth and the structural transformation that goes with it will continue for at least the next two decades. Population growth has fallen from 24 percent per decade in the early period to a projected 16 percent in the decade after 2001. By 2026, 61 percent of the population will be within in the 15–60 age bracket, the prime income-earning years. This gives India a remarkably low dependency ratio by international standards and a robust percentage of the population able to contribute to a growing economy.[3]

India's economic structure has changed. (See figure 2.2.) At the time of independence, more than half of India's GDP and two-thirds of its labor force were in agriculture. By 2005–2006, an estimated 54 percent of GDP came from services. Manufacturing figured relatively little in the early years of expanded growth, but moved ahead smartly after 2000 and passed agriculture in its share of GDP in 2004.[4] In both services and manufacturing, much of the growth came from sectors that were deeply intertwined with the international economy and are likely to remain so.

India's economic boom is largely based on long-term productivity growth. Both the information technology surge and the expansion in manufacturing have contributed to this phenomenon. Two important studies estimate that productivity accounts for more than half of India's growth since the mid-1990s.[5]

The shorthand name given to India's economic reform program after 1991 was "ending the 'license-permit raj.'" This involved reducing the regulatory burden on the domestic market and lowering barriers to trade and investment. Because private business, and especially multinational corporations, are politically controversial in many parts of India, this process has involved a good deal of "reform by stealth," decisions cautiously made and hesitantly announced. The garment industry has been removed from the list of industries reserved for small and medium-sized enterprises. In principle, "one-stop shopping" is available to foreign investors in India (though the operation of this system can still be complicated). By international standards, India is still a heavily administered and relatively closed market, but the trend is clearly toward allowing India's economy to be pushed forward by market forces.

These policy changes were accompanied by a steady increase in savings and investment, especially after 2000. Domestic capital formation reached 31 percent of GDP in 2005–2006, up from 23.4 percent in 1999–2000. The private sector accounted for 75 percent of this investment, and private capital formation accounted for nearly all of the increase in capital formation as a share of the economy.[6]

Indian-style "privatization" was one important dimension of this expansion of the private sector. India has only rarely sold public-sector assets to private owners; instead, it permitted the private sector to enter areas of the economy hitherto reserved for the public sector. Telecommunications and domestic air transport were public-sector monopolies until private companies were allowed to join the market in the 1990s, with dramatic results.

In the telecommunications field, private operators were initially restricted to "value-added" services, but private "value-added" services soon passed the "basic" ones reserved for the government. India's telephone subscribers crossed the 300 million mark in March 2008, representing teledensity of 26 percent, twice the level achieved two years earlier. Only 10 percent of these subscriptions were for landline service, still dominated by the public sector. Mobile phone subscriptions were increasing by 8 million–10 million per month, one of the fastest rates in the world. As any visitor to India can see, everyone from vegetable vendors to taxi drivers to yuppies now seems to have a cell phone glued to his ear.

On the air travel front, private airlines were allowed into the market in 1991. By 2006, they had collectively taken over 80 percent of the domestic air travel market and had begun making similar inroads into travel between India and most of its neighbors. Prices fell to the point where they were easily competitive with higher-end rail tickets. Soaring fuel prices temporarily reversed this trend and put both private- and public-sector airlines in financial trouble, but the changed structure of the industry will remain. Anecdotal evidence attests to the improvement in service that accompanied this newly competitive market. The changes in both the telecommunications and air travel industries contributed to the efficiency and user-friendliness of the Indian economy in ways that go beyond the numbers.[7]

India's corporate leaders have modernized their management and expanded their reach. Infosys and Wipro were early starters in information technology and are now global leaders in the field. Tata, one of India's oldest companies, has been successful in both manufacturing and services. Tata Consultancy Services is a world leader in business process outsourcing. The Tatas have expanded their long-standing presence in truck manufacturing to lighter vehicles, and have just launched a pathbreaking "people's car," the Nano, that sells for the equivalent of about $2,500. They have become a world leader in steel, one of the areas where the business started out. The two offshoots of Reliance, rising above a colorful "robber baron" history and a messy family split, are major players in the energy and telecommunications markets. These companies are not just setting a different standard for private corporate performance in India: they are also leading India's economy into the world.

These developments in corporate India reflect a wider trend: greater international openness. Foreign exchange regulations were dramatically simplified, leaving individuals able to travel, businesses to import, and foreign investors to remit earnings with few bureaucratic obstacles and only modest delays. International trade reached 34.1 percent of GDP in 2005–2006, up from 23 percent in 2000–2001 and more than double the 1990–1991 level (14.7 percent).[8] (See figure 2.3.) According to the World Bank, India's Tariff Trade Restrictiveness Index fell from 27.1 percent in 2000–2004 to 15.0 percent in 2006–2007. This is a dramatic drop, though India's tariffs are still high compared to the global average of 7.47 percent.[9]

Figure 2.3 Indian International Trade as Percentage of GDP, various periods 1990–2006

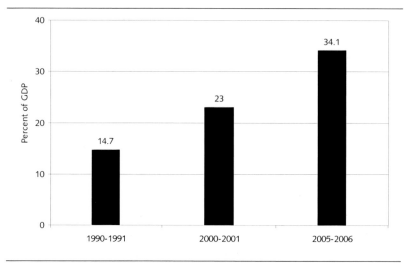

Source: World Bank, "Country Snapshot: India," *World Trade Indicators 2008*, http://info.
  worldbank.org/etools/wti2008/2b1.asp?pillarID=1&indList=66,69,75,72,118,152,161,190&ci
  d=86&comparator=0&vr=Value&timeperiod1=t1&timeperiod2=t2&timeperiod3=t3&timeperio
  d4=14.

Inbound and outbound foreign investment rose as well. In 1995–2000, foreign direct investment (FDI) came to $2.0-3.5 billion per year; by 2007 it had reached $19.5 billion. Overseas investment by Indians also rose, more unevenly, to $11.9 billion by 2007.[10] Still, investment represented a smaller percentage of the economy and of overall capital formation in India (3.5 percent) than in the rest of the developing world (12.8 percent) or in China (9.2 percent). This is in keeping with the growing but still low trade-intensity of the Indian economy.[11]

These trends all suggest a bright future for India's economy. But there is a dark side as well. The best-known problem, and one of the hardest to tackle because it is so diffuse, is the sheer complexity of doing business in India. Every business has its own anecdotes. Veteran India watchers comment that the problems were much worse in years past. But India is still a difficult environment. The World Bank's survey of doing business abroad ranks India 116th out of 122 countries surveyed.[12]

One illustration is land acquisition. Acquiring the land needed for major industrial developments or Special Economic Zones has been fraught with controversy. Legally, land transactions are the responsibility of India's states, as is the Indian counterpart to eminent domain.

Beyond the legal procedures, removing land from agricultural use, especially where poor farmers are involved, is a toxic political issue. In late 2008, Tata was unable to resolve in a timely way the politically driven protests over its proposed establishment of a factory in West Bengal for the Nano car, and decided to move the enterprise to Gujarat. Ironically, the area around the proposed plant site in West Bengal then saw protests by local farmers whose relatives had hoped to find jobs in the new plant.

Another long-term challenge is job creation. From 2000 to 2005, growth in employment in India roughly matched growth in the labor force, and it exceeded growth in population. Interestingly, rural employment has grown faster than urban employment (3.2 percent, compared with 1.6 percent), with self-employment growing fastest in cities and rural areas.[13] The challenge will be to increase the productivity boost from redeployment of India's labor force. The Goldman-Sachs study cited in endnote 5 of this chapter estimates that movement of surplus labor from agriculture to industry and services contributed about 1 percentage point to annual GDP growth.[14] This is a modest percentage, considering the huge supply of underemployed agricultural labor and the enormous productivity differences between agriculture and the rest of the economy (estimated at 1:4).[15] India's economic leaders are just beginning to focus on the implication of this situation: that India needs to produce a larger and more consistent pool of skilled labor to sustain its recent growth. This includes not just university and technical education, but also better skills development at the low end of India's labor force. Without this skills upgrade, India will have a severe political and social price to pay.

A related issue, which has received little public attention, is the need for greater research and development to sustain the productivity surge. India currently spends about 0.8 percent of GDP on research, about 75 percent of it funded by the government. Both the overall share and the weight of research within private industry are substantially below emerging markets like South Korea and Singapore.[16]

Infrastructure development outside the telecommunications sector has lagged behind the needs of the booming economy, and behind India's major international competitors (notably China). Deficiencies in electric power and transportation facilities are especially acute. Industry estimates of the needed infrastructure investment cluster around $100 billion to $150 billion per year. This represents some 10 percent of

GDP, or double the percentage that has been invested in infrastructure in recent years.[17] Mobilizing capital will require new ways of linking the public and private sectors.[18] The global financial crisis is bound to aggravate India's fiscal pressure, making private financing even more important.

The problem of the "second India"—those left out of India's prosperity—will affect India's politics as well as its economic prospects. Agriculture, which sustains 60 percent of India's population, grew an average of only 2.6 percent a year during this period, at a time when overall economic growth was over three times that level and prosperity was becoming very visible elsewhere.[19] The disparity between rural and urban India will continue unless job creation accelerates and significantly reduces the number of people dependent on farming. Agricultural growth alone cannot do the job. Senior Indian officials speak about their hope of raising agricultural growth from 2 to 4 percent, but do not expect it to reach the 8–9 percent range the economy as a whole has experienced.[20]

India's economic opening has created opportunities for its farmers, but has also made India's rural economy and its national politicians vulnerable to adverse price movements. Spiking international food prices in the summer of 2008 did little to benefit farm incomes in India, but much to harm urban pocketbooks. The Indian government's response was understandable—a temporary ban on rice exports—but illustrates the conflicting pressures on political leaders.

India's economic surge has affected different Indian states very differently. A few states, especially in the south and west, have surged ahead since 1980, with accelerating growth since 1990. (See figure 2.4.) The poorest states are predominantly in the most densely populated parts of northern India. They have grown, but more slowly than the rest of the country. India's richest state, Gujarat, has a per capita GDP 4.7 times that of the poorest state, Bihar.[21] This invites a political backlash, with poorly performing states using their large parliamentary delegations to demand a greater share of central government resources. The increasingly important role of single-state political parties in India's political system, and the prominence and political ambitions of the charismatic chief minister of India's largest state, Uttar Pradesh, will amplify their political voice.

Despite these challenges, the story of India's economic emergence since 1990 bodes well for its future economic expansion and for its

Figure 2.4 India's Annual Growth in Per Capita GDP by State, 1991–1999 (percentage per year)

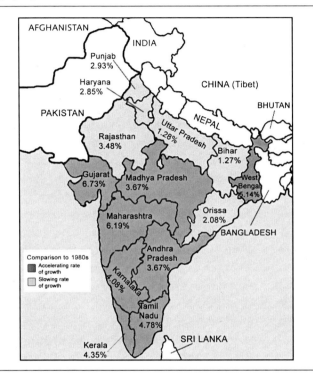

Adapted from Teresita C. Schaffer, "Partnering with India: Regional Power, Global Hopes," in *Strategic Asia 2008–09: Challenges and Choices*, ed. Ashley J. Tellis, Mercy Kuo, and Andrew Marble (Seattle: National Bureau of Asian Research, 2008), 206, figure 2.

Source of data: Montek S. Ahluwalia, "State Level Performance under Economic Reforms in India" (paper presented at Center for Research on Economic Development and Policy Reform conference on Indian Economic Prospects, Stanford Univeristy, May 2000), table 2.

Note: States are shown as they existed in 1999.

relationship with the United States. Private trade and investment tend to strengthen governmental ties with the United States. India's future growth and the continuing integration of India with the global economy are an essential foundation for a healthy U.S.-India partnership.

U.S.–INDIAN ECONOMIC TIES: FROM AID TO TRADE AND INVESTMENT

To assess where the economic engine is taking India-U.S. relations, we look first at the changing focus of U.S.-India economic relations, and then at the issues that dominate relations today: trade, investment, information technology and the services economy, and the Indian-American community.

During the first 25 years after India's independence, the governments dominated the economic relationship. India was one of the largest recipients of international development assistance. According to a
formula worked out in the World Bank board, it received 50 percent
of the funds dispensed by the World Bank's soft-loan wing, a percentage that was reduced after 1971. India was by far the largest recipient
of food aid from the United States under Public Law 480, popularly
known as the Food for Peace Program, and was a major recipient of
regular development aid, receiving 12.3 percent of all U.S. foreign assistance in 1970.[22] Aid represented a relatively small percentage of India's total resources, as is often the case in large countries. But there
were times, such as the poor crop years of the mid-1960s, when U.S.
assistance was critical to averting famine. Lyndon Johnson's effort to
increase U.S. leverage by manipulating a "ship to mouth policy" is still
remembered in India with distaste.

U.S. aid to India during this period had two "crown jewels." The first
was its contribution to the first Indian green revolution, the expansion
of high-yielding varieties of grains that, when given adequate fertil-
izer and water, dramatically increased food production and eventually
made India self-sufficient in basic foodgrains. Besides the increase in
production, U.S. scientists like Norman Borlaug and John Mellor created lasting ties with their Indian counterparts. The Indian Council of
Agricultural Research, led by M. S. Swaminathan, was a major recipient of U.S. support, and it remains to this day one of the best-known
faces of India's effort to feed its large population.

The second enduring legacy of U.S. aid during the pre-1970 period
was its involvement in India's scientific and technological research and
training establishments. India encouraged each of its major donors to
develop one of the Indian Institutes of Technology (IIT). The United
States was deeply involved with the IIT in Kanpur. Exchanges of pro-
fessors went on long after the golden years of U.S. aid. At the same
time, the United States funded, initially with surplus rupees generated by sales of its food aid, scientific collaboration in a broad array of
fields, creating a remarkable network of professional linkages. These
institutional connections had an impact far beyond the dollar value of
the assistance involved, and are the parents of the scientific cooperation that India and the United States are trying to cultivate today.

The United States cut off development assistance (but not food
aid) to India in 1971 over India's intervention in the war that sepa-

rated Pakistan and Bangladesh. Development aid resumed in 1978, but never regained its former size or high profile. U.S. assistance to India today consists almost entirely of technical assistance and goes primarily to the social sectors, such as family planning and health, and to agriculture. In 2006 India received $172.8 million in aid, only 0.6 percent of all U.S. economic aid given that year and substantially below aid to such countries as South Africa, Ethiopia, and Colombia.[23] Apart from a few high-profile issues, such as HIV-AIDS, aid has become a subject for discussion by technical experts rather than one that engages national leaders.

After India launched its economic reforms in 1991, the key elements in U.S.-India economic relations shifted decisively. The main economic story was no longer aid but private transactions: trade, investment, and information technology. Government policy discussions remained essential to remove obstacles in all these areas, but the prime movers, and the results by which success would be measured, were in the private sector. The United States is India's largest trade and investment partner, though both the trade and investment relationships are asymmetrical. India accounts for just over 1 percent of U.S. trade and 0.3 percent of U.S. overseas investment.[24] These levels, coupled with the potential for increase, make India a significant partner for the United States, with enough economic heft to stay on the radar screen of both the U.S. government and U.S. corporations, but not at the top rung.

India's merchandise trade with the United States increased in line with India's overall trade: its imports from the United States nearly quadrupled in value (to $11.7 billion) and its U.S. exports doubled (to $18.8 billion) between 2001 and 2007. The United States remains India's largest export market, with 15 percent of India's exports in 2007. All these figures represent a much larger share of India's GDP than they did in the past, and trade counts for more in India's foreign policy as well. China passed the United States as India's largest merchandise trade partner in 2006, but patterns of trade are quite different. India runs a substantial deficit with China, and its exports are heavily concentrated in unprocessed products, chiefly iron ore. By contrast, India's trade with the United States is in 2-to-1 surplus, and more than half its exports are manufactured goods, including some of India's most sophisticated products. The United States is India's largest market by far for pearls, gems, and jewelry; apparel; machinery, including auto parts; and pharmaceuticals. Together, these four broad categories account for

96 percent of India's exports to the United States.[25] These figures do not include information technology and related exports, which add another $20 billion in foreign exchange earnings to the totals above. The United States buys 67 percent of India's IT-related exports.[26]

In general, the private trade relationship works best; bilateral government discussions on economic issues are harder; and the multilateral level is the most difficult aspect of U.S.-India economic ties. The agenda of trade disputes between the United States and India is long and durable. One U.S. trade official commented, "Nothing ever goes away." Two examples— intellectual property and the Doha Round, in particular the issue of agricultural trade—illustrate the kinds of issues that have been regular bones of contention, and also the way India's trade policy is and is not changing as its economy expands.

Like other countries at an early stage of industrialization, India traditionally sought to avoid being hemmed in by restrictions on the transfer of intellectual property and made ample use of such devices as compulsory licensing and process rather than product patents. Under pressure from the U.S. chemical industry, the U.S. government pushed hard on this subject. U.S. legislation passed in 1974 put India at perpetual risk of U.S.-imposed sanctions for what the United States considered inadequate intellectual property protection. In 1995, India joined both the World Trade Organization (WTO) and the agreement on Trade Restricting Intellectual Property (TRIPS) at the conclusion of the Uruguay Round of trade negotiations. The TRIPS agreement, amplified by a bilateral agreement between India and the United States implemented at the same time, called for India to adjust its intellectual property regime to a tougher international standard over a period of ten years. It was a complex and highly technical set of arrangements. There were frequent arguments about whether it was being fully implemented, and U.S. officials remain concerned that the research described in patent applications is not well protected. But by the end of the transition period, India had changed its patent regime for chemicals—the most contentious issue—from process to product patents, and much of the venom had gone out of the intellectual property dialogue.

During this period, India began to produce and export more products with significant intellectual property, such as pharmaceuticals. This did not instantly transform India's policy, but it led to a more pragmatic Indian approach to intellectual property issues. Today U.S.-

Indian intellectual property discussions are aimed at preventing future problems more than rehashing old ones.

The second issue, the Doha Round of trade negotiations, has been a highly emotive bone of contention. A full review of the issues in play goes beyond the scope of this book. The issue of agricultural trade illustrates the limitations on U.S. and Indian cooperation, especially when dealing with politically sensitive issues. On trade issues, operating in a multilateral arena seems to intensify U.S.-India problems.

In previous trade rounds, agricultural trade negotiations were generally a duel among developed countries with important agricultural exports, pitting those that explicitly subsidized exports (principally the European Union) against those that did not, including the United States. The fact that its trade partners regard U.S. farm programs as a thinly veiled subsidy made the dispute nastier. For decades, most of the developing countries sat on the sidelines, recognizing that both sets of developing-country farm policies made cheap food aid more available.

In the Doha Round, formally launched in 2001, the United States sought a grand bargain: better market access for its key exports, especially agriculture, which had benefited little from previous trade rounds, in exchange for further U.S. liberalization of imports from developing countries, some of them politically sensitive in the United States. The actual negotiating structure was more complex and included many non-agricultural market access issues, but agriculture was key. The United States had more ambitious goals for agriculture than most of its negotiating partners. This time, the United States had reached an accommodation with the EU regarding the level of cuts in farm programs, and the main negotiations were with developing countries. India took up the cudgels on behalf of its own large agricultural population. It also saw in the trade round an opportunity to assert effective leadership of the developing countries on an issue of great political salience.

India's objectives in the Doha Round were quite different from those of the United States: to gain better access to developed country markets for its products that faced peak tariffs, such as textiles, and to liberalize movement of people, without giving up key protections for its own market. On agriculture, India's approach was mainly defensive. It had few exports that would be directly affected by the outcome of agricultural trade talks. Its largest agricultural commodity export is cotton, which accounted for about $4 billion or 3 percent of total exports in 2007.[27] The key issues were food security and the all-important farm vote that accounts for more than half of India's electorate. India defended its right to restrict access to its market even for agricultural products it does not produce. It would be almost impossible for any Indian leader to move away from the traditional approach to agriculture, and the Doha Round did not appear to offer sufficient benefits on India's other key issues for the government to take that risk.

Agriculture had been controversial in the Doha Round since the Cancun ministerial meeting in 2003, and there had been near-breakdowns in 2006 and 2007. Agricultural negotiations centered on three "pillars"—market access, export competition, and removal of trade-distorting domestic programs. The first and third of these were of particular interest to India. In an effort to develop common ground, negotiators worked through a "Group of Four" consisting of the United States, the EU, Brazil, and India. This proved frustrating for all concerned. Indian officials had difficulty reaching compromises and also had trouble accepting U.S.-drafted papers as the basis for negotiation. In July 2008, the negotiators deadlocked.

The politics of multilateral trade, as perceived in India, made this issue harder to resolve. Especially at the WTO, economic issues become political statements. India's commitment to strategic autonomy means that Indian politicians find it useful to show that they have resisted American pressure. In this case, the commerce minister who led the negotiations, Kamal Nath, reaped the domestic political benefit of showing that he had been leading the developing countries.

This came at a cost, however. For India, the prospect of having the Doha Round fail is not particularly alarming. Expectations were low, and the Indian government was convinced that no deal was better than an unfavorable one. But for the U.S. administration, a failure at Doha meant that the hope of expanding market access for U.S. agriculture and services would go unrealized. The United States saw India as the primary culprit in the breakdown of the Doha talks. This revived the doubts U.S. trade officials have had for years about whether India and the United States can work together on multilateral economic issues. The real cost to India of this episode may come elsewhere, in U.S. unwillingness to push for a larger Indian role in regional institutions.

Both the intellectual property dispute and the disagreement over agricultural trade and the Doha Round have their roots in the Indian government's long-standing "export pessimism." India recognizes that services exports are one of its biggest success stories, and it is gradually coming to see expanded trade as an opportunity with respect to knowledge-intensive manufactured goods. Other manufactures and agricultural trade, however, are not yet viewed in that light. India's industrialists have not yet entered the domestic debate on agricultural policy, unlike in the United States, for example, where representatives of export-oriented industries argue against restrictive policies on the grounds that these cut off opportunities for new exports. The changing structure of India's economy will eventually help shift the official attitude from its current defensive stance. But this process, and the politics that go with it, will lag behind the objective indicators, and multilateral trade is likely to remain a thorny issue for the United States and India.

Investment, like trade, is primarily a private activity, with governments playing a supporting role. The United States is a major source of investment in India. Exactly where it ranks is hard to measure, as many investments into India are routed through Mauritius to take advantage of an India-Mauritius investment treaty. However, according to U.S. government figures, foreign direct investment from the United States constituted 13 percent of India's total in 2006.[28] The dollar value of FDI from the United States is roughly comparable to U.S. investment in Indonesia, Chile, Thailand, or Argentina.[29]

Services, IT-related investments, and telecommunications together accounted for the lion's share of incoming investment—38 percent of FDI in India in 2007/2008.[30] Manufacturing and petroleum-related investment have been increasing. The liberalization of ceilings on foreign investment in sectors such as insurance and banking has made it easier for foreign companies to invest in these industries. The Indian government continues to adjust FDI rules to encourage more foreign investment. In January 2007, the government relaxed restrictions in several sectors, including civil aviation, construction, and petroleum and natural gas.[31]

The United States is also the main destination for India's increased investment overseas. Several of India's blue-chip companies, including Tata Motors, Infosys, and Wipro, are today listed on stock exchanges in the United States. The investment surge by Indian companies started in the IT sector but has spread to industries as diverse as pharmaceuticals and auto parts. Some Indian companies are significant employers in the United States. Tata, for example, initially came to the United States in 1945 as a steel company, and now has 16,000 employees representing 16 Tata Group companies in 80 locations across the country.[32]

As with trade, investment has also generated disagreements that have had to be resolved at the government level. The issue of investment access to industries traditionally restricted in India illustrates both the difficulties and the changes that have taken place on the Indian scene.

India historically limited a number of major sectors of the economy either to the public sector or to domestic investors, with FDI either banned or restricted. The United States made liberalizing investment into a major campaign. Two of the lead sectors for this campaign were life insurance, long limited to one public-sector provider, and retail trade, traditionally restricted to small business. In both cases, foreign companies sought to enter a market where even domestic participation was restricted.

The driving force for both issues was the interest of major U.S. companies, including New York Life and the American International Group in the insurance industry and Wal-Mart among retailers. In both cases, India changed its policy, but less completely and more slowly than had been hoped. The Indian parliament in 2000 revoked the government's monopoly on insurance and allowed foreign investment up to 26 percent in insurance companies. Several American companies were quick to invest, and by 2006, 27 foreign companies had entered the market. The insurance market expanded, bringing in new customers and new products and expanding its employment in India. Revenues rose sharply, new entrants to the market turned a profit in short order, and the private market share reached 34 percent for life insurance and 26 percent for general insurance. Expectations that the foreign investment cap would be raised to 49 percent had not materialized by 2008. But all things considered, this was a success story, and the issue of private-sector insurance is no longer controversial.

With retail, the issue was the impact of foreign retail giants on India's many small outlets. The Indian government moved ahead in stages, starting in 2006 by permitting foreigners to enter the retail sector only for stores that sold a single brand, in which they were permitted to own up to 51 percent. Large Indian corporations have been out in front of their foreign competitors in the effort to open up retail. This follows the classic pattern followed by the Indian government when it wants to change the system: rather than abolish regulations that have been in place for decades, it may pick out a specialized segment of the market and allow new players to enter it. In telecommunications and air travel, the result was a market revolution in fairly short order. The politics of retail are more complicated, so the market will be slower to transform. Wal-Mart, one of the first to urge the opening of the retail market, got no benefit from early liberalization measures. Its presence in India remains focused on buying, and it hopes for a future break-through on retail trade.

The two governments maintain close to a dozen formal consulta-tion mechanisms on economic issues ranging from technical stan-dards and regulatory issues to broad policy questions. The one that best illustrates the combined private-sector–public-sector focus that the U.S. government is trying to achieve is the CEO Forum, consisting of half a dozen CEOs from each country, who meet together with three or four cabinet officials from each side. The agenda is generated by the business participants. The fact that so many cabinet officials continue to attend the meetings testifies to the quality of the discussions. Par-ticipants on both sides see the group as an effective mechanism for focusing attention on the issues of greatest concern to the businesses involved in trade and investment, and in some cases for coaxing deci-sions out of slow-moving bureaucracies.

Americans are accustomed to this kind of hybrid group, but it is a new experience for India. Economic relationships with India's other major partners tend to be more government-oriented. With China, for example, it is routine for official visits to conclude with a promise to double the value of trade within a set number of years; and even with Japan, the focus is more on governmental encouragement for eco-nomic relations and on official financing for major projects. The more private orientation of economic ties with the United States is one of the strengths of the U.S. connection. As long as trade and investment continue to move forward on their own momentum, some of that mo-mentum will extend to official relations as well.

INDIAN-AMERICANS AND THE IT CONNECTION

The prominence and prosperity of the Indian-American community have also helped to transform U.S.-India relations. The community became a highly visible constituency in the United States during the 1980s. In 1980, the U.S. Census showed nearly 400,000 Indian-Americans in the United States. The 2000 figure was more than 1.6 million, of whom over half were U.S. citizens. They are the most prosperous ethnic group in the country. They are also the most highly educated segment, with 63.9 percent of adults holding a bachelor's degree or above. Among Asian communities, Indian-Americans have the highest percentage in management or professional jobs and the highest labor force participation.[33]

The formation of the U.S. House of Representatives Caucus on India and Indian-Americans in 1993 is a benchmark for the community's political "coming of age." In 2008, the caucus boasted 176 members, and its counterpart in the Senate had 37. Indian-Americans were discovered by candidates for state, congressional, and national office as fund-raising targets. Former U.S. representative Stephen Solarz, representing a district in Brooklyn with few Indian-Americans, developed a strong interest in South Asia, and was the first congressman to tap this community seriously for campaign support. Others have followed. Indian-Americans have joined the collection of ethnic committees that work with presidential campaigns. Their political action committees (PACs) are active and prominent. Congressmen and senators come enthusiastically to meetings of their community associations. They are part of the fabric of American political life. The largest number of Indian-Americans live in California, and the state with the largest percentage (2 percent) is New Jersey.[34] Maryland elected the first Indian-American state legislator, Kumar Barve, in 1990; Louisiana elected the first governor, Bobby Jindal, in 2007.

The community's best-known economic connection is the one linking the U.S. and Indian information technology industries. India's IT industries got their start in the 1980s and took off after liberalization started in 1991. U.S.-India trade in this area increased substantially during the dot-com boom of the late 1990s, with the large influx of work needed to fix the Y2K computer bug. U.S. firms continued to work with Indian IT industries as they tried to cut costs during the economic slowdown in 2000–2001.[35] These connections were driven almost entirely by the private sector and industry groups such as The Indus Entrepreneurs, the U.S.-India Business Council, and the Indian industry association NASSCOM.

Figure 2.5 India's IT Industry 1998–2007

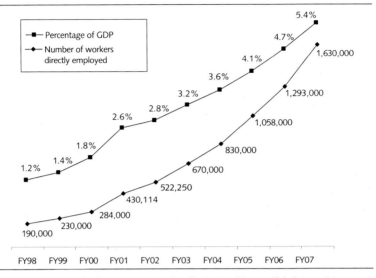

Adapted from Teresita C. Schaffer, "Partnering with India: Regional Power, Global Hopes," in *Strategic Asia 2008–09: Challenges and Choices*, ed. Ashley J. Tellis, Mercy Kuo, and Andrew Marble (Seattle: National Bureau of Asian Research, 2008), 205, figure 1.
Source of data: NASSCOM, "Indian IT Industry: NASSCOM Analysis," August 2007, http://www .nasscom.in/upload/5216/Latest_IT_Industry_Factsheet_Aug_07.pdf.

In a short time, information technology and the industries it enables have gone from being an exotic hothouse plant to becoming the fastest-growing industry in India, a major employer, and the country's largest foreign exchange earner. As a proportion of India's GDP, the technology sector has grown from 1.2 percent in FY1998 (see figure 2.5) to 5.5 percent in FY 2008, and employment rose more than tenfold, from 190,000 to 2 million, during the same period. IT exports in 2008 were expected to top $40 billion, a 28 percent increase from exports in 2007. The United States continues to be the largest market for India's IT sector, with 67 percent of India's exports in 2007, although European and Asian markets are rising. India's IT industry association estimates that the market for "global sourcing" is worth $1.7 trillion and is growing at 7.3 percent per year. India's share of the global market is 65 percent for overall IT services and 45 percent for business process outsourcing (BPO). Both figures are continuing to grow rapidly.[36] In the wake of the global financial crisis, projections are down by one-third or more, but the industry still expects to sustain growth of between 10 and 20 percent.

Within the IT sector, services are the largest export earner, and outsourced services are the fastest-growing segment and continue to be the primary driver of growth. Outsourcing presently accounts for approximately 27 percent of IT exports, and BPO export revenue was expected to total a little more than $10 billion in FY 2008.[37]

The financial sector is a particularly eager user of outsourced services. A survey by Deloitte and Touche found that banks in the United States were sourcing 6 percent of IT-related spending overseas, primarily in India and China, and that this percentage was likely to grow to 30 percent by 2010. In early 2007, Citigroup announced that it would be eliminating nearly 5 percent of its global workforce and relocating 9,500 jobs to "low-cost" locations.[38] A majority of those jobs would be focused on equity research, investment banking, and back-office transaction-related services.

Outsourcing and other IT-related trade have grown at record-breaking rates since 2000. It is an unusually rapidly changing field, however. Outsourcing is growing in sophistication, with U.S. companies sending more complex aspects of their IT work to India. Some outsourced functions are shifting from low-level data entry jobs, such as call centers and payroll processing, into higher-level value-added services, such as product design and software development. Leading Indian IT companies are developing an international presence and, in the process, bringing jobs back to the United States, especially where proximity to clients is critical. Although the U.S.-India connection is likely to be a durable one, it is easy to foresee the possibility of parts of India's industry shifting to lower-cost suppliers, or an Indian equivalent of the dot-com bust that took place in the United States during the 1990s. In other words, just as India has found both opportunities and risks in playing on a world stage, its IT industry could do the same.

Outsourcing has been one of the most controversial issues in U.S.-India economic relations. During U.S. political campaigns at both the federal and state level, outsourcing has become a magnet for political discontent. Legislation has been introduced at the federal level to discourage moving U.S. jobs overseas. In February 2004, for example, Senate Democrats announced their intention to introduce the Jobs for America Act, requiring companies to give public notice three months before implementing any plan to outsource 15 or more jobs. In March 2004, the Senate overwhelmingly approved a measure banning firms from outsourcing work on federal contracts. There have also been calls to extend Trade Adjustment Assistance (TAA), which provides relief and retraining to workers displaced by international trade, to workers displaced by outsourcing. As of the end of 2008, no such bills had passed. There have also been calls for changing provisions of the tax code that allegedly treat outsourced operations more generously than U.S.-based contracting out for services. The early 2009 economic stimulus package contained some modest changes in the tax treatment of outsourcing, but in general there has been little action on this front.

Since the turn of the twenty-first century, more than 20 state legislatures have introduced bills designed to make various forms of offshore outsourcing illegal. The proposed measures range from requiring companies to disclose how many jobs they outsource when bidding for state contracts, to making it illegal for those who contract with the state to outsource. While none of these plans have become law, New Jersey offers a unique example. eFunds, a company that contracted with the state, was going to move its call center from Wisconsin to Mumbai. A state legislator threatened to cancel the contract with the firm, and a deal was reached. eFunds would move its call center to Camden, New Jersey, and the state would subsidize the company by paying it the savings it lost by not outsourcing to India.[39]

Outsourcing brings the vibrant U.S.-Indian economic relationship into the rough and tumble of U.S. politics, just as trade brings the United States into the Indian political debate. The momentum of economic change should eventually make it easier for India to adjust its trade policy. This is not necessarily true in the United States, where the acceleration of growth in the cutting-edge industries will also entail painful adjustments in the job market.

The trade, investment, and IT issues with which both countries are wrestling show that each needs the other to pursue its goal of prosperity in a global market. The U.S. service industries have made a big bet on India, in the same way that other U.S. industries made concentrated investments in China or Mexico. Indian companies are now involved with some of the most sophisticated segments of corporate America, whether through the supply of parts, the development of the software that provides their "nervous system," or the provision of internal services and communications. Pharmaceutical companies are starting to "out-license" to India new potential products that look promising but may not justify the higher cost of testing and developing in the United States. The resulting research efforts involve serious scientific work on both sides of the ocean and a deepening integration of their research establishments. This could generate huge job creation in both countries. It also integrates production in the two countries in ways that go beyond the trade statistics. And it will push the two governments to work together, less they lose the productive energy of this business-level integration.

LOOKING AHEAD

The scale and durability of India's relations with the United States will depend on India's economic prospects. A decade and a half of unprecedented economic growth helped transform the relationship. India's hopes for faster and more widely distributed growth can best be realized if India expands its international economic reach and becomes more fully a trading nation. This would deepen the transformation that has already occurred.

The global financial crisis that began in 2008 is leading to a recession, probably quite severe, in most of the world. India will face a period of reduced growth, partly as a result of its greater vulnerability to imported economic troubles. At the same time, India, China, and a handful of emerging markets are likely to produce most of the economic growth in the global economy. Hard economic times often generate trade disputes and protectionism. They may also, as we will see in chapter 10, provide an occasion for new forms of economic cooperation. The economic turbulence ahead is likely to reinforce the economic connections that are bringing the United States and India together.

NOTES

1. Sadiq Ahmed, *India's Long-Term Growth Experience: Lessons and Prospects* (Los Angeles, Calif.: Sage Publications, 2007), 21; Ministry of Finance, Government of India, "Economic Survey of India 2007–2008," http://indiabudget.nic.in/es2007-08/chapt2008/tab13a.pdf, A-5.

2. Ministry of Finance, "Economic Survey of India 2007–2008," http://indiabudget.nic.in/es2007-08/chapt2008/chap103.pdf, 244.

3. Office of the Registrar General and Census Commissioner, Government of India, *Census of India 2001: Population Projections for India and States 2001–2026* (revised December 2006), http://www.censusindia.net/Projection _Report.pdf; National Commission on Population, Government of India, *Report of the Technical Group on Population Projections*, Working Group Report, May 2006, 139 ff.

4. Ministry of Finance, "Economic Survey of India 2007–2008," S-5, http:// indiabudget.nic.in/es2007-08/chapt2008/tab13a.pdf .

5. See Tushar Poddar and Eva Yi, "India's Rising Growth Potential," *Global Economics*, Paper no. 152, January 2007, Goldman Sachs Global Economic Website, http://www2.goldmansachs.com/ideas/brics/book/BRIC-Chapter1 .pdf ; see also Ahmed, *India's Long-Term Growth Experience*.

6. Ministry of Finance, "Economic Survey of India 2007–2008," table 1.1 (A3) and 1.6 (A10), http://indiabudget.nic.in/es2007-08/tables.htm.

7. Rajiv Shankar, "Merged Air India-IA Revenue Projected at 15,000 Crore by 2010," domain-b.com, February 22, 2007, http://www.domainb.com/ industry/aviation/20070222_air_india.htm; Byas Anand, "New Airlines Garner 40% Share," TNN (TFF News Navigator), November 11, 2006, http:// timesofindia.indiatimes.com/articleshow/402116.cms; Siddharth Srivastava, "India's Airlines Look to Fly High," *Asia Times* (New Delhi), January 4, 2007, http://www.atimes.com/atimes/South_Asia/IA04Df01.html.

8. Ministry of Finance, "Economic Survey of India 2007–2008," http:// indiabudget.nic.in/es2007-08/tables.htm, tables 1.3B (A3) and 7.1A (A80).

9. The TTRI is based on MFN applied tariffs. World Bank, "Country Snapshot: India," *World Trade Indicators 2008*, http://info.worldbank.org/etools/ wti2008/2b1.asp?pillarID=1&indList=66,69,75,72,118,152,161,190&cid=86 &comparator=0&vr=Value&timeperiod1=t1&timeperiod2=t2&timeperiod3 =t3&timeperiod4=14.

10. Reserve Bank of India, Government of India, "India's Overall Balance of Payments," *Annual Report 2006–2007* (Mumbai: Reserve Bank of India, August 30, 2007), http://www.rbi.org.in/scripts/AnnualReportPublications .aspx?Id=788; Reserve Bank of India, "Table 161: Foreign Investment Inflows," http://rbidocs.rbi.org.in/rdocs/Publications/PDFs/80341.pdf.

11. United Nations Conference on Trade and Development (UNCTAD), "Country Fact Sheet: India," *World Investment Report 2006*, http://www .unctad.org/en/docs/wir2006_en.pdf.

12. World Bank, *Doing Business in South Asia in 2006* (Washington, D.C.: World Bank, 2006), http://www.doingbusiness.org/documents/2006-South _Asia.pdf, 1.

13. Organization for Economic Cooperation and Development (OECD), "Labor Markets in Brazil, China, India and Russia," *Employment Outlook 2007*ow/44187019.cms (Paris: OECD, 2007), Table 1.A.1.3, http://www .oecd.org/dataoecd/57/9/38965029.xls.

14. Poddar and Yi, "India's Rising Growth Potential," 3.

15. Ahmed, *Long-Term Growth Experience*, 23.

16. Amit Shovon Ray, *Emerging through Technological Capability: An Overview of India's Technological Trajectory*, Indian Council for Research on International Economic Relations, Working Paper 227, November 2008, http:// www.icrier.org/publication/WorkingPaper227.pdf.

17. There were at least half a dozen infrastructure-financing conferences planned for the second half of 2008. The industry estimates on which they are based are all in the same range; see the documents announcing the second Global Infrastructure Leadership Forum, scheduled for Washington in December 2008, http://www.asiatradehub.com/India/intro.asp.

18. Author's interviews with senior Indian economic officials, February 2008.

19. Computed from data from the Ministry of Finance, *Economic Survey 2007–2008*, http://indiabudget.nic.in/es2007-08/chapt2008/tab13a.pdf.

20. See, for example, the speech by Planning Commission Deputy Chairman Montek Singh Ahluwalia, reported in "Planning Will Focus on Inclusive Growth: Montek," *The Hindu Businessline*, April 8, 2007, http://www.thehindubusinessline.com/2007/04/08/stories/2007040804060300.htm.

21. Catriona Purfield, "Mind the Gap: Is Economic Growth in India Leaving Some States Behind?" International Monetary Fund (IMF) Working Paper, 2006, table 1, http://www.imf.org/external/pubs/ft/wp/2006/wp06103.pdf.

22. U.S. Agency for International Development (USAID), "Economic Assistance, Total (Historical $) 1970," *U.S. Overseas Loans and Grants, Obligations and Loan Authorizations (The Green Book)*, http://qesdb.cdie.org/gbk/index.html.

23. U.S. Agency for International Development (USAID), "Ten Year Program Report Economic Assistance, Total (Historical $)," *U.S. Overseas Loans and Grants, Obligations and Loan Authorizations*, http://qesdb.cdie.org/gbk/index.html.

24. U.S. Census Bureau, "Trade in Goods (Imports, Exports and Trade Balance) with India," *Foreign Trade Statistics*, http://www.census.gov/foreign-trade/balance/c5330.html; U.S. Bureau of Economic Analysis, "U.S. Direct Investment Abroad: Selected Items by Detailed Country, 2004–2007," http://www.bea.gov/international/xls/longctry.xls.

25. Export Import Data Bank, Ministry of Commerce and Industry, Government of India, http://commerce.nic.in/eidb/default.asp.

26. NASSCOM, "Indian IT-BPO Sector: India's IT-BOP Performance in 2006," http://www.nasscom.in/Nasscom/templates/NormalPage.aspx?id=11028.

27. Export-Import Data Bank, http://commerce.nic.in/eidb/default.asp.

28. U.S. Department of State, Bureau of Public Affairs, "India," *Background Notes*, http://www.state.gov/r/pa/ei/bgn/3454.htm.

29. U.S. Bureau of Economic Analysis, "Direct Investment Positions for 2007: Country and Industry Detail," *Survey of Current Business*, July 2008, Tables 1.1 and 1.2, http://www.bea.gov/scb/pdf/2008/07%20July/0708_dip.pdf.

30. Department of Industrial Policy and Promotion, Government of India, "Factsheet on Foreign Investment, August 1991 to March 2008," http://www.dipp.nic.in/fdi_statistics/india_fdi_March2008.pdf.

31. Reuters, "India Lifts FDI Caps in Key Sectors," *Financial Express*, January 30, 2008, http://www.financialexpress.com/news/India-lifts-FDI-caps-in-key-sectors/267054/.

32. David Good, "From Strength to Strength," Tata Group Worldwide, 2008, http://www.tata.com/0_tata_worldwide/america/articles/20080312_strength .htm.

33. Terrance J. Reeves and Claudette E. Bennett, *We the People: Asians in the United States*, Census 2000 Special Reports, U.S. Census Bureau, U.S. Department of Commerce, December 2004, http://www.census.gov/prod/2004pubs/ censr-17.pdf.

34. Indian Embassy, "Indian-American Population", [map], http://www .indianembassy.org/ind_us/census_2000/ia_population_map_2001.pdf.

35. Simon Long, "Virtual champions," *The Economist (US)*, June 3, 2006; Jim Gordon and Poonam Gupta. "Understanding India's Services Revolution" (paper prepared for IMF-NCAER conference "A Tale of Two Giants: India's and China's Experience with Reform," International Monetary Fund, New Delhi, November 14–16, 2003), http://www.imf.org/external/np/apd/ seminars/2003/newdelhi/gordon.pdf. SB.

36. NASSCOM, "India's IT-BPO Performance," http://www.nasscom.in/Nasscom/templates/NormalPage.aspx?id=11028 ; NASSCOM, "Key Highlights of the IT-BPO Sector Performance, in FY 2007-2008," http://www.nasscom. in/upload/5216/Strategic_Review_Feb2008.doc; NASSCOM, "Strategic Review February 2008," http://www.nasscom.in/upload/5216/Strategic_Review _Feb2008.doc. Years refer to India's fiscal years (FY 2007 begins in April 2006). Note that U.S. and Indian figures on information technology and outsourcing differ greatly; the data collectors use different definitions and have data collection protocols that result in much larger figures from Indian than from U.S. sources. This analysis is based on Indian figures, which seemed to reflect more fully the international linkages of the industry.

37. NASSCOM, "Key Highlights of the IT-BPO Sector Performance, in FY 2007-2008," http://www.nasscom.in/upload/5216/Strategic_Review_Feb2008 .doc.

38. Paul McDougall, "Big Surge for Bank Offshore Outsourcing, Deloitte Study Predicts," *InformationWeek*, March 19, 2007, reprinted on Wall Street & Technology Web site, http://www.wallstreetandtech.com/showArticle .jhtml?articleID=198001851; "Citigroup to Ramp Up India Headcount," *Economic Times,* April 11, 2007.

39. Chidanand Rajghatta, "American Firm Reverses Outsourcing to India," *The Times of India*, April 22, 2003, http://timesofindia.indiatimes.com/ articleshow/44187019.cms.

3

ENERGY
WHERE ECONOMICS MEETS STRATEGY

In November 2007, the International Energy Agency (IEA) released its World Energy Outlook report. Remarkably, it was devoted entirely to two countries that are not members of the organization: India and China. Its hundreds of pages of facts and figures documented a conclusion already familiar to those who follow energy markets or Asia: that these two giants would transform energy markets over the next 30 years.

For India, this is the inevitable result of the economic growth that is central to its emergence as a regional and global power and to its partnership with the United States. An expanding economy creates new requirements and vulnerabilities. India's growth requires ever-increasing amounts of energy, more and more of it imported. Energy is where India's economic, security, and foreign policy prospects come together.

The Indian government's most formal analysis of its energy prospects, the report of the Expert Committee on Integrated Energy Policy released in August 2006 by the Planning Commission, defines energy security very broadly. It argues that "India's energy security, at its broadest level, has to do with the continuous availability of primary commercial energy at a competitive price to fuel our economic growth and to provide reliable access to modern forms of primary and secondary energy and energy services needed for lifeline support to more than 50 percent of our population."[1] The report deals in detail with India's international energy relationships, but it considers fundamental price mechanisms in the domestic market and the smooth functioning of international energy markets more important than establishing equity positions in oil-producing facilities overseas. Striving for social justice is built into the definition.

In practice, India's energy policies represent a political and bureaucratic compromise between this marketed-oriented statement and India's traditional policies, with their heritage of a dominant state role and a mercantilistic approach relying more on ownership of assets than on the market. Politically, Indian governments have to be concerned about energy prices for farmers and the poor. State-centered energy markets have moved slowly toward market-based pricing. Internationally, expanding and diversifying supply and protecting the sea-lanes by which it travels to India have become a major foreign policy and security driver, but one whose effectiveness ultimately depends on how the country meets its domestic policy challenges.

The U.S. concept of energy security bears a strong resemblance to the vision spelled out in the Planning Commission's report. An article by the U.S. State Department's principal energy official, Paul Simons, describes the U.S. objective as "sufficient, affordable, and reliable energy supplies on terms and conditions that support economic growth and prosperity." The main tools for achieving that goal are diversification of supply, a coordinated international response to market disruptions, dialogue with producers, and efficiency measures to reduce global dependence on oil. The two most important differences with the Indian concept of energy security are a much greater reliance on the market and a global focus.[2]

India's energy needs lie at the heart of some of the most important interests it shares with the United States. India's economic growth is one of the foundations of the emerging partnership. Its preoccupation with maritime security, the direct consequence of its dependence on imported oil, brings U.S. and Indian security interests together. But energy issues are also central to the most difficult foreign policy differences between the two countries. The U.S. response has primarily taken the form of an elaborate government-to-government energy dialogue, an exercise more useful as a way of deepening bilateral contacts than as a vehicle for solving India's energy supply problems.

To understand where energy fits into the U.S.-India relationship, this chapter will first look at India's energy market. It will then review the international dimensions of India's energy strategy, and the U.S.-India bilateral energy dialogue, and the way India does and does not fit into international energy institutions.

ENERGY AND THE INDIAN ECONOMY

The basic numbers are sobering. India used 537.3 million tons of oil equivalent (MTOE) in 2005. Leaving aside the noncommercial materials used by rural households, such as wood, dung and charcoal, the largest energy source is coal, accounting for 53 percent of India's commercial energy use, most of it for electricity generation and nearly 90 percent of it domestically produced. In second place is oil, which accounts for 34 percent of the country's commercial energy use. Imports represent 70 percent of this total, and they are expected to top 90 percent by 2030. As in other countries, oil is especially critical for the transport sector, despite the conversion of taxi and bus fleets in many of India's cities to compressed natural gas (CNG). Gas represents less than 8 percent of the commercial energy market, but is growing faster than other fuels. Imports are likely to increase from today's 7 percent to 49–58 percent by 2032.[3]

India's drive to expand access to energy for its one billion-plus population reflects not just the raw statistics of its economic growth, but also the numbers of people living in poverty. An estimated 57 percent of the rural population has no electricity. Per capita electricity generation is about 20 percent of the world average and only 4 percent of the level in the United States. Road transport, the most oil-intensive mode, currently moves 80 percent of India's passengers and 60 percent of its freight. This guarantees that oil will continue to be vital for many years.[4]

India's economic growth since the early 1990s has benefited from a healthy balance of payments, but high energy prices put this under pressure. Oil and gas constitute India's largest import, accounting for $61 billion or 33 percent of India's import bill in 2006. Petroleum products are also India's largest export, at 15 percent of the total. The net oil import bill in 2006 came to $42.9 billion, equivalent to one-third of India's merchandise exports.[5] Looking ahead to 2030, the IEA estimates that net oil imports will triple in volume if current energy policies continue.[6] Since those estimates were made, oil prices tripled and then fell back to below their earlier levels. The most recent IEA projections anticipate an oil supply crunch. This will almost certainly mean that prices trend up over the medium to long term.

Add to this the inevitable changes in India's energy market in the next two to three decades, and it is easy to understand India's preoccupation with energy. There are several analyses of India's energy outlook in circulation, one produced by the Indian government, another by the Energy and Resources Institute (TERI), a highly respected Indian think tank, and the third by the International Energy Agency and the U.S. Energy Information Agency. The details and assumptions are slightly different in each one, but their message is consistent: India's energy requirements will grow inexorably with GDP, especially if there is no change in current energy efficiency policies. The most conservative estimate comes from the IEA, which projects energy demand growth of 3.6 percent per year; the highest estimates come from the Planning Commission, which estimates that for every percentage point in GDP growth, India's energy requirements will increase by between 0.7 and 0.95 percent, representing annual growth of 4.9–6.6 percent at the 7 percent trend growth rate. At the rates projected by the IEA, overall commercial energy requirements would double in 25 years. At the rates projected by TERI and the Planning Commission, they would double in a decade or less. To make matters worse, oil discoveries have slowed down since 2005. The IEA concludes that India's domestic crude oil production is likely to fall by almost half by 2030.

The electricity problem is especially toxic, a combination of demand growth estimated at 7 percent per year and meager resources. The State Electricity Boards (SEBs) that run India's electric system have become a byword for fiscal red ink, owing largely to poor bill collection and to the persistent practice by state politicians of offering free electricity to farmers. Compounding this problem is the electoral calendar. India is never more than a few months away from a major election in one of its states, with electricity prices a predictable part of the political mix. Over the past five years, the central government's efforts to strengthen the finances of the SEBs have borne some fruit, but the combination of high energy and food prices will make that very hard to sustain.[7]

These projections all agree that the most effective way to expand effective energy supply is to improve the efficiency of domestic energy use. TERI finds that the most ambitious efficiency scenario could save as much as 30 percent in energy use by 2031 compared with the "business as usual" scenario. This would nearly compensate for the increased demand that would result if GDP growth increased 10 percent. Depending on one's assumptions about India's economic growth, the cumulative gain from efficiency would amount to between 600,000 and one million tons of oil equivalent, or between one and two times today's annual energy consumption. The IEA projections are similar.[8]

However, despite these tremendous potential benefits, a national drive for energy efficiency may prove excruciatingly difficult. India's energy sector is dominated by the government. Fragmented responsibilities among three central government ministries, responsible respectively for coal, power, and petroleum and natural gas, and the state governments, responsible for producing electricity, make coherent policy almost impossible. As we will see again in the discussion of climate change in chapter 10, even benign change creates powerful political losers, and this is especially true in a sector so dominated by subsidies.

The public sector is still the dominant player in India's energy industry. The Oil and National Gas Corporation (ONGC), the government's oil exploration and production enterprise, is one of the most profitable companies in India and accounts for more than 78 percent of India's oil and gas production.[9] A majority of India's refineries are owned by the Indian Oil Corporation (IOC), one of the 20 largest petroleum companies in the world, which features on the Fortune 200 list. The Gas Authority of India Ltd. (GAIL) is the leading gas transmission and marketing firm in India and is one of the ten most profitable companies in the country. Together ONGC, IOC, and GAIL form three of the crown jewels of the Indian government's public-sector undertakings.

The Bharatiya Janata Party (BJP) government, soon after the turn of the century, tried to build up the private energy industry by selling a portion of the assets of the public-sector corporations. The ensuing furor from its own politicians, the opposition, and the state-owned energy sector probably put an end to any thought of privatization for years.

Since then, however, the private sector has become a more important player, as private companies expanded their presence in parts of the energy market, following the pattern we have already seen in telecommunications and air travel. Private energy companies are most prominent in refining. Reliance Industries Ltd. operates the third-largest refinery in the world, is a major exporter, and is constructing another major refinery. Essar has recently entered the refining business and now operates India's second-largest refinery at Vadinar in Gujarat. Private operators, including both of these companies, are also creating a presence in the "upstream," or exploration and production, business.

The government's New Exploration Licensing Policy (NELP) was intended to standardize the process of awarding exploration licenses, so as to bring foreign and private companies into the process on a basis acceptable both to them and to the Indian government. It has a mixed record. Reliance and Essar have been awarded several blocks; Reliance then had certain licenses lifted for nonperformance. Private oil companies complained about the government's decision not to factor in technical expertise for shallow-water sites. This may help to explain the low response in the bidding round that concluded in early 2008: more than 20 percent of the blocks were unbid, and one-third had only one bid.[10]

The key policy tool is pricing, which is being asked to accomplish contradictory goals. In 1998, India began phasing out its Administered Pricing Mechanism, which subsidized the prices of four politically sensitive commodities (including kerosene) in what was supposed to be a four-year transition to market-based prices.[11] Continued steep increases in the price of crude oil undermined this goal and led to a continuation of some of the key subsidies, while paradoxically leaving India with higher consumer prices for many products than other Asian countries.[12] As oil prices hit a record high of more than $140 per barrel in the summer of 2008, the contradictory pressures on price policy grew even more acute. At first, the newspapers were full of stories about government efforts to keep consumer prices down and to take the pressure off the public-sector companies by canceling the import duty on crude oil. Yet in a matter of weeks, due to mounting pressure from state-owned energy companies, the government hiked petrol, diesel, and kerosene prices for the first time in years. Falling oil prices a few months later created political pressures to reduce domestic selling prices again.

The government is caught in a classic squeeze between its own fiscal exigencies, those of the public-sector companies, and its fear of political retribution for raising consumer prices. The subsequent fall in oil prices eased the problem but did not eliminate it, and the prospect of volatile international oil prices will bedevil India's internal market for the foreseeable future. Ultimately, the efficiency scenarios that show such remarkable savings in energy rely on prices to change people's behavior. Politically, it is always easier to look overseas for solutions to this problem. It is a conclusion Americans will find all too familiar.

INDIA'S INTERNATIONAL STRATEGY

India's energy needs have influenced strategic thinking and even the bureaucratic structure of India's national security policy. The Indian Ocean, India's energy highway, has assumed major importance in India's strategic thinking. The navy's standing as a guarantor of national security has similarly risen. As we will see in the next chapter, much of the Indian military's investment in power projection and equipment is intended to build up its naval capabilities. Among the regions that India has paid special attention to in its "outer security perimeter," the Middle East is its major energy supplier and Southeast Asia is the site of important Indian energy investments.

India's international energy policy aims above all at diversifying energy supplies and making them more secure. It uses three principal tools: contracting for long-term supplies; expanding India's ownership stake in international upstream energy assets; and using India's refinery capacity and exports of product to build up relationships with energy producers. In principle, India's policy also calls for building cooperative relationships with potential competitors in the energy market, principally other Asian countries and especially China. This aspect of policy is less well defined, and the international institutions through which it might be carried out are not well adapted to the task.

India's energy imports come primarily from the Middle East, where 67 percent of its oil supplies originate. (See figure 3.1.) Saudi Arabia is its largest supplier. The top six suppliers (figure 3.2) account for 80 percent of India's oil imports. Virtually all of India's regularly contracted supply of liquid natural gas (LNG) comes from the Middle East (Qatar). India also imports modest amounts of oil from Sudan, Russia, Malaysia, and a sprinkling of Latin American and other African countries.[13] India's critical oil transit routes are equally concentrated. Some 60 percent of India's imported oil in 2005 passed through the Strait of Hormuz, and 24 percent came through the Indian Ocean (including supplies coming around the Cape of Good Hope). India's refining capacity is heavily concentrated on India's west coast, fairly close to the

Figure 3.1 Sources of India's Oil Imports, 2004–2005 (in percentages)

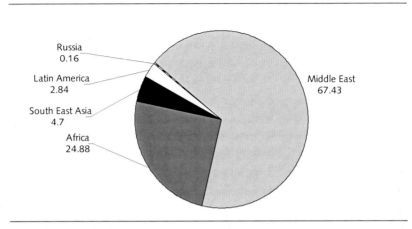

Russia
0.16

Latin America
2.84

South East Asia
4.7

Africa
24.88

Middle East
67.43

Source of data: Planning Commission, Government of India, Integrated Energy Policy, http://planningcommission.nic/in/reports/genrep/rep_intengy.pdf, 59.

Figure 3.2 India's Major Oil Suppliers, 2004–2005

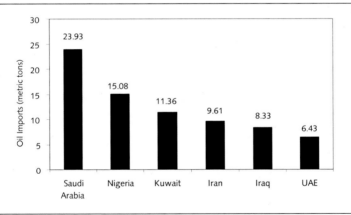

Source of data: Planning Commission, Government of India, Integrated Energy Policy, http://planningcommission.nic/in/reports/genrep/rep_intengy.pdf, 59.

Pakistan border; and virtually all its functioning capacity to handle liquid natural gas is on the west coast.[14]

Adding new suppliers has been a priority for Indian policymakers, and they are willing to deal with regimes that the United States and other countries find objectionable. Iran, for example, looms large in

India's energy strategy: it now supplies about 10 percent of India's oil imports, has the potential to supply large quantities of gas, and is located between India and potential suppliers in Central Asia. Dealings with Iran figure in all elements of India's energy strategy—long-term contracts, pipelines, reciprocal upstream/downstream investments, and cultivating governments in key energy supplier countries. The United States has not made an issue of India's energy purchases from Iran as such, but its political ties with Tehran and proposed pipeline investment have caused heartburn in Washington. The raw numbers of actual and potential energy supply will make even India's most pro-American officials reluctant to pull back from the energy relationship with Iran.

In trying to add new suppliers or investment partners, India has approached anyone with oil to find or sell. Nigeria is India's second-largest supplier, with 16 percent of the market. Sudan and Myanmar are more recent additions to the list. Their importance as suppliers is nowhere near that of the top six sources, but the importance that Indian officials attach to increasing the number of suppliers and spreading out their geographic base is considerable.

With both old and new suppliers, India's energy officials see long-term supply relationships and pipelines as a way of reducing price fluctuations and ensuring that supplies remain available. So far, the only successful long-term contract has been for LNG. India has negotiated contracts with Qatar and Iran, but only the Qatar contract is being implemented. The difficulty in implementing the other contracts and in negotiating or extending new ones stems from the challenge of setting a price in today's volatile energy market. The Qatar contract has a price formula that has become quite advantageous to India. India would like to match this price in other contracts, but it is well below the norm in today's market, and the contract will probably not be extended without significant modification.[15]

An even stronger mechanism for strengthening the security of gas supply lies in pipelines, which can be linked to supply contracts. One study of the views of Indian security officials found a consensus that pipelines, while not without risk, are the best potential tool for securing gas supply.[16] Indeed, some energy sources are out of reach for the Indian market unless the transportation infrastructure is created.

Three pipelines are under active consideration. Most problematic from the U.S. perspective is the proposed Iran-Pakistan-India pipeline that would span all three countries, with an estimated cost of $7.4 billion for infrastructure. This project has been in some stage of negotiation since the mid-1990s. If fully implemented, it would supply India with 90 million cubic meters of LNG per day. By way of comparison, this would be equal to nearly 20 percent of India's anticipated 2030 consumption as estimated by the Energy Information Agency.[17] There are many obstacles to moving ahead with this proposal, including major differences over the gas price and concerns about the security of supply coming through Pakistan. The complicated politics of this proposal are spelled out more fully in chapter 8. The important point to note here is that Iran's potential contribution to solving India's energy problems is large. The project may fail for inherent commercial reasons, but if these problems can be overcome, the U.S. will not have an easy time deflecting India from it.

The other pipeline proposals are less politically controversial with the United States, but have implementation problems. There have been proposals for a 1,830-kilometer undersea pipeline from Qatar. Undersea construction has long been considered too expensive to compete with the land route from Iran, but new technologies may bring the cost down and interest has recently revived.[18] Another proposed pipeline would originate in Turkmenistan and cross Afghanistan and Pakistan before reaching India. Its price tag and capacity are broadly comparable to the Iran pipeline. The political risk for India is substantial: the government of Turkmenistan has not been a consistent supporter of the idea, and crossing both Afghanistan and Pakistan incorporates a significant risk of sabotage. Yet another proposal that India was actively pursuing involves a pipeline from Myanmar, possibly crossing Bangladesh. This has been thwarted by both the anti-India political environment in Bangladesh and Chinese gas politics in Burma.

The second international tool for securing energy from a diversified basket of suppliers lies in upstream investments: expanded exploration and production overseas, with an equity stake in the facilities involved. Most of India's international upstream investments have been in oil. The principal state-owned upstream operator is the international branch of ONGC (ONGC Videsh Ltd., or OVL). As of June 2008, OVL had participated in 29 exploration and production projects in 15 countries, of which 9 projects in 6 countries had been acquired in the two preceding years alone. OVL is either the operator or a joint operator in 12 of these projects. Many of the countries involved have difficult business environments (such as Nigeria and Iraq) or have serious policy problems with the United States (Sudan, Cuba, Iran, Myanmar, and Syria). As the lead public-sector operator, OVL is also the one most frequently working in countries where India's energy relationship is dominated by the government, such as Russia.[19]

India's other international upstream operators work on a much smaller scale. Most of them are primarily "downstream" companies—those devoted mainly to refining and processing—seeking to round out their portfolios by adding an upstream element. The most important is Reliance, which has upstream investments in somewhat more conventional locations—Yemen, Oman and Malaysia. Taken together, India's upstream investments were estimated to produce 120,000 barrels per day in 2006, equivalent to about 5 percent of India's total oil and gas imports.[20] India's oil producers hope this will increase. IOC, a public-sector company best known for its refining and retail operations in India, aims to bring in 2 million tons of crude oil per year from its overseas holdings by 2012. It is looking in Africa and the former Soviet Union, and it is interested in purchasing not just concessions but a company with the talent and track record to exploit them.[21]

These investments have been a commercial success but have not yet achieved the scale to make them a major contributor to India's energy security. Indian companies' assets still represent a small percentage of global energy assets; one estimate puts India's share at 1 percent.

Some have argued that the strategy of seeking energy security by acquiring a stake in overseas and production facilities is based on the assumption that Indian-owned assets will be dedicated to the Indian market. Thus far, this has proved only partly true. In some cases, notably ONGC's holdings in Sakhalin, distance from India makes direct sales expensive, so ONGC's share of production can swapped for oil from nearer sources. There has been some tendency for overseas upstream operators to sell their overseas production to their own refineries in India, though other Indian purchasers do not necessarily get preferential treatment.[22] Perhaps the most painful example of the shortcomings of this strategy is in Myanmar. A 30 percent stake in the Shwe field by two state-owned Indian companies, ONGC and GAIL, did not prevent Myanmar from contracting to sell the gas from that field to China. India's offers of soft loans to sweeten the deal were apparently bested by China, and a pipeline to China is under discussion instead of the one India had hoped to build via Bangladesh.

India's upstream strategy becomes more interesting when joined to its international downstream strategy. Energy products have become India's largest export, accounting for $18 billion, or nearly 15 percent of India's goods exports, in 2006–2007.[23] Although there is refining capacity in the public sector, Reliance is in the process of building what will be the largest refinery in the world. The capacity of India's refineries and their ability to handle heavy and sour crudes is an attractive asset in setting up two-way energy deals with countries that would like to import product refined in India. The largest customer for Indian petroleum products is Abu Dhabi.

Reciprocal investment commitments are part of this strategy as well. One example is Russia. India has a 20 percent stake in the Sakhalin-1 oilfields in Siberia and is now negotiating to partner with Russian oil giant Rosneft for a block in the Sakhalin-3 field as well. In return, Rosneft will invest in India's downstream industries, such as small grassroots refineries, modernization and upgrading of refineries, gas-based petrochemical plants, and gas processing plants including liquefaction plants in India, Russia, and third countries.[24] Similarly, ONGC and the Hinduja Group are negotiating to join the development of the South Pars phase-12 gas field and the Azadegan oil field in Iran. ONGC has offered Iranian firms an equity stake in its proposed refinery and a liquefied natural gas terminal in Southern India. ONGC plans to build a 300,000 barrels-a-day refinery in Andhra Pradesh and a 7.5-million-ton LNG terminal in Karnataka. It is no coincidence that the top executive leading the private-sector Hinduja Group in its energy ventures is Subir Raha, the revered ex-chairman of ONGC who made it India's most profitable company.[25] These arrangements are still under discussion and may take a long time to mature, but they illustrate the kinds of linkages that both private and public companies in India are trying to put together with the tacit backing of the government.

Reliance is also building refineries overseas, with current or planned facilities in Iran and Yemen. Essar and two public companies, IOC and ONGC, are likewise building international downstream capacity. Besides their contribution to energy security, these investments give the parent companies an outlet that is not constrained by Indian price regulations.

The government has sought to reinforce these corporate activities with strong government-to-government ties in energy-producing countries. It has made a point of trying to establish productive energy trade and investment relations with as many countries as possible. These include a number of countries with which the United States has serious political difficulties. Saddam-era Iraq was a prime example. India participated in the oil-for-food program to the tune of $1.1 billion per year. More recent examples include Iran, Burma, and Sudan. India's commitment to diversifying energy supply will make India unwilling to heed U.S. pleas to cut back on relations with these regimes.

Cross-border sales of electricity receive little public attention, but they could be a significant means of diversifying India's energy supply. India currently buys electricity from Bhutan and Nepal. The amounts are small—a total of 1.8 billion kilowatts in 2005, or less than half a percent of national consumption—but locally significant. In the past, efforts to finance dams in Nepal based on massive potential exports to India have foundered over concerns about excessive concentration of Nepal's financial risk and environmental dangers. A World Bank study urged India to reexamine the situation, noting that by constructing run-of-the-river generating plants, it could mitigate the environmental and diffuse the financial risk. Similarly, Tajikistan, Kyrgyzstan, and Turkmenistan have hydropower potential far in excess of their current demand, though getting it to India would involve going through Afghanistan and Pakistan, raising the same security and political problems as the pipeline.[26]

One persistent theme in India's international energy policy is competition with China. China's overseas strategy resembles India's in its emphasis on diversification and on acquiring an ownership stake in producing assets around the globe. Indian strategists talk about the importance of developing a cooperative relationship with China, under which both would ensure orderly access to the world's energy market rather than trying to undercut one another.

Thus far, both have paid lip service to this ideal, but the list of cooperative ventures is short. A 2006 Memorandum of Understanding was supposed to set forth the rules for Chinese-Indian joint ventures in the energy field. The only places where such a joint venture is in place, however, are Syria, where a Chinese-Indian partnership bought the assets of Petro Canada, and Colombia, where Chinese firm Sinopec and ONGC formed a joint-venture company.

On the other hand, there is a growing list of places where a Chinese public-sector company has beaten an Indian counterpart to the finish line. Besides Myanmar, mentioned above, Chinese companies bought

Royal Dutch/Shell assets in Angola, outbid India in Sudan, and bested IOC and ONGC in Nigeria, Ecuador, and Kazakhstan. This last example is especially important because it involves a pipeline, and Central Asia's energy resources generally lack transportation. With India-China energy competition becoming more common, host countries may pit the two against one another. China has also been more prepared than India to throw major government resources into the effort, as for example in its growing aid budget for oil-producing countries in Africa.

The real potential for international cooperation may lie not in individual energy transactions but in the way countries and energy companies approach the overall functioning of oil markets. Despite a tradition of state-dominated economic policy and the dominant position of public-sector companies in its energy economy, India's economic leadership recognizes that owning international energy assets and reciprocal trade and other special arrangements can go only so far in satisfying the country's energy needs. Ultimately, the marketplace will determine whether India's demand for energy is satisfied and how energy is distributed within India.

U.S.-INDIA ENERGY RELATIONS

India's energy policy revolves around balancing efficiency and equity in its domestic market and expanding its international sources of supply. U.S. international energy policy is built on strengthening the market, but the domestic politics of energy in the United States are driven chiefly by the desire for low prices. In both countries, these policies involve internal contradictions that are almost impossible to reconcile. Despite contradictory political pressures, both countries share a strong interest in reliable international energy markets and safe transit of energy resources across the world's oceans and pipelines.

Leaders of both countries often refer to this common interest, though Indians are more likely to stress reliability of supply and Americans the functioning of the marketplace. They have tried to turn energy into a significant strand of their bilateral relationship. The principal instrument for this has been an "Energy Dialogue," launched in 2005 between the two governments, which periodically brings officials together to explore concrete areas of cooperation.

The energy dialogue has created good working relationships at the top and at senior working levels of the two governments. In a pattern familiar to anyone who has worked in government, the senior representatives, the U.S. secretary of energy and the deputy chairman of India's Planning Commission, use the energy dialogue meetings to force decisions on recalcitrant issues and to develop common strategies for dealing with complex bureaucracies on both sides. Much of the work is done in five working groups, covering oil and gas; coal; electric power and energy efficiency; new technology and renewables; and civil nuclear cooperation. Private companies participate. The working groups have generated real collaboration at the technical level, especially on better and cleaner utilization of coal. They have opened the way to U.S.-funded feasibility studies for potentially important energy-related projects. India has one of the more active cooperative relationships with the U.S. Department of Energy, albeit not at the same level as China and Japan.

Side by side with the energy dialogue and its bilateral working groups, India has participated in two high-profile research ventures with the United States. Both seemed prestigious and promising at the start; both have run into funding problems that raised questions about the U.S. commitment and ultimately about where India fits into this type of international collaboration.

India invested in the Department of Energy's FutureGen project, launched in 2003, which originally aimed to develop a zero-emissions coal-based generating plant and which included private-sector companies as well as a number of countries as partners. After a promising start, FutureGen ran into major cost overruns, and a restructuring has been announced, which may transform it from one major project into several smaller ones. India had been unhappy at the project managers' reluctance to test this design with the high-ash coal common in India; the announcements about the restructuring do not make clear where the foreign participants will fit in.

The International Thermonuclear Experimental Reactor (ITER) is not a U.S. project but a partnership of six parties, including both the United States and India. It is intended to demonstrate the scientific and technical feasibility of fusion energy. The United States has been somewhat ambivalent about it for some time and in early 2008 cut its funding.

The energy dialogue is oriented toward work that is important but technical. It is not set up to deal with the major policy issues that energy supply and high energy prices raise for both governments. The substance of the U.S.-India energy dialogue covers efficiency issues that can shape future energy demand. However, India is unlikely to give the United States or any other foreign country a seat at the table where decisions on pricing and subsidies are made. The dialogue is not set up to deal with the structure of international cooperation. The question of security of supply would under the best of circumstances be a difficult one, incorporating as it does the tensions between market and nonmarket mechanisms and the problem of trading with politically controversial suppliers.

More fundamentally, there are limits to what a bilateral dialogue can do to address energy issues. The energy market is global, and the big energy issues need to be addressed in a larger regional or global context. This dimension is largely absent from the U.S.-India energy dialogue, and this is where both countries need to start looking for new mechanisms for cooperation and crisis management.

The major forum where consumer countries deliberate on this type of policies is the IEA, and, as noted above, India is not a member. Founded in 1974 in response to the OPEC oil price increases, the IEA carries out a comprehensive program of energy cooperation aimed at improving the response to supply disruptions, promoting energy policies that are rational in the global context, operating information systems, and encouraging alternative sources of energy and better stewardship of the environment. Two of its members are major energy exporters. The treaty establishing the IEA, the Agreement on an International Energy Program, made membership in the Organization for Economic Cooperation and Development (OECD) a requirement for membership in the IEA. This was logical in 1974, when the major oil importers were developed market economies and they already had an institutional link through their OECD membership. In today's world, it is an anachronism.

Asia has been a priority area for the IEA's work with nonmembers, including research programs, technical and policy workshops, and support for information systems and other statistical materials. Energy security and response to supply disruptions have been a particular focus of IEA's outreach to Asia. India was the first country to sign a comprehensive cooperation agreement, the Declaration of Cooperation, in 1998. Since then, China, Russia and ASEAN (the Association of Southeast Asian Nations) have followed suit. Cooperative efforts of this sort keep Indian energy officials in close touch with counterparts in Asia and in the rest of the world, and provide an opportunity for exchange of technical data and policy thinking. This halfway house does not integrate India into the IEA energy security system, however.[27]

India participates in other international forums for discussing energy diversification and security as well. Its ministers regularly attend the International Energy Forum (IEF), an organization with 70 member countries that promotes dialogue between producers and consumers, with the participation of executives from energy companies. The IEF has tried to develop a data exchange designed to add transparency to energy markets, the Joint Oil Data Initiative, but it has had difficulty getting data from members. India hosted one of the IEF's Asian roundtables.[28] India participated in the two G-8 summit meetings at which energy was a significant theme, at Gleneagles in 2005 and at St. Petersburg in 2006. It also belongs to the Asia Pacific Partnership on Clean Development and Climate, a smaller grouping that focuses on developing new clean-energy technologies. The other Asian regional forums, the Energy Working Group of Asia Pacific Economic Cooperation (APEC) and the ASEAN Energy Group (affiliated with the "ASEAN Plus 3"), are offshoots of regional groups to which India does not belong.

India has been looking for forms of Asian energy cooperation that can prevent destructive competition between itself and China. Coordinating domestic energy policies has little appeal, though there may be interest in exchanging views on "best practices" applicable to particular sectors. In the IEF, India has looked for measures that producers and consumers can take together, including reciprocal upstream and downstream investments. Indian energy analysts have focused on measures that might moderate swings in the market. They have suggested establishing a regional benchmark crude oil that can serve as a pricing yardstick and perhaps create counterpressures to eliminate the price premium that is common in Asian energy markets. Another proposal is the creation of regional storage facilities capable of handling up to 30 percent of daily volume in Asian trading to smooth the delivery process. Similarly, deficiencies in infrastructure or transportation might lend themselves to cooperative solutions.

Creation and management of strategic petroleum reserves could be another form of Asian energy cooperation. A reserve equivalent to 90 days' net imports, through a strategic reserve and/or the imposition of reserve requirements on industry, is a requirement for IEA membership.[29] At present, Japan and Korea are the only Asian IEA members, and both maintain substantial reserves. Other Asian countries have begun creating reserves, but lack a system for regional management of supply disruptions. India has decided to create a strategic reserve and has identified locations for it but is starting at a relatively low level (15 days' supply). China has begun creating a reserve whose goal is to reach 90 days' supply eventually. Cooperation in the drawdown or management of these reserves might be a very useful device for increasing regional energy security, though it is not likely to get very far until the countries of the region have established a more comparable level of strategic stocks.[30]

LOOKING AHEAD

Energy figures in U.S.-India relations in two ways: as a factor in India's economy, and as a subject in need of international cooperation. On this second dimension, the international machinery falls short of the task. Including India fully in international energy cooperation should be a priority for U.S.-India energy relations in the future. The United States is well aware of the need. As we will see in chapter 10, it has been looking for a formula that would bring India into the IEA, as part of its effort to bring emerging market countries to a greater role in the world's economic institutions. The United States and India should join forces in looking for mechanisms to supplement this, especially on the Asian regional level. This can provide a valuable bridge between bilateral and international cooperation in a field where India and the United States have very similar interests.

NOTES

1. Planning Commission, Government of India, *Integrated Energy Policy: Report of the Expert Committee,* August 2006, http://planningcommission .nic.in/reports/genrep/rep_intengy.pdf, 66.

2. See Paul E. Simons, Deputy Assistant Secretary of State for Economic and Business Affairs, "Energy Security as a Global Partnership," in *eJournal USA,* http://usinfo.state.gov/journals/ites/0706/ijee/simons.htm.

3. Energy Statistics, International Energy Agency, "2005 Energy Balances for India," http://www.iea.org/Textbase/stats/balancetable.asp?COUNTRY _CODE=IN (accessed May 13, 2008); Sustainable Development Department, South Asia Region, World Bank, *Potential and Prospects for Regional Energy Trade in the South Asia Region,* (Washington, D.C.: World Bank, June 2007), http://go.worldbank.org/5ELYB9XXX0 (or http://www-wds.worldbank. org/external/default/WDSContentServer/WDSP/IB/2007/11/21/000310607

_20071121125527/Rendered/PDF/415820SAR1Energy1Trade1Nov10701PU
BLIC1.pdf).

4. Leena Srivastava, "India's Energy Sector" (paper presented at conference
on India's Energy Sector: Where Economics Meets Strategy, Center for Strategic and International Studies, Washington, D.C., July 11, 2008).

5. Export Import Data Bank, Ministry of Commerce and Industry, Government of India, http://commerce.nic.in/eidb/default.asp, accessed June 3,
2008.

6. International Energy Agency, *World Energy Outlook 2007: China and India Insights* (Paris: IEA, 2007), 168.

7. Derived from Planning Commission, Government of India, *Integrated
Energy Policy*, 19-20, http://planningcommission.nic.in/reports/genrep/
rep_intengy.pdf; Leena Srivastava, "National Energy Map for India: Technol-
ogy Vision 2030: Summary for Policy-makers," The Energy and Resources
Institute (TERI) and Office of the Principal Scientific Adviser, Government
of India (New Delhi, 2007), http://www.teriin.org/projects/Summary.pdf;
International Energy Agency, *World Energy Outlook 2007: China and India
Insights*, Summary 8, main report 492; Sustainable Development Department,
South Asia Region, World Bank, *Potential and Prospects for Regional Energy
Trade in the South Asia Region*, http://go.worldbank.org/5ELYB9XXX0, 7.

8. Srivastava, "National Energy Map for India: Technology Vision 2030,"
http://www.teriin.org/projects/Summary.pdf, 14; International Energy Agency, *World Energy Outlook 2007: China and India Insights*, 600–603.

9. Oil and Natural Gas Corporation, *Profile, Oil and Natural Gas Corporation
Ltd., India, 2008–2009*, June 2008, http://www.ongcindia.com/profile_new
.asp.

10. Ted Jones, "Energy Reform" (presentation at conference on India's Energy
Sector: Where Economics Meets Strategy, Center for Strategic and Interna-
tional Studies, Washington, D.C., July 11, 2008); Ministry of Petroleum and
Natural Gas, Government of India, "Notice Inviting Offers for Exploration for
Oil and Natural Gas under the New Exploration Licensing Program, Seventh
Round (NELP-VII)," December 27, 2007, http://petroleum.nic.in/nelp1.pdf.

11. Neha Misra, Ruchika Chawla, and Leena Srivastava, "Towards Effective
Petroleum Subsidies," *Energy Security Insights* 3, issue 1 (April 2008), http://
bookstore.teriin.org/docs/newsletters/Energy-Security-3 (1).pdf.

12. See Neha Misra, Ruchika Chawla, Leena Srivastava, and R. K. Pachauri,
"*Petroleum Pricing in India: Balancing Efficiency and Equity*, (New Delhi:
TERI, 2005), http://bookstore.teriin.org/book_inside.php?material_id=389,
7–11; and Dagmar Graczyk, "Petroleum Product Pricing in India: Where
Have All the Subsidies Gone?" Working Paper, International Energy Agency,
Focus on Asia Pacific, October 2006, http://www.iea.org/Textbase/work/2006/
gb/papers/Petroleum_Product_Pricing.pdf.

13. Figures are for 2004–2005. Planning Commission, Government of India,
Integrated *Energy Policy*, http://planningcommission.nic.in/reports/genrep/
rep_intengy.pdf, 59.

14. Bethany Danyluk, Juli A. MacDonald, and Ryan Tuggle, *Energy Futures in Asia: Perspectives on India's Energy Security Strategy and Policies* (report prepared by Booz Allen Hamilton for Director, Net Assessment, Office of the Secretary of Defense, June 2007), 3-3-5.

15. Rajnish Goswami, Wood Mackenzie, interview with author, London, October 5, 2007.

16. Danyluk, MacDonald, and Tuggle, *Energy Futures in Asia*, 4–30.

17. Ali Mostashari, "The Political Economy of the Iran-Pakistan-India Gas Pipeline," *Iran Analysis Quarterly* 4, no. 1 (January-March 2007): 26–33; U.S. Energy Information Agency, "International Energy Annual 2004," *Energy Report* (Washington, D.C., updated 2006), cited in Danyluk, MacDonald, and Tuggle, *Energy Futures in Asia*, 2–6.

18. Indrani Bagchi, "India Eyes Underwater Pipeline," *Times of India*, May 12, 2008, http://timesofindia.indiatimes.com/articleshow/msid-3030893 ,prtpage-1.cms; Sustainable Development Department, South Asia Region, World Bank, *Potential and Prospects for Regional Energy Trade in the South Asia Region*, http://go.worldbank.org/5ELYB9XXX0, 61.

19. Oil and Natural Gas Corporation, *Annual Report 2006–07*, New Delhi, http://www.ongcindia.com/download/annual_report06_07.pdf, 24–26.

20. Danyluk, MacDonald, and Tuggle, *Energy Futures in Asia*, 4–17.

21. Interview with B. M. Bansal, Director for Business Development, Indian Oil Corporation, quoted in "Indian Oil Sets Aside $3 Bn for Overseas Acquisition," *Bloomberg/Mumbai*, December 19, 2007, http://www.business-standard .com/general/printpage.php?autono=308015.

22. Danyluk, MacDonald, and Tuggle, *Energy Futures in Asia*, 4–21.

23. Export Import Data Bank, Department of Commerce, Government of India, http://commerce.nic.in/eidb/ecom.asp (accessed May 2, 2008).

24. "Energy deals between India, Russia by Feb: Deora," *Times of India*, November 27, 2007, http://timesofindia.indiatimes.com/World/Rest_of_World/ Energy_deals_between_India_Russia_by_Feb_Deora/articleshow/2574105 .cms.

25. Naxal Watch, comment on "India's ONGC Videsh, Hindujas Fail to Clinch Iran Deal," IntelliBriefs, comment posted January 07, 2008, http://intellibriefs .blogspot.com/2008/01/indias-ongc-videsh-hindujas-fail-to.html

26. Central Intelligence Agency, "India," *World Factbook*, https://www.cia .gov/library/publications/the-world-factbook/print/in.html, accessed August 28, 2008; Sustainable Development Department, South Asia Region, World Bank, *Potential and Prospects for Regional Energy Trade in the South Asia Region*, http://go.worldbank.org/5ELYB9XXX0, 1, 9.

27. Nobuo Tanaka, Director, International Energy Agency, "The Next 10 Years Are Critical—The World Energy Outlook Makes the Case for Stepping up Co-operation with China and India to Address Global Energy Challenges, (press release following the release of the IEA's *World Energy Outlook 2007*), November 7, 2007, http://www.iea.org/Textbase/press/pressdetail .asp?PRESS_REL_ID=239.

28. International Energy Forum Secretariat, "The Joint Oil Data Initiative," *Newsletter,* April 2008, http://www2.iefs.org.sa/IEFS%20Newsletters/NL_11th.pdf, 22.

29. International Energy Agency, *IEA Response System for Oil Supply Emergencies* (Paris: IEA, 2007,) http://www.iea.org/Textbase/nppdf/free/2007/fs_response_system.pdf.

30. Ivo J. H. Bozon, Subbu Narayanswamy, and Vipul Tuli, "Securing Asia's Energy Future," *McKinsey Quarterly,* no. 2 (2005), http://www.mckinseyquarterly.com/article_print.aspx?L2=3&L3=49&ar=1599. See also Yo Osumi, "China and India's Energy Development in Global Perspective" (presentation at IEA workshop, Beijing, March 2006), http://www.iea.org/textbase/speech/2006/yo_apec.pdf; Norio Ehara, "IEA Collaboration with India and China on Oil Security" (presentation at IEA conference on Oil Supply Disruption Management Issues, Siem Reap, Cambodia, April 2004), http://www.iea.org/textbase/work/2004/cambodia/bj_session3.2-Ehara%20presentation.pdf; and Vijay Sakhuja, "A Regional Approach to Strategic Oil Reserves," *Opinionasia,* December 25, 2006, http://www.opinionasia.org/Aregionalapproachtostrategicoilreserves.

4

SHAPING A SECURITY RELATIONSHIP

In April 2001, Foreign Minister Jaswant Singh of India, visiting Washington for the first time since the George W. Bush administration took office, called on the U.S. national security adviser, and President Bush dropped in on the meeting. The conversation turned to missile defense, one of the new administration's major defense priorities. To the surprise and delight of the administration, Singh welcomed the idea, especially the move away from the Cold War system of defense based on Mutual Assured Destruction.[1]

A few weeks later, the Indian government publicly welcomed the statement of U.S. national security policy the day after its proclamation by President Bush in a speech announcing the U.S. decision to develop a missile defense system. India was one of only three countries to give this move an early boost. The statement by the Ministry of External Affairs reserved most of its praise for the planned unilateral reductions in the U.S. nuclear arsenal and for the shift in strategy away from Mutual Assured Destruction, rather than for missile defense as such. Regardless of the careful drafting, Singh's receptivity to the concept and the prompt and warm statement publicly opened the door to a warmer relationship with the United States. A week later, the United States sent Deputy Secretary of State Richard Armitage on a special trip to brief India about where missile defense fit into U.S. strategic thinking, a trip from which China was pointedly excluded.

Since then, the transition in U.S.-India security relations has accelerated. The reflexive suspicion that characterized the U.S. security establishment's attitude toward India during the Cold War has been replaced by a presumption that security cooperation with India is valuable and normal. India has moved from the periphery of U.S. strategic concerns to a more central position. India's attitude of concern and wariness toward the United States has been replaced by serious engagement. The economic ties examined in the last two chapters laid the foundation for the new U.S.-India connection; the security dialogue discussed in this chapter and the revival of nuclear and high-tech trade, discussed in the next chapter, are the best evidence of how these ties have been reoriented.

This chapter begins by reviewing the strategic context of the new security relationship, first for India and then for the United States. It then examines the content and structure of the new U.S.-India security relationship, focusing in particular on joint operations and exercises, defense trade, and counterterrorism operations. The establishment of a serious security relationship is well under way, and the fundamental convergence of U.S. and Indian security interests that made this possible is likely to carry it forward. How far it will go depends in part on how both countries manage expectations, an issue that will come up in greater depth in the next chapter.

INDIA'S STRATEGIC GOALS

The Indian government rarely issues statements of grand strategy. Its national security policy has been based on dominating South Asia, countering any major threat that intrudes into this space and deterring major threats from beyond.[2] Historically, India has behaved as a continental power. Its wars have been primarily land engagements (with China and Pakistan). Its military structure reinforces this tendency: the army is by far India's largest military service, accounting for nearly half the defense budget, and has been the dominant one bureaucratically as well. India spends a relatively low 2.3 percent of its GDP on defense, but it has made substantial capital investments since the mid-1990s.[3]

Indian strategic policy starts from the premise that India's immediate neighborhood—the inner ring of its security environment—is a dangerous place. Senior security managers often make the point that their greatest national security challenge stems from internal insurgencies connected to problems in their neighbors' territory. Pride of place goes to Pakistan. Support for the insurgency in Kashmir is the traditional problem, but in the years since India and Pakistan started their most recent peace process, major terrorist incidents elsewhere in India have become the most painful manifestation. The three-day attacks in Mumbai in November 2008 that left more than 170 people dead are a classic case in point.

Weak governance and inadequate border management in Bangladesh feed the complex mosaic of ethnic troubles in India's northeast and create a risk of illegal immigration. Indian security managers believe these Bangladesh-based problems and domestic organizations that have engaged in terrorism receive at least indirect support either from Pakistani intelligence or from organizations that operate in Pakistan. The Naxalite disturbances in central India have a loose connection with the Maoists who have recently emerged as the main governing party in Nepal. The ethnic conflict in Sri Lanka has not fed insurgency in India in the same way, but the Liberation Tigers of Tamil Eelam assassinated Indian Prime Minister Rajiv Gandhi in 1991, and India's three-year experience maintaining a peacekeeping force there was costly and traumatic for the Indian army. Sri Lanka's conflict sent waves of refugees into southern India, and the insurgents' naval wing, the Sea Tigers, represents a maritime threat right off India's southwest coast. These problems are not looked on as "strategic," but they are a larger day-to-day preoccupation for India than the "strategic" problems.

Pakistan is India's most immediate potential military adversary, with whom India has fought three real wars and one half-war. Historically, the size and configuration of India's armed forces were to a large extent driven by the potential threat from Pakistan. Because of its smaller size, Pakistan relies on asymmetric warfare, including use of insurgents. For the same reason, it has insisted on retaining the option to use nuclear weapons first, unlike India's no-first-use policy.

In the past, India had planned to approach the contingency of a major conflict with Pakistan by cutting the country in two and threatening Pakistan's heartland. With nuclear weapons in play, however, this strategy could risk a Pakistani nuclear response. India and Pakistan have instituted nuclear risk reduction measures intended to reduce the likelihood of war by accident or miscalculation. The striking feature of India's military posture toward Pakistan since 2001 is its forbearance in not responding militarily to terrorist incidents that involved high levels of casualties.

Indian military planning for limited war in a nuclear environment focuses on two ends of the operational spectrum. One is a limited response to future engagements that resemble the Kargil campaign of 1999—short, sudden, intense border clashes.[4] The yearlong mobilization on the border that followed the attacks on India's parliament in December 2001 is an example, though the Indian military felt that this tactic did not serve them well. The other approach, which the Indian army is just putting into operational form, is a kind of "offensive defense" known as Cold Start. This involves creating eight integrated battle groups capable of undertaking a major action without requiring an extensive buildup. The concept is intended to achieve a decisive result quickly in a subnuclear environment, before either Pakistan or the outside world has an opportunity to respond.[5]

India has twice intervened militarily in neighboring countries. In 1971, India's action in response to the impending disintegration of the two-wing Pakistan and the massive flow of refugees that accompanied it helped give birth to independent Bangladesh. In 1987, India sent a peacekeeping force to Sri Lanka on the invitation of its government. It would take a radical deterioration in government authority, together with population movements posing a clear security danger, for India to consider a fresh intervention in one of its nonnuclear neighbors.

These are the most urgent issues facing India's security managers. From the point of view of India's relations with the United States, however, they are the subject of political dialogue rather than strategic or military collaboration. U.S. ties with Pakistan have inhibited U.S.-India relations for years. India has periodically tried to persuade the United States to downgrade relations with Pakistan, but it has little expectation of succeeding. For the United States, heading off a major India-Pakistan military engagement, and limiting the minor ones, is a major objective of policy toward both countries.

The strategic thinking that is most pertinent to India's security relations with the United States starts outside this inner perimeter. Indian strategic thinkers have for years spoken of India's expanded strategic space as extending from the Middle East to Malacca. In this outer circle, India's immediate goal is to protect its lifelines for trade, investment, and energy, both from large strategic threats and from such dangers as terrorism and piracy. This strategic environment is centered on maritime and littoral security, and naval and air power are key. India's large procurement budgets for the navy and air force aim to build up its power projection capability to give India presence and capacity throughout this extended region.[6] Even India's most hawkish security analysts do not foresee circumstances in which India would use it for offensive purposes beyond the subcontinent.[7]

India sees the Indian Ocean as a single strategic environment, with its navy as the dominant littoral force. India does not want to see its primacy challenged. Indian policy has moved away from its earlier quest for arrangements like the Indian Ocean Zone of Peace, which were intended to exclude or limit the presence of the navies of global powers. The defensive mission of U.S. forces in the Indian Ocean, coupled with excellent national and service-to-service relations, have led Indian military planners to look on the U.S. presence as benign.

Naval planners refer to a zone of "positive control," within 500 kilometers of the coast, in which the navy must be capable of sea denial; a zone of "medium control," 500–1,000 kilometers from the coast, in which India can engage potential threats through air and naval power, including submarines; and a more distant zone of "soft control."[8] India's maritime doctrine also highlights nuclear deterrence as a key function, and argues for the eventual introduction of nuclear submarines into the Indian navy.[9] For the air force, power projection is paramount, and China is the primary threat.

India's ability to deal with large-scale humanitarian disasters like the 2004/2005 tsunami is regarded as a critical tool for building regional linkages, including securing regional acceptance of a robust Indian military posture. India's growing political relations with Southeast Asia and Japan are in sync with its military goals. Interestingly, the Indian military's only joint regional command is the Andaman and Nicobar Command, with responsibility for the area to India's southeast. It has developed effective joint interoperability in carrying out its responsibilities for the security of the eastern approaches to India from the Indian Ocean and protecting the eastern parts of India's Exclusive Economic Zone.[10]

The long-term challenge to India's east stems from China, still regarded as its main strategic rival. At the same time, with dramatic improvements in their political and economic ties, India hopes to build a peaceful and profitable relationship. The two countries share a long but generally quiet border in the high Himalayas. India's goal is to prevent a recurrence of the 1962 Chinese surprise attack, and to counter one effectively should prevention fail. India's forces are well trained and well suited to the terrain, but, more fundamentally, both political trends and the rugged, sparsely populated terrain make a conflict in this region quite unlikely.

In the longer term, Indians worry about possible Chinese plans for an eventual military presence in the Indian Ocean. India's official policy statements play down the Chinese threat, but the government is suspicious of Chinese activities in neighboring countries like Burma and Bangladesh as well as Pakistan. Nationalist commentators and other strategic thinkers identify Chinese ambitions in the Indian Ocean as an emerging threat that demands a stronger Indian military posture, including a deterrent arsenal that includes thermonuclear weapons.

The area to India's west is more troublesome, and at least as important in India's strategic outlook. India's dependence on oil imports from the Middle East will rise in the next two decades. China's assistance to Pakistan in building a new port in Gwadar, on the Arabian Sea coast near the Iranian border, is seen as a clear indication that China seeks a presence near the energy lifelines on which both India and China depend. The volatility of the oil-producing countries makes this supply line vulnerable. India's large diaspora of workers in the Persian Gulf region is both a source of remittances and a vulnerability.

India hopes that its security relationship with the United States will help it deal with security challenges outside the inner perimeter of South Asia, both politically and militarily. A former senior military official argues that "India principally wants the [United States] to partner it in shaping the strategic space in the region, which could otherwise be usurped by other regional players."[11] It wants the political stature that comes from being taken seriously by the United States. It wants access to the full range of U.S. technologies, civilian and military, including the opportunity to produce top-of-the-line military equipment originating in the United States. It expects to maintain its other sources of military supply, notably Russia, while examining how much it wants to buy from the United States. It would like to participate in the U.S. supply chain and sees itself as a low-cost producer of parts of systems or software. It wants to understand, and to learn from, U.S. capabilities in the fields of greatest relevance to India's strategic interests.

Indian leaders recognize that U.S. strategic goals in the Indian Ocean largely dovetail with India's. As a result, for the first time since India became independent, they are apparently comfortable making parallel security arrangements in a region where India has always considered itself preeminent. The major short-term contingencies India faces, in the words of one observer, are "Kargils and tsunamis"—short but intense land border engagements and more diffuse humanitarian disasters in which India's military assets become a tool for building a more peaceful and cooperative expanded neighborhood.

U.S. STRATEGIC GOALS

U.S. strategic goals in the region center on China and its future role in Asia, maritime security, and security in the area from the Middle East through the Pakistan/Afghanistan border area, where the United States has a major military role. Of these, the first two have figured importantly in the relationship with India, and the third has been a complication.

Neither Indian nor U.S. security officials cite China as a motivation for their security relationship, and China has figured remarkably little in the two countries' strategic dialogue. The rise of China is "the elephant in the room," however. Both India and the United States see China as a long-term security challenge; neither wants to see Asia dominated by a single country. At the same time, neither wants to exacerbate China's concerns about "encirclement" or treat China as an enemy. U.S. officials speak of encouraging China to develop in a benign fashion, as part of a larger regional and global network, including a robust and friendly India. India, for its part, does not want to be considered a pawn in any other country's relations with China. The rise of China is perhaps the most important long-term question mark about the future of Asia, so it inevitably shapes the context of U.S.-India security relations.

The Middle East and especially the Persian Gulf represent the greatest immediate security worry for the United States. India has major interests in the Gulf and in Iran, but it has not been a shaper of events there. It has had grave misgivings about U.S. policy in the region and turned down a U.S. invitation to station a division in Iraq in 2003. Iran is a particular bone of contention: India's strategic interest in Iran's energy supplies and its preference for avoiding confrontation there contrast with the Clinton and Bush administrations' policy of isolating Iran. The Obama administration's outreach to Iran was welcomed in India, but there are still significant differences in how the United States and India deal with Iran. Nonetheless, shoring up U.S. political and military relations to the immediate east of the Gulf is one of the arguments for strengthening the U.S.-India relationship.

U.S. interest in the security of the Indian Ocean coincides with India's security concerns and has been a subject of both official and unofficial discussions. The U.S. Maritime Strategy released in 2007 by the U.S. Navy, Marine Corps, and Coast Guard specifies that "credible combat power will be continuously postured in the Western Pacific and the Arabian Gulf/Indian Ocean." In other words, the two principal centers of U.S. sea power are both in India's area of strategic interest. Both in its conceptual discussion and in its references to implementation, the strategy document stresses the importance of working with regional powers, through alliances and "informal arrangements." In one arresting phrase, the document asserts that "although our forces can surge when necessary to respond to crises, *trust and cooperation cannot be surged.* They must be built over time so that the strategic interests of the participants are continuously considered while mutual understanding and respect are promoted."[12] (Emphasis in original.) Freedom of navigation, prevention of piracy, countering proliferation of weapons of mass destruction (WMD), and shoring up failing states are priorities for both countries. Especially since 9/11, terrorism is a major preoccupation, as violent groups have made their presence felt along the Indian Ocean littoral in places like Sri Lanka, Malaysia, Indonesia, and Singapore.

India figures prominently in the "Global Maritime Partnership" discussed in recent years especially by senior U.S. Navy officials. The concept is a loosely connected network of countries that share major interests in maritime safety, stopping piracy, preventing nuclear proliferation to rogue states, and humanitarian relief, and have enough experience working together to be capable of responding to a wide range of contingencies as the need arises. It extends beyond the navies of the region to include commercial shipping, both as a source of information on the maritime environment and potentially as a source of lift in times of emergency. It would be a purely voluntary association, without legal or encumbering obligations. The U.S. chief of naval operations, in a 2005 speech at the Naval War College, used the phrase "thousand-ship navy" to describe the idea.[13]

The United States hopes to achieve both operational and strategic goals through its expanded security relations with India. It is looking for interoperability, through common operating experience and if possible through use of common equipment. This applies particularly to the two navies in the Indian Ocean, and the two governments have made a particular point of underlining their desire to cooperate on maritime security. But the idea of partnership through interoperability extends as well to the other services. The United States hopes to learn from India's areas of special expertise and to strengthen India's already considerable skill in peacekeeping operations. It hopes through all these forms of concrete cooperation to increase the mutual confidence between the two defense establishments so as to make possible serious strategic dialogue and cooperation in possible larger-scale future contingencies. It would also like expanded access to Indian military infrastructure; however, the Indian government has not yet signed what Americans look on as a more or less routine agreement on logistical cooperation.

The big prize, which the United States hopes can be brought within reach by working on less glamorous short-term issues, would be to cement U.S.-India policy cooperation on the big issues that affect Asian security and those aspects of global security in which India is playing a role. These include in particular more formal Indian participation in counterproliferation mechanisms. They also include working in parallel, if not together, on peaceful engagement with China.

THE NEW SECURITY RELATIONSHIP

In the Cold War years, U.S.-India security ties were thin, formal, and largely devoid of substance even in the best of times. They were a low priority for both countries. The United States sold modest amounts of military equipment to India, and it conducted regular but limited training and other exchanges. The priority for the United States during most of this period was its alliance with Pakistan, and Pakistani sensitivities impeded U.S. arms sales to India. The period of greatest promise followed the 1962 India-China war. India's shattering defeat at Chinese hands came as a shock to Washington as well, and cast India as a country fighting Communists. But despite prompt U.S. military shipments, and despite India's disappointment at the Soviet response, this episode provided no lasting momentum for expanding U.S.-India defense ties.

The 1965 India-Pakistan War prompted the United States to cancel military supply to both countries. Given Pakistan's greater dependence

on U.S. arms, the action hurt Pakistan far more than India, but it also
sparked Indian doubts about U.S. reliability as a supplier that persist
to this day.

India's principal defense relationship during these years was with
the Soviet Union. In the early 1960s, the Soviet decision to supply India
with its MiG-21 aircraft established the USSR as a supplier of sophisticated equipment. It soon became by far India's largest supplier of imported equipment. Soviet willingness to have some of their equipment
manufactured in India contributed to India's industrial development.

The groundwork for a changed U.S.-India relationship was laid
nearly a decade before the Cold War ended. Two 1983 decisions by the
Reagan administration opened the door: a science and technology cooperation agreement and an offer to sell India TOW anti-tank missiles
and 155 mm howitzers. India decided not to buy either, but the fact
that the United States was willing to approve them showed that policy
was shifting. In 1984, the United States and India signed a Memorandum of Understanding on technology transfers. A few months later,
the United States agreed in principle to work with India on a Light
Combat Aircraft (LCA), the first significant joint defense production
agreement in two decades.[14] Implementation moved excruciatingly
slowly, and approval of export licenses for particular items needed for
this enterprise was difficult.[15] However, it did signal U.S. understanding of the importance that India attached to defense production.

The first comprehensive effort to define a new defense relationship
came with the proposal for army-to-army cooperation put forward
in 1991 by Gen. Claude Kicklighter, the general commanding army
forces at the U.S. Pacific Command. The Kicklighter proposals focused
primarily on consultative mechanisms, strategic dialogue, training and
other exchanges, and visits at both senior and staff levels. The Agreed
Minute continued with this procedural emphasis, providing a framework for considering the stepped-up pace of activities that eventually
followed.[16]

This was followed in 1995 by an Agreed Minute on defense cooperation signed by the two defense ministers, which structured the "getting to know you" phase of defense relations between the United States
and India. It provided for an increasingly comprehensive program of
exercises, of which the most successful, according to one U.S. observer,
involved both nations' Special Forces. There were modest successes in
collaboration on testing and evaluation, and a handful of defense sales

contracts. But real strategic dialogue was slow in developing. Differences in bureaucratic structure and priorities made it hard to mesh the two systems. Most importantly, there were still significant policy barriers to U.S.-India defense relations.

The Indian nuclear test of 1998 and the resultant sanctions brought India-U.S. military cooperation to a halt. Military cooperation was one of the last areas to revive when sanctions were lifted. When this happened, both governments benefited from the extended series of talks between Foreign Minister Jaswant Singh and U.S. Deputy Secretary of State Strobe Talbott that had followed the 1998 test. As we will see in the next chapter, these discussions reached few of the decisions the United States had sought, but they did provide some experience in dealing seriously and candidly with strategic issues at the top levels of government.

The 2001 Indian statement on U.S. missile defense described at the beginning of this chapter encouraged the newly inaugurated Bush administration to continue building up security relations with India. After September 11, India was the first country to offer the United States use of its facilities in its fight against terrorism.[17] In the end, Pakistan's location and its decision to abandon the Taliban government made it the primary regional partner for U.S. operations in Afghanistan, but unlike earlier periods of close U.S.-Pakistan relations, the United States continued to build up ties with India even as it worked with Pakistan. In short order, security became the most active part of the U.S.-India government dialogue. One Indian observer deeply involved in U.S.-India relations commented that the biggest change India observed was the "transformation of the Pentagon." As he and others saw it, the U.S. defense establishment, having been wary of India, became enthusiastic about collaboration.

A June 2005 agreement establishing a "New Framework for the U.S.-India Defense Relationship" set forth a general policy context for this expanding relationship. It cited the two countries' "common belief in freedom, democracy, and the rule of law." It also stipulated four key interests that both countries seek to advance in their defense cooperation: maintaining security and stability; defeating terrorism and violent religious extremism; preventing the spread of weapons of mass destruction and associated materials, data, and technologies; and protecting the free flow of commerce via land, air, and sea-lanes. The United States and India expanded their joint exercises, exchanges, and multinational operations. The proposed program included specific references to counterproliferation, missile defense, disaster relief, and defense trade.[18] Other formal statements put particular emphasis on maritime security.[19]

The expansion of security ties included a formal U.S.-India strategic dialogue, carried out primarily through the Defense Policy Group, chaired by the Indian secretary of defense and his U.S. counterpart, the undersecretary of defense. This was at first a rather stiff and bureaucratic exercise, which had some difficulty moving toward what former undersecretary of defense Douglas Feith referred to as a "strategic conversation."[20] Initially, the group's meetings featured either briefings on global U.S. policies, such as the U.S. defense posture, the war on terror, and missile defense, or discussions of noncontroversial issues connected with the region, such as the situation in the Straits of Malacca and the Indian Ocean. Major common concerns like China, and major areas with potential differences like the Middle East, played relatively little part.

Two operational aspects of the security relationship are an easier way to measure its progress: (1) the pace of exercises and other joint operations, and (2) defense trade, including collaboration on production and research. Where the security relationship is headed, however, will be determined more by the strategic visions of both countries and the degree to which these converge.

Joint exercises between U.S. and Indian forces are now a regular feature of the defense landscape. Since 2002, they have steadily grown in number and sophistication. Naval exercises are the most consistent and the most complex. The "Malabar" series of naval exercises in the Indian Ocean started with basic maneuvers and communication drills, and expanded to include exercises in fleet air defense, antisubmarine warfare, simulated interdiction, and amphibious operations. The 2005 exercise in this series allowed the United States and India to begin interoperability training with aircraft carriers in full strike formation. This marked a substantial increase in complexity and sophistication, though the United States and India have not yet carried out six-week exercises of the sort that are done with NATO allies. As the two navies have worked together, they have also developed enough understanding of each other's operating procedures that the exercise planning process has been greatly simplified.[21]

In April 2007, India and the United States participated in a one-day trilateral naval exercise with Japan. The exercise lacked the technical sophistication of the bilateral exercises, but its multilateral character added a significant new dimension.

The Indian and U.S. air forces have held exercises regularly since 2004. Both forces spent nearly two weeks at the Cope 2006 exercise in India simulating combat and aircraft maintenance procedures. The exercise marked the first time that the United States shared its coveted Airborne Warning and Control System (AWACS) technology with India and trained Indian fighter pilots to use the radar technology.

Armies from both countries have also held regular exercises in counterinsurgency. The bilateral exercise called Yudh Abhyas in Hindi, or "training for war," started in 2002 with a platoon of Indian and U.S. soldiers. It has since ballooned to feature hundreds of troops, including 140 Indians who flew to Hawaii for the exercise in 2006. The United States has been particularly interested in learning from specialized institutions in India such as its mountain and jungle warfare schools.

More unusual but in the long term more significant are joint operations that the two countries have carried out. In 2002, India agreed to escort sensitive U.S. cargoes through the Strait of Malacca. This operation signaled the end of its long-standing opposition to U.S. naval presence in the Indian Ocean. In late 2004 and early 2005, India and the United States worked together to provide relief from the tsunami that struck the Indian Ocean. This was clearly a seminal event for India-U.S. cooperation. The sense of common purpose engendered by this operation is cited, especially in India, as emblematic of the new security relationship. On a more practical note, the United States was impressed with the speedy reaction and professionalism of the Indian forces. The Indians, for their part, took pride in their performance and recognized this as an opportunity to demonstrate India's skill as well as its good intentions to countries around the Indian Ocean, some of whom had previously had grave misgivings about India's growing power-projection capability. At the same time, the operation brought home to Indian planners their weaknesses in medium and heavy lift, and the importance of interoperability with the United States. Since that time, Indian and U.S. military personnel have worked together on other humanitarian missions, such as the deployment of the hospital ship USNS *Mercy* in the summer of 2006.

One of the reasons for the 2002 escort operation was to prevent pirate attacks. Cooperation against piracy to India's west, in the Arabian Sea and Gulf of Aden, has been more complicated. A combination of U.S. bureaucratic structures and Indian sensitivity about how it engages formally with the United States have limited U.S.-India cooperation, even in an area of prime interest to both countries and both navies.

Piracy in these waters began to surge in 2008. The International Maritime Bureau in November 2008 estimated that there had been 92 attacks on ships that year, including 36 hijackings.[22] The principal U.S. mechanism for dealing with piracy in this area is through Combined Task Force 150, a multinational group established during the Afghan military operations of Operation Enduring Freedom, including participation from countries both inside and outside the region. Responsibility for U.S. military operations in the Indian Ocean is currently divided between the Pacific Command, whose area of responsibility includes India and the waters to the east of the India-Pakistan border, and the Central Command, which is responsible for Pakistan and the waters to the west of that same line—what one American observer called "an invisible line of buoys in the water." This structure will become even more complicated as the newly created United States African Command takes on more operational responsibilities. Participation in the task force is through Central Command. Pakistan is a member of the task force and did a stint in command of it. There have been tentative discussions about whether and how India might be connected with the task force's operations, but they have run aground over the complexity of U.S. military command arrangements and sensitivities about India-Pakistan relations. In addition, India prefers working under a United Nations umbrella if it is to be involved in this type of multilateral undertaking.

Meanwhile, India has been actively involved in monitoring piracy operations. In November 2008, Indian naval vessels preempted a would-be pirate attack. That same month the missile destroyer INS *Tabar*, fired upon by what it believed was a pirate "mother ship," destroyed the vessel. Thai maritime authorities and the International Maritime Bureau subsequently announced that the ship was a hijacked civilian vessel, on which the hijackers had apparently positioned a large quantity of ammunition that blew up when the *Tabar* engaged it. This underscores the need for a closer operational relationship among the naval forces patrolling against pirates in the Arabian Sea.

Defense trade is the other highly visible issue in the security relationship. For many Americans, it serves as the easiest yardstick for measuring a major military relationship. After 1980, India diversified its sources of defense equipment, and by the dawn of the new century, Israel emerged as its second-largest source of imported armaments. Some of the most important items India bought from Israel included U.S. components and therefore required U.S. permission. Trade with Israel thus helped open the door to U.S. export licenses.

Indians and Americans have different views of how military supply fits into a broader security relationship. The United States sees it as a normal way to build security relationships. It helps to lock in both interoperability between the two countries' armed services and their institutional relationships. Integrating a U.S.-supplied system creates linkages up and down the military chain of command through training and other joint activities, in ways that benefit both sides and reinforce the service-to-service relationship. In addition, the U.S. government is sensitive to the commercial benefits of defense sales for the U.S. defense industry. Maintaining the health and profitability of the defense industrial base, and in some cases sustaining the export business that keeps production lines going, also affect U.S. government decisions on defense sales.

For India, U.S. willingness to supply sophisticated equipment is an important indicator of whether it looks on India as a serious partner. But India's litmus test works in only one direction. In the way India organizes its military and defense ministry, it tends to look at defense trade as a supply question, separate from training and doctrine. One result of this practice is that India's training and doctrine retained important links with Western European countries during the Cold War, despite the preponderance of Soviet equipment in the Indian inventory.

Senior officers in the Indian military services have for some time been attracted by the quality of U.S. equipment. It was expensive to buy, but Russian equipment was much more expensive to maintain. Still, India had misgivings about expanding its dependence on the United States. Indian defense scientists, many of them strongly predisposed to develop their own technology and boost India's technological self-reliance, play an important part in the procurement process. As India's regional and global ambitions came to require more sophisticated weaponry, the trade-off between self-reliance and the timely availability of already-tested technology became more acute.

1965

The "reliability" issue remains a major concern on the Indian side, dominating many conversations about procurement with officials, in-dustry representatives, and even nonofficial analysts. The 1978 U.S. cancellation of fuel supply contracts for the nuclear power plant at Tarapur impressed on the government that the U.S. Congress could cancel even contracts that had been in operation for years. More re-cently, the cancellation of military supply licenses after India's nuclear test in 1998 had the same impact. The U.S. transfer of the helicopter carrier USS *Trenton* to India in January 2007, together with six H-3 Sea King helicopters and six landing craft, was an important milestone. Determined to show that it could be responsive to an important Indian request, the United States had moved quickly to obtain the necessary legislative approval and complete the transfer.

Besides these philosophical differences, some of the same bureau-cratic disconnects that plague other aspects of the relationship affect military supply. India's procedures for formalizing and releasing a for-mal request for bids work extremely slowly, but the expected response times assume that suppliers can respond very quickly. Each side—with some reason—finds the other's bureaucratic processes clogged and opaque.

The defense framework agreements in 1995 and 2005 created an ex-pectation that defense trade would expand. The signature in 2002 of a General Security of Military Information Agreement (GSOMIA) after 15 years of dilatory negotiations, and India's strengthening of export controls in conjunction with the Next Steps in Strategic Partnership, discussed more fully in chapter 5, removed the biggest bureaucratic obstacles on the U.S. side.

Actual trade started slowly. One of the most significant early moves was the 1995 U.S. offer to provide counterbattery radars. The system would have made a major difference in India's capability to deal with firing across the Line of Control from Pakistan. The deal got bogged down in the Indian bureaucracy and was not finalized until 2002, but U.S. willingness to provide this state-of-the-art equipment helped change India's view of what the United States would be like to deal with as a defense supplier.[23]

Between 2002 and 2008, the United States approved technical as-sistance and manufacturing license agreements with India worth more than $700 million. Besides the transfer of the USS *Trenton* and the counterbattery radars, items supplied included six C-130J transport aircraft, a VIP aircraft protection system, antiterrorism equipment and sensors for use in Kashmir, and General Electric engines for use in the Light Combat Aircraft.[24] Each of these items was important, and several had an important impact on India's capabilities.

The U.S. industry believes that there is tremendous potential for future business, especially in light of growing Indian defense spending. As of early 2007, U.S. suppliers had taken a serious interest in or were in the process of bidding on some $13 billion worth of business in India, including supply of more than 100 Multi-Role Combat Aircraft (MRCA), flight control systems, attack helicopters, transport helicopters, transport aircraft, and parts for modernizing existing fleets. U.S. suppliers are structuring their proposed sales to minimize the "reliability" question, such as building a multiyear supply of spare parts into the initial purchase. The United States announced its willingness to allow U.S. manufacturers to offer coproduction of their aircraft, without which U.S. bids could not be competitive. The negotiation of a contract of this magnitude, should it be awarded to a U.S. supplier, will once again be an extended exercise in communication across countries and across bureaucratic cultures. It will also be an essential stepping-stone in enabling the two defense establishments to work together. Working out the precise nature of coproduction will also require difficult negotiations. India will be looking to participate in producing state-of-the-art equipment and will take U.S. willingness to supply it as a political signal.

Agreements on military security and export controls were also the first steps toward a more productive relationship in defense-related research. The slow pace of activity in the 1980s and 1990s moved a bit faster as the U.S.-India relationship intensified. An annual conference on cyber security started in 2002.

One of the most interesting areas for collaboration, or at least consultation, is missile defense. In the year after India's statement on missile defense, India came to explore missile defense as a technology that might have important security benefits for itself. It had few good options for dealing with threats in a nuclear environment. In 2002 India began participating in analytical missile defense exercises with the United States. One American participant in this process observed that the Indian team was adept at structuring the exercises so as to derive lessons pertinent to India's security situation, unlike participants from certain other countries who treated the exercise as a theoretical undertaking and passively played along with whatever scenario the U.S. team brought to the table.[25]

Beyond missile defense consultations and the possibility of aircraft coproduction, there has been more talk than action on defense production and research. Part of this reflects the deliberate pace of India's defense procurement and production apparatus. Ideas for either procurement or production that the Indian services begin exploring today may not fully mature for a decade. One consequence is that the kind of response the U.S. government gives to an early query may have an impact that lasts a decade or more, especially during this period where the patterns for defense trade may be shifting. As we will see in the next chapter, India's capacity to carry out major manufacturing operations on a large scale is picking up. As that happens, the industrial part of this process will speed up, but India's expectations will grow as well.

Counterterrorism has been a less successful part of this emerging security relationship. India and the United States both regard terrorism as a major threat, but their experience and priorities are different. For the United States, terrorism was primarily a threat outside its own territory until 9/11. Many of the standard tools the United States uses against terrorism predate 9/11, including maintaining and sanctioning the list of state sponsors of terrorism and the list of foreign terrorist organizations. Some of the organizations designated as "terrorist" achieved that status in part because of attacks on Indians, including Sri Lanka's Liberation Tigers of Tamil Eelam, the Babbar Khalsa (Sikh separatist organization), and several Islamic groups that operate in Pakistan. But the countries or organizations designated by the United States more typically were those that attacked Israeli or American targets. The attacks on New York and Washington in 2001 brought terrorism home to Americans.

For India, terrorism started as a domestic phenomenon. India's experience with violent insurgency goes back at least to the Naxalite insurgencies of the 1950s. During the 1980s, separatist Sikhs used terrorism, including hijacking and blowing up aircraft. Insurgent groups in the ethnic mosaic of India's northeast resorted to terrorism as part of their campaign to gain autonomy. The Liberation Tigers of Tamil Eelam, the spearhead of the ethnic insurgency in Sri Lanka, sent a suicide bomber in 1991 to assassinate former Indian prime minister Rajiv Gandhi. The Kashmir insurgency that started in the 1990s put a spotlight on the Pakistan connection, and Indian security officials believed

Pakistan was at least indirectly involved in many of the other terrorist threats against them.

In the 1980s and 1990s, counterterrorism training and information exchange took place through intelligence channels. Aircraft hijackings in the Middle East led to training of Indian and other intelligence officers in the United States for antihijacking operations and hostage negotiations. Later in the 1980s, intelligence exchanges expanded. In 1985, Sikh separatists blew up an Air India airliner flying out of Canada. In the aftermath, U.S. agencies exchanged information with India on other Sikh separatists, but not on groups based in Pakistan. By the 1990s, the focus shifted more to operations in India, including several kidnappings of foreigners in Kashmir—a group of Israeli tourists in 1992 and four Westerners, including an American, in 1995. This last incident was the object of a massive combined investigation by both governments. The incident led the United States to formally designate one Pakistan-based organization as a terrorist group; more designations followed in later years.

The trend throughout this period was toward closer cooperation between Indian and U.S. investigative authorities. Pakistan remained off limits, however. On at least one occasion, the result badly undercut the pattern of mutual assistance that was developing. According to an account published by a former Indian intelligence official, U.S. forensics experts consulted by Indian investigating officials identified a timer used in a series of deadly bombings in Mumbai in 1993 as part of a U.S. consignment to Pakistan in the 1980s. The U.S. experts, however, would not permit these findings to be used in the trial of the bombing suspects. They did not return the timer, claiming later that it had been destroyed by mistake.[26] This left a legacy of resentment and mistrust.

Following the 1999 hijacking of an Indian aircraft en route to Afghanistan, the United States and India created a Joint Working Group on Counterterrorism in January 2000.[27] This brought counterterrorism collaboration out of the closet, but may have inadvertently made it more difficult. As long as the process was dominated by intelligence agencies, it operated out of public view, with the pragmatic thrust that had characterized other areas of intelligence cooperation.[28] The Joint Working Group was officially acknowledged, and its work took place in a more public environment. Greater visibility helped create public awareness of how the U.S.-India partnership was progressing, but it also made the group's work more vulnerable to political sensitivities.

The working group started cautiously, but after September 11, the pace picked up. By mid-decade, more policy-oriented issues were added to the relatively noncontroversial operational agenda that had dominated until that point. Areas of joint activity included training in preventive, protective, and consequence management capabilities for both conventional and WMD terrorism. The two countries cooperated on forensics, financial issues like money laundering, and transportation security. They examined together the linkages between terrorism and such other ills as arms and narcotics trafficking. When the group met in 2007, the agenda included bioterrorism; border issues between India and Bangladesh, Sri Lanka, and Nepal; joint training; use of biometric identity documents; and links between Kashmiri organizations and other terrorist groups. At the same time, military cooperation channels also took up the issue of counterterrorism. An important tool was the ratification in 2005 of a Mutual Legal Assistance Treaty.[29] Indian officials were interested in learning from U.S. expertise and experience.

The difference between the U.S. and Indian "enemies lists" inhibited cooperation against terrorism, however. Counterterrorism success stories tended to be operational and procedural ones, divorced from considerations of the specific countries India and the United States were concerned about. India was not interested in joining an international campaign against the high-profile targets of U.S. anti-terrorism policy, such as Iran and Saddam Hussein's Iraq. The United States was ambivalent about Pakistan's role. Especially after 9/11, the United States took a harder line against the radical organizations based in Pakistan and operating in Kashmir or elsewhere in India and designated four of them as terrorist organizations. However, U.S. policy toward Pakistan was driven by the security relationship that undergirded U.S. military operations in Afghanistan. As we will see in chapter 6, the differences between U.S. and Indian approaches to terrorism in Pakistan were inseparable from their respective policies toward Pakistan and suffered from the same differences in goals.

DOWN THE ROAD

During the 1990s and early 2000s, the United States and India worked cautiously and incrementally in developing defense relations, with a few major breakthroughs hastening the pace. The United States accepted that it needed to do most of the "confidence building," though India's decision to strengthen its export controls was an important contribution.

The agreement on civil nuclear cooperation, discussed in the next chapter, was intended as a major contribution to confidence building. The hope on both sides is that it will spark a much deeper transformation of the security relationship. Smaller successes—in defense trade and in expanding the ambit of military exercises—and overcoming the inevitable bureaucratic challenges of implementing the nuclear agreement will make the two countries' security establishments more comfortable working together.

More than any other aspect of the bilateral U.S.-India relationship, security ties are created and carried out by governments, and as such they reflect those governments' domestic political strengths and the crosscurrents of international politics. The basic policy convergence that has made possible today's expansion in security relations seems quite robust on the U.S. side. U.S. policy and strategy in the area from the Persian Gulf to the Pacific will continue to depend on good relations with a network of important powers, and India will be a critical part of that network. Pakistan will be a complicating factor, as will the different U.S. and Indian perspectives on Iran, but the areas where U.S. and Indian interests converge today will remain strong.

From India's perspective, the future is more of a question mark. India's caution in developing security ties with the United States is not simply the product of a complex bureaucracy resistant to change. It also reflects Indian policymakers' difficulty in deciding how publicly they are willing to be associated with the United States on regional security issues. They see the U.S. Navy as a benign presence in the Indian Ocean, as we have noted—but U.S. naval visits still arouse occasional controversy in India. On a whole series of issues—piracy, nuclear nonproliferation, and others—India and the United States have the same aims, but working together to achieve them seems exceptionally complicated.

This difficulty is compounded by differences in operating style and in organization between the two militaries. As noted earlier, the jurisdictional boundaries between the U.S. Pacific, Central and African Commands chop up India's strategic space. They also inhibit strategic conversation and cooperation. The United States expects the regional commands to be the primary point of contact with foreign military leaders. For India, this appears to equate its national military leaders with U.S. officers of lesser protocol standing whose responsibilities are only regional. This in turn reinforces the impression that the United States is unwilling to grant India a genuine relationship among equals. On the Indian side, military-to-military contact is much less common than it is for Americans, and it took years to overcome the presumption that all dealings by the U.S. military with their Indian counterparts needed to go through the Indian Ministry of External Affairs first.

Some of this ambivalence will recur in the discussion of nuclear nonproliferation in the next chapter, and in the discussion of how the United States and India think about different regions of the world in the second half of this book. The staying power of the U.S.-India security partnership ultimately depends on how successfully the two countries can address not just the issues on which they agree, but also those on which they disagree.

NOTES

1. Jaswant Singh, *A Call to Honour: In Service of Emergent India* (New Delhi: Rupa, 2006), 328–330.

2. See presentation by MG Dipankar Banerjee (Ret.) in K. P. Vijayalakshmi, Arvind Kumar, Sonika Gupta, and S. Chandrashekar, eds., *Report on the National Workshop on Changing Contours of Indo-U.S. Relations*, (International Strategic and Security Studies Programme, National Institute of Advanced Studies, Indian Institute of Science, Bangalore, 2006), 137.

3. Ministry of Defense, Government of India, "Defense Expenditures," http://mod.nic.in/aboutus/welcome.html; Ministry of Finance, Government of India, *Economic Survey of India 2008*, http://indiabudget.nic.in/es2007-08/chapt2008/tab13b.pdf, table A-6; Laxman Kumar Behera, "India's Defence Budget 2009–10: An Assessment," Institute for Defence Studies and Analyses (IDSA) Strategic Comments, February 18, 2009, http://www.idsa.in/publications/stratcomments/LaxmanBehera180209.htm.

4. Lt. Gen. K. Natraj, "Indian Army Doctrine," October 2004, http://indianarmy.nic.in/indianarmydoctrine.htm.

5. Subhash Kapila, "India's New "Cold Start" War Doctrine Strategically Reviewed," South Asia Analysis Group, Paper 991, May 4, 2004, http://www.southasiaanalysis.org/papers10/paper991.html.

6. Between 2004 and 2006, the air force received 36–44 percent of procurement funds and the navy 23–24 percent; the army, vastly larger than either, was held to 26–29 percent of procurement funds. See International Institute for Strategic Studies, *Military Balance* 106, no. 1(June 2006): 224–227.

7. See, for example, Brahma Chellaney, *Asian Juggernaut: The Rise of China, India and Japan* (New Delhi: HarperCollins, 2006), which argues for a realist policy and for preventing Chinese domination of Asia, but makes no argument for any kind of offensive goals.

8. Vijay Sakhuja, "Indian Navy: Keeping Pace with Emerging Challenges," in *The Evolving Maritime Balance of Power in the Asia-Pacific: Maritime Doctrines and Nuclear Weapons at Sea*, ed. Lawrence W. Prabhakar, Joshua H. Ho, and Sam Bateman (Singapore: World Scientific, 2006), 98.

9. Reshmi Kazi, "Indian Naval Aspirations," Institute for Peace and Conflict Studies, New Delhi, August 10, 2004, http://www.ipcs.org/Nuclear_articles2 .jsp?action=showView&kValue=1484&issue=1015&status=article&mod=a.

10. A. Vinod Kumar, "Will the Joint Doctrine Result in Synergy on the Ground?" Institute for Defense Studies and Analyses, June 2006. http://www .idsa.in/publications/stratcomments/VinodKumar080606.htm.

11. Brig. Arun Sahgal (Ret.), quoted in Rahul Bedi, "U.S.-India Defense Relations," *SPAN*, New Delhi, March-April 2005. See also Juli A. Macdonald, *The Indo-U.S. Military Relationship: Expectations and Perceptions* (report prepared for Director, Net Assessment, Office of the Secretary of Defense, U.S. Department of Defense, October 2002), 16.

12. U.S. Navy, Marine Corps, and Coast Guard, "A Cooperative Strategy for 21st Century Seapower," October 2007, http://www.navy.mil/maritime/ MaritimeStrategy.pdf.

13. *Defense News*, September 2, 2005; see also Vice Adm. John Morgan Jr. and Rear Adm. Charles Martoglio, "Global Maritime Network," http://www.military .com/forums/0,15240,81652,00.html; see also testimony by Adm. Michael G. Mullen, Chief of Naval Operations, before the U.S. Senate Armed Services Committee, March 29, 2007.

14. Dennis Kux, *India and the United States: Estranged Democracies 1941– 1991* (Washington, D.C.: National Defense University Press, 1992), 393–416.

15. This reflects the author's experience as Deputy Assistant Secretary of State for South Asia, 1989–1992. The Light Combat Aircraft had its maiden flight in July 2003, 19 years after the cooperation agreement was signed.

16. Col. Steven B. Sboto, U.S. Army, "India and U.S. Military Cooperation and Collaboration: Problems, Prospects and Implications" (unpublished thesis submitted to National Defense College, New College, New Delhi, India, 2001), 7–9. The text of the Kicklighter plan and the 1995 Agreed Minute are included as annexes.

17. Author's interview with retired senior State Department official (n.d.).

18. Embassy of India, "New Framework for the U.S.-India Defense Relationship," press release, June 28, 2005.

19. See, for example, the March 2006 Fact Sheet on the U.S.-India Defense Relationship issued by the U.S. Department of Defense in the context of President Bush's visit to New Delhi, http://www.defenselink.mil/news/Mar2006/ d20060302us-indiadefenserelationship.pdf.

20. Author's conversation with Douglas Feith, September 13, 2006.

21. Author's conversations with Ashley Tellis (August 2006) and Air Chief Marshal (Ret.) S. P. Tyagi (April 2007); Gurpreet S. Khurana, "India-US Combined Defence Exercises: An Appraisal," *Strategic Analysis* 32, no. 6 (November 2008): 1048–1049.

22. "VLCC Hijacked by Pirates," November 18, 2008, Web site of International Maritime Bureau, http://www.icc-ccs.org/index.php?option=com_content &view=article&id=319:vlcc-hijacked-by-pirates&catid=60:news&Itemid=51.

23. Author's interview with former U.S. State Department official, December 2007.

24. K. Alan Kronstadt, "India-U.S. Relations," Congressional Research Service, CRS Report for Congress, Washington, D.C., updated July 1, 2008, 22; "F 16, C-130 Right Choices for India," *Financial Express*, February 19, 2008, http://www.financialexpress.com/news/F16-C130-right-choices-for-India-Lockheed/274762/; unpublished summary of defense trade provided by U.S. Department of State; see also Bedi, "India-U.S. Defense Relations."

25. Ashley J. Tellis, "The Evolution of U.S.-Indian Ties: Missile Defense in an Emerging Strategic Relationship," *International Security* 30, no. 4 (Spring 2006): 137–146; interviews with U.S. government officials.

26. B. Raman, "Indo-U.S. Counterterrorism Cooperation," in Sumit Ganguly, Brian Shoup, and Andrew Scobell, eds., *U.S.-Indian Strategic Cooperation into the 21st Century: More than Words* (New York: Routledge, 2006), 157–158.

27. Singh, *A Call to Honour*, 318.

28. This is not the first time that intelligence contacts have been able to work together in ways that were not possible in public. As far back as the 1950s, even before the India-China war, the United States and India exchanged information about China's nuclear development and Tibet. (Author's correspondence with a retired Indian security official, October 2008.)

29. U.S. Embassy New Delhi, "U.S.-India Treaty on Mutual Legal Assistance in Criminal Matters Ratified," press release, October 3, 2005, http://newdelhi.usembassy.gov/pr100305a.html.

5

NUCLEAR AND HIGH-TECH COOPERATION
GETTING BEYOND THE TABOOS

On October 1, 2008, the United States Senate passed legislation giving final authorization for U.S. civil nuclear cooperation with India. A week later, President Bush took a few minutes off from the financial meltdown that had convulsed the U.S. economy and signed the bill into law. A collective sigh of relief went up from the many people who had worked on the agreement in the United States and India. A series of decisions on U.S.-India security relations had been slowed down to see if the nuclear deal would pass. The legislation was the culmination of three years of intense effort. It launched a new era, with new political and commercial opportunities, in which India and the United States would be challenged to put more substance behind their hopes for a new partnership.

The nuclear issue exemplifies the roller coaster of U.S.-India relations since the end of the Cold War. India decided not to sign the Non-Proliferation Treaty (NPT) in 1968. Its "peaceful nuclear explosion" in 1974 put India into nuclear isolation and triggered tighter international restrictions on peaceful nuclear commerce. Two subsequent events in particular made nuclear matters a major obstacle to India-U.S. cooperation. The first was the 1978 U.S. decision to oblige the American supplier of fuel to a U.S.-built civilian power plant in Tarapur, India, to cancel its supply contract, a decision required by legislation passed soon after the 1974 test. This development overwhelmed the U.S.-India agenda at the time, and it has been regarded by Indians ever since as a textbook case of the United States changing the rules after a contract is written, as well as evidence of U.S. efforts to keep India down. The second decisive event was India's avowedly military nuclear tests in 1998, triggering Pakistan's tests three weeks later. Those tests put U.S.-India relations temporarily in the deep freeze but also occasioned the first serious strategic dialogue between the two countries.

From 1999 onward, as we have seen, the United States and India developed increasingly rich bilateral ties in security, economics, and a wide range of intellectual and scientific areas. However, cooperation in fields with potential applications to nuclear technology, missiles, or space remained off limits. These became a kind of litmus test for U.S.-India partnership, for both symbolic and substantive reasons.

Initially, the United States tried to address the resulting tensions incrementally. Progress toward loosening specific export restraints inched forward under the Clinton administration and early Bush administration. But export controls throughout the high-tech area were linked to the basic problem of India's nuclear status. In any case, step-by-step liberalization was not dramatic enough to transform the U.S.-India partnership. This led the Bush administration in its second term to propose a historic agreement for civil nuclear cooperation, changing a nonproliferation policy that U.S. administrations of both parties had strongly backed. This initiative was finally approved in October 2008.

This chapter focuses on this small group of high-tech issues. It starts by tracing the history of the turnaround in U.S.-India nuclear relations, together with the loosening of export restrictions on "dual use" items the United States considers to be connected with missile programs. It then reviews progress and prospects on space cooperation. In both areas, the United States and India are now on the threshold of a major expansion in their relationship. How this will affect their partnership will be shaped primarily by the answers to three questions, which are examined in the final section of this chapter. First, will the opening of cooperation in these areas serve only as a bilateral breakthrough, or will it lead to a reshaping of international efforts to stop onward nuclear proliferation, with more vigorous participation by India? Second, how will the agreements be implemented, and how will the United States and India deal with potential commercial competition? And finally, where does scientific cooperation outside the government fit into the U.S.-India relationship?

GETTING TO YES: HIGH-TECH TRADE AND THE
NUCLEAR AGREEMENT

India and the United States have been at odds for decades over nuclear cooperation. In the United States, the grand bargain embodied in the NPT enjoyed nearly universal support for almost four decades. Under the NPT, only the five countries that had tested nuclear weapons before 1967 were considered "nuclear weapons states." For all other parties to the treaty, weapons were forbidden, but they were to receive help in developing peaceful uses of the atom.

The promise of peaceful nuclear cooperation became more restrictive over time. India's nuclear program was one of the principal reasons for this. India's 1974 nuclear test led the United States to enact domestic legislation limiting U.S. civilian nuclear trade and cooperation more tightly than the strict requirements of the NPT. A major element in this structure was the Nuclear Non-Proliferation Act of 1978, which among other things required that any non-weapons state (as defined by the NPT) place all its nuclear facilities under international safeguards ("full scope safeguards") in order to be eligible for civilian nuclear cooperation with the United States. Safeguarding the facility at which cooperation would take place was not sufficient.

The United States also spearheaded the creation of a number of institutions consisting of NPT members with significant nuclear and related technological capabilities and designed to ensure that members all followed the same approach to nuclear cooperation that had been enacted into U.S. law.[1] The ones most directly concerned with nuclear trade were the Zangger Committee, formed soon after the NPT went into effect, and the Nuclear Suppliers' Group (NSG), created in the wake of India's 1974 test, whose members included most of the countries capable of making equipment used in peaceful nuclear technology. The intent was to restrict trade in items that could contribute to a nuclear weapons capability and to harmonize the rules among all suppliers. A number of other institutions performed a similar function of standardizing export controls and exchanging information on potential transactions for sensitive nonnuclear exports. These included the Australia Group (chemical and biological weapons and their precursors), the Wassenaar Arrangement (dual-use equipment and technology applicable to conventional armaments), and the Missile Technology Control Regime (MTCR). The dominant theme in U.S. policy in this area shifted from peaceful cooperation to control.

The NPT-related institutions became the major forum for cooperation on preventing international proliferation of nuclear know-how (as well as a range of sensitive nonnuclear technologies). Nonmembers of these institutions were urged to cooperate in counterproliferation efforts; indeed, United Nations Security Council Resolution 1540 obliges all countries to "take and enforce" effective measures to prevent proliferation. But the structure of the NSG and its sister institutions meant that India was treated by the nonproliferation system mainly as an object of controls, not as a country that could contribute to nonproliferation or help shape the controls.

India in its early years was ambivalent about nuclear development. One strand in Indian thinking was drawn to a peaceful civilian nuclear program and sought an end to nuclear weapons worldwide. Another strand, in which the country's nuclear scientists were better represented, did not want any aspect of nuclear development placed off limits. Once China exploded a nuclear device in 1964, the weight of opinion swung behind the drive to develop nuclear technology for all purposes.[2]

When India exploded a nuclear device in 1974, the term it used—"peaceful nuclear explosion"—signaled its continuing ambivalence about nuclear weapons. This explosion and India's decision not to join the NPT reflected India's emerging nuclear policy. India was not willing to accept a discriminatory system that treated it as a junior partner, especially one that gave senior status to China; and India was determined to develop whatever technology it might find important.

This put India in a nearly unique category, later reinforced by its avowedly military nuclear tests in 1998. India was one of only three nonmembers of the NPT (the others were Pakistan and Israel). It could not join the NPT as a nuclear weapons state because that would require amendment of the treaty, a process requiring a level of consensus that could not realistically be met. Nor could it join as a non-weapons state unless it gave up its nuclear weapons capability. This option would have been massively unpopular and would have brought down any government. By the time the 1998 tests were completed, India had two nuclear neighbors, China and Pakistan, and had a troubled history with both. India could not implement full scope safeguards, as doing so would involve dismantling its military program. It took pride in its nonproliferation record: it had not transferred sensitive nuclear technology or know-how outside of India. But it was not welcome in international nonproliferation institutions, and their linkage to the NPT meant that the normal vehicles for international cooperation against proliferation were seen as part of the discriminatory structure that India had rejected in the first place.

After India's 1998 tests, the United States imposed the sanctions required by U.S. law. These effectively closed down trade with a wide range of organizations connected with defense production (the "entities list") and also suspended senior-level contacts with India's defense establishment. But the United States also began looking for a way to address its nuclear differences with India.

The first attempt came in the strategic dialogue between Deputy Secretary of State Strobe Talbott and Foreign Minister Jaswant Singh. The two men entered the discussions with different objectives: in Talbott's case, to persuade India to agree to some form of restraints on its nuclear program; in Singh's, to gain acceptance for India as a country with nuclear weapons. The United States explored a number of proxies for nuclear limitations, referred to as "benchmarks." It sought India's and Pakistan's signatures on a Comprehensive Test Ban Treaty (CTBT); stopping production of fissile materials and participation in still-embryonic talks on a Fissile Material Cutoff Treaty (FMCT); and institution of export controls meeting the highest standard of effectiveness. The most difficult discussions centered on the fourth benchmark, which the United States referred to as "strategic restraint." The U.S. intention was to obtain some public articulation of India's defense posture that would give concrete meaning to the limitations implied by India's stated goal of "minimum credible deterrence."

None of these benchmarks was met in the way the United States had hoped during the Singh-Talbott discussions. Prime Minister Atal Bihari Vajpayee made a carefully qualified pledge regarding the CTBT in his 1998 speech to the United Nations General Assembly.[3] The U.S. Senate's refusal to ratify the U.S. signature on the treaty effectively ended any serious consideration of the CTBT in the Indian government, however. The Fissile Material Cutoff Treaty remained on the table, but India did not agree to end production of fissile material while the treaty was under negotiation. Under the "strategic restraint" heading, the United States hoped that India would adopt what amounted to an arms control regime, including limits on the numbers and types of missiles it maintained. India rejected the whole idea of negotiating its strategic posture with an outside power, and argued that its no-first-use doctrine represented a meaningful voluntary restraint on its nuclear posture. It did reassure the United States that it was serious about reducing tensions with Pakistan, hence reducing the risks inherent in the regional dynamics.

Overall, as Talbott recognized, India came closer to its goals than the United States did. By the end of the discussions it was clear that the United States was moving to strengthen relations with India despite the latter's nuclear weapons. The talks contributed significantly to the two countries' strategic understanding; as Talbott later recalled, they made a major contribution to overcoming the "visceral distrust of the United States." However, they failed to provide a means of addressing their nuclear disagreements.[4]

With the transition to the Bush administration, a broad strategic dialogue continued through the Indian and U.S. ambassadors in Washington and Delhi and through a brisk pace of high-level visits and defense contacts. On the high-tech side, the focus shifted to finding a way to make U.S. export controls less burdensome. India and the United States launched a High Technology Cooperation Group in 2002 to provide a forum in which officials and business representatives could work together to facilitate high-tech trade. In operational terms, the key initiative was the "Next Steps in Strategic Partnership" (NSSP), formally launched in January 2004. The initiative, designed as a series of reciprocal steps, focused on three areas: civilian nuclear regulatory and safety issues; space cooperation; and expanding high-tech commerce.

In July 2005, the two governments announced the completion of the NSSP. India had passed the Weapons of Mass Destruction and their Delivery Systems (Prohibition of Unlawful Activities) Bill in 2005, which put its export control regime in conformity with U.S. and international export controls.[5] This made it possible for the United States to announce a significant liberalization of its export licensing policies. In particular, it removed the Indian Space Research Organization (ISRO) from the so-called entities list of organizations banned from receiving U.S. exports; it eliminated the requirement for an export license for certain "low level dual-use items" and for unilaterally controlled nuclear items sold to most end users; it applied a policy of "presumption of approval" for licensing dual-use items not controlled by the NSG when the end user was a safeguarded facility; and it announced that its would expand bilateral commercial satellite cooperation.[6] The

Get
Tellis
stuff

United States offered India limited cooperation on nuclear safety and security issues.

U.S. government figures indicate that these actions substantially simplified and expanded trade. The percentage of U.S. exports to India requiring export licenses fell from 25 percent in 1999 to 0.2 percent in 2008. Processing times for export license applications fell from 52 days in 2003 to 33 in 2007, in line with the processing time for licenses to the UK, Israel, and France.[7] Indian importers were eligible to apply for the Trusted Customer Program administered by the U.S. Commerce Department, which simplified processing of licenses.

U.S. export control procedures are technically complex and difficult for first-time users to understand, so the impact of this liberalization has still not fully registered on the perceptions of the Indian government, or of businesses in both countries. There was a widespread perception that export licensing requirements were a form of sanctions, despite many U.S. efforts to explain that the United States requires licenses for the export of certain sensitive items no matter who is buying them.

The NSSP agreement was a substantial accomplishment, but a step-by-step approach was too modest and technical to be a "game-changer" in U.S.-India relations. Moreover, the NSSP dealt with only one category of U.S. export controls—those affecting items with dual civil and military use. Export controls on munitions were still in place, although their impact on India was clearly diminishing. And controls on nuclear exports still remained a factor, with U.S. policy linked to the NPT and nonproliferation institutions. As long as India was in nuclear isolation, progress on export controls and related issues would continue to be hemmed in.

The United States then decided to shift its focus to nuclear cooperation. In July 2005, six months into the second Bush administration, Prime Minister Manmohan Singh visited Washington, and the two leaders announced a dramatic new initiative on civil nuclear cooperation. The United States pledged to make the necessary changes in its domestic law—and to work toward changes in the practice of international institutions—to "achieve full civil nuclear energy cooperation with India." For its part, India would reciprocally agree to "assume the same responsibilities and practices and acquire the same benefits and advantages as other leading countries with advanced nuclear technology." It would formally separate its military and civilian nuclear facilities;

place those designated as civilian under international safeguards; sign an Additional Protocol with the International Atomic Energy Agency (IAEA); work with the United States for the conclusion of a Fissile Material Cutoff Treaty; refrain from transferring enrichment and re-processing technologies to states that do not have them; ensure the continuing harmonization of India's export controls with those of the Missile Technology Control Regime and the Nuclear Suppliers' Group; and continue its "unilateral moratorium on nuclear testing."[8]

For the United States, this reversed decades of nonproliferation policy. The principal U.S. motivation was to energize the partnership with India, which it saw as a potential geopolitical link to a number of sensitive areas in Asia in the medium to long term. India's standing as the world's largest democracy also figured in this reasoning. The administration believed that it could make the necessary changes in U.S. law and practice without undercutting the NPT itself, and that this could help "bring India into the nonproliferation mainstream." In particular, India's commitment to keep its export controls aligned with those of the nonproliferation institutions and its acceptance of an Additional Protocol with the IAEA, with the attendant obligation to report all exports of sensitive items included in the IAEA's "trigger list," would strengthen the international network of anti-proliferation controls. The administration hoped that, having made this dramatic change in policy on India's behalf, it could look forward to India's active participation in international counterproliferation work once the agreement was in place.[9]

India's aims in pursuing a nuclear deal with the United States were simpler. It sought equality of treatment with "leading countries with advanced nuclear technology," meaning the recognized nuclear weapons states. It aimed to end the discriminatory treatment inherent in the NPT and to avoid restrictions on its military facilities. And it sought access to the civilian nuclear marketplace for its nuclear industries.

India's interest in developing civilian nuclear energy was very much related to its voracious appetite for energy. Nuclear power in 2007 supplied only 2.6 percent of India's electricity. Even India's ambitious plans for the development of nuclear energy will not bring this share above 7–10 percent by 2030.[10] But India has limited uranium reserves, and its current production capacity for nuclear power-related equipment is also limited. Without access to the international market, expansion of nuclear energy would be difficult, slow, and expensive, so the impact of the nuclear agreement on India's energy needs is more important than the numbers would suggest.

Moving the agreement toward implementation proved to be a roller coaster. The process was complex, from India's announcement in March 2006 specifying which nuclear facilities would be designated as "civilian," to the passage of the first piece of U.S. enabling legislation, the Hyde Act, in December 2006, to the negotiation of a bilateral cooperation agreement on the peaceful uses of nuclear energy (known popularly as the "123 agreement") between India and the United States in July 2007, to India's decision to put the entire nuclear agreement on hold because of opposition from the government's leftist coalition partners, to the Indian government's decision to go forward and its successful survival of a parliamentary vote of confidence in July 2008, to the approval of a safeguards agreement by the IAEA Executive Board, to the NSG's agreement in September 2008 to change its rules on India's behalf, to the passage of the final implementing legislation by the U.S. Congress on October 1, 2008. At each step controversy swirled in both countries, reflecting the different objectives the two governments were trying to serve.

At each stage India struck a hard bargain. The touchstone of each negotiation was whether the agreement allowed India full equality with the recognized nuclear weapons states. Among the thorny issues were whether the United States would allow India to reprocess fuel supplied by the United States; whether the United States would sell reprocessing equipment; whether the United States would guarantee India against interruptions of fuel supply; what was meant by safeguards "in perpetuity" on India's civilian nuclear facilities; and, especially, what would be the consequence if India chose to abandon its unilateral, voluntary pledge not to test a nuclear device. Each of these issues was seen in India as a test of whether the United States really meant to allow India equality. Each ran into a specific obstacle in U.S. law or practice. In the case of the "right to test," the Hyde Act, which made it possible to negotiate the nuclear agreement, stipulated that an Indian nuclear test would end cooperation.

Both countries' negotiators devised a number of creative workarounds for these problems. They dealt indirectly with the issue of future nuclear tests, spelling out an elaborate set of procedures for terminating the bilateral cooperation agreement, without ever mentioning the word "testing." As the key U.S. negotiator, Under Secretary

India wants to be France

of State Nicholas Burns, said, "India retains the right to test, and the United States retains the right to respond."[11]

In India, the heat of the debate demonstrates the continuing strength of the commitment to strategic autonomy among India's elites. Three constituencies opposed the agreement. India's nuclear scientists and officials viewed the whole enterprise with resentment and skepticism. Having suffered from U.S. sanctions and having developed India's program in spite of them, the nuclear establishment looked with extreme suspicion on any hint that the United States might be able to cut off supplies again. The bilateral cooperation agreement reassured them, although as its negotiating record was made public, their concerns received a new airing. The second source of objections was the main opposition party, the Bharatiya Janata Party or BJP. It was simply acting as an opposition; there is good reason to believe that it would cheerfully have negotiated and accepted an equivalent agreement had its leaders been in office.

The third set of opponents nearly killed the agreement. The government's allies from the Communist and other leftist parties objected not because of their devotion to India's nuclear program but because they opposed the close relationship with the United States that it represented. Their threat to bring down the government delayed India's consideration of the nuclear deal by a year. In the end, the government went ahead, and the leftists' vote of no confidence was rejected. The government's success owed more to horse-trading and a display of political courage by the prime minister than to policy arguments. By the time the vote of confidence took place, it was clear that the idea of a nuclear cooperation agreement with the United States had broad public support in India.

On the U.S. side, it is a mark of how far U.S.-India relations had progressed that not even the agreement's critics challenged the wisdom of crafting a partnership with India. The principal issue, rather, was the impact of this particular agreement on the nonproliferation system. Opponents argued that reversing four decades of nonproliferation policy would accelerate what one of them called a "slow leakage" out of the global consensus embodied in the NPT. By rewarding India for challenging the system, they believed the agreement would make it easier for others to follow suit and would hand a useful debating point to the most irresponsible countries that had already taken steps in that direction, such as North Korea and Iran.[12]

A second line of argument concerned India's relationship with Iran. The U.S. administration was satisfied that despite India's strategic interest in Iran's energy supplies, Delhi's ties with Tehran were actually modest. But congressional critics of the agreement, including some of India's stalwart supporters who also shared a deep concern about Iran, insisted heatedly that India join in U.S. efforts to isolate Iran, and wrote into the Hyde Act a requirement for the administration to report regularly on India-Iran ties.

The arguments that developed in Delhi and Washington, in other words, were mirror images of one another. Whatever one government said to soothe its domestic critics could be counted on to stir up critics in the other capital.

In the end, the agreement moved forward. The International Atomic Energy Agency approved an India-specific safeguards agreement. On September 5, 2008, the Nuclear Suppliers' Group agreed to waive its rules for India, based in part on a formal restatement by India of its voluntary commitments to strengthen its participation in the nonproliferation system and its "voluntary, unilateral moratorium" on testing.[13] A few weeks later, the U.S. Congress voted by large bipartisan margins to approve the U.S.-India cooperation agreement. The NSG decision had already ended India's nuclear isolation, authorizing other suppliers such as Russia and France to sell civil nuclear supplies to India. The final legislation made it possible for U.S. suppliers to participate.

SPACE COOPERATION

Space cooperation has a history similar to high-tech trade and nuclear cooperation: U.S. involvement in the early years of the program, followed by a freeze on cooperation starting in the 1970s due to U.S. export controls. Like its nuclear program, India's space program is a subject of national pride. It started in 1962, spearheaded by the legendary Indian physicist Vikram Sarabhai, with the foundation of the Indian National Committee for Space Research (INCOSPAR). In 1969, INCOSPAR was renamed the Indian Space Research Organization and space became a full-fledged program. The first launch from India took place in 1963, with a U.S.-made sounding rocket. The first Indian-made satellite was launched in 1975 from a Soviet-made launch vehicle, and the first successful launch on an Indian-made space launch vehicle took place in 1980. At the outset, the purposes of the space program were explicitly civilian and dedicated to practical applications that could improve the lives of Indians.[14]

Over the years, India expanded its capabilities in the construction and operation of both satellites and launchers. Its INSAT satellites, first launched in 1983, have been used for telecommunications and educational applications in geosynchronous orbit. More recently, the CARTOSAT series has been devoted to similar purposes. For earth observation, the principal indigenous satellites are the Indian Remote Sensing (IRS) satellite series, first successfully launched in 1988 and used in sun-synchronous orbit. India developed indigenous launch vehicles for both types of satellite. The success of these satellites in telemedicine and educational applications and their contribution to identifying scarce water resources in India are prized achievements. India is beginning a program of exploration of the oceans from space. The major launch vehicles in current use are the Polar Satellite Launch Vehicle (PSLV), whose first operational use was in 1996, and the Geosynchronous Satellite Launch Vehicle (GSLV), first used for an operational launch in 2004.

The Indian space program is expanding its work in these traditional focus areas. But, as ISRO chairman G. Madhavan Nair explained in a presentation in Washington in January 2008, the Indian space program is at a turning point and is looking to advance in two areas. The first is space exploration. India has undertaken a moon mission, the Chandrayaan. The first satellite destined for the moon was launched in October 2008, with U.S. cooperation. The second will be a joint Indian-Russian mission, with India managing the orbiter and Russia the roving landing vehicle.[15] ISRO also aims to put together a manned space mission by about 2016, with a fully autonomous orbital vehicle and two or three crew members.[16]

The second goal is expanding India's commercial space program and making it available to a growing number of international participants. ISRO has carried out a number of commercial launches on PSLVs for customers including Italy, Indonesia, Argentina, and Israel. India's simultaneous launch of eight nano-satellites from the same vehicle that launched the Israeli satellite in January 2008 will help build a record on which to base expanded commercial business. In addition, ISRO, through its marketing arm, has developed a good business selling remote sensing images and leasing transponders. It reported more than $200 million in revenues from its commercial activities in 2007–2008.[17]

International cooperation has always been an important element in the space program, despite the emphasis on developing India's skills. In the early years, U.S. scientists from the National Aeronautics and Space Administration (NASA) helped India create a launch site in Tiruvananthapuram, and some 300 foreign—mostly U.S.—sounding rockets were launched from there. The first rocket launched from India was a Nike-Apache rocket from the United States, carrying a payload and instruments from Europe. During the 1960s and 1970s, the United States worked with India on the Satellite Instructional Television Experiment (SITE), which stationed a U.S. satellite in geosynchronous orbit above central India, providing education, information, and entertainment to some 2,400 villages. This experiment was regarded as both a technical and an educational success, and it helped inspire the subsequent indigenous effort to use satellites for educational outreach.[18]

Russia too was an early participant in India's space program, with deep involvement in the IRS program and an Indian astronaut spending a week aboard the Salyut 7 space station in 1984. India's other important collaboration was with France and eventually with the EU. During the 1990s, a number of INSAT satellites were launched on Ariane rockets from Kourou in French Guyana. These were all at least in principle two-way collaborations. One of India's best known scientists has argued, for example, that Indian engineers contributed substantially to the building of the Viking liquid propulsion engine for the French Ariane rocket.[19]

By the mid-1970s, however, export controls had become an obstacle to cooperation. The United States would not participate in Indian launch activities, though it was willing to launch Indian satellites from the United States. With the creation of the Missile Technology Control Regime in 1987, the limitations became more stringent. The MTCR treated anything related to launching a spacecraft or maintaining it in flight as a potential contribution to a missile program. Exports to India were prohibited if they could contribute to a missile or civilian space launch vehicle capable of delivering a payload of 500 kilograms to a range of at least 300 kilometers. The MTCR stated that its guidelines were "not designed to impede national space programs or international cooperation in such programs as long as such programs could not contribute to delivery systems for weapons of mass destruction," but this distinction has been hard to maintain.[20] The Indian nuclear tests of 1998 put all space cooperation with the United States in the deep freeze.

Despite the civilian orientation of India's space program, there was extensive exchange of people and knowledge between ISRO and the Defense Research and Development Organization (DRDO), which developed India's indigenous missile program. Elements of both of India's launch vehicles reappeared in India's missiles.[21]

Members of the MTCR retained some discretion about how to implement their commitments. However, on at least one occasion, the tight U.S. rules prevented Russia from carrying out its plans for space cooperation with India. In 1992–1993, the United States took strong exception to Russia's decision to provide India with cryogenic engines for use in placing a satellite into a geosynchronous transfer orbit. The United States banned both participating organizations— Russia's Glavkosmos and India's ISRO—from any contacts with the United States. Russia, which was just emerging from the wreckage of the Soviet Union, eventually cancelled the contract.[22]

The 1990s marked the apex of U.S. and international restrictions on cooperation with India's space program. Since 2001, the United States and India have been working to establish a basis, and a new set of ground rules, for space cooperation. As discussed earlier, the NSSP helped liberalize space cooperation by removing three elements of ISRO from the "entities list."

ISRO and NASA signed a framework agreement setting forth the terms for cooperation on February 1, 2008, an important milestone. U.S. participation in the Chandrayaan 1 lunar mission, launched on October 21, 2008, marked a new beginning of U.S.-India cooperation in missions launched on Indian space vehicles. This remote-sensing mission, designed to map the moon and assess its mineral resources, carried two U.S. instruments, mini-synthetic aperture radar and a moon mineralogy mapper, along with four devices from the European Space Agency and six Indian devices. India and the United States also plan to collaborate on less controversial projects involving collection and use of space-based data. The two countries are working to fill gaps in data derived from the United States' Landsat remote sensing program. They have continued using satellite communications to reach remote areas for such humanitarian purposes as telemedicine and tele-education, including one project targeting Afghanistan.[23] In addition, NASA and the National Oceanic and Atmospheric Administration (NOAA) have been working with India on monitoring emissions for environmental purposes and on monitoring rainfall patterns and monsoon shifts. India and the United States are both members of the International Charter for Space and Major Disasters, which provides for members to pool space resources in case of a major disaster.[24]

India also continues to work with other international partners. The ISRO Annual Report lists space cooperation agreements with 28 countries, from space powerhouses (United States, EU, Russia) to small countries with no real space presence. The EU and Russia are the biggest players. France has a special place in India's meteorological research, and Russia has been a partner in all stages of India's space work. ISRO is participating in Russian efforts to advance its Global Navigational Satellite System and in the EU's Galileo global navigation system.[25]

Sanctions and technology denials against India's space program slowed India's development of indigenous space technology but did not stop it. India has continued work on different kinds of launch vehicles, and it has tested its own cryogenic engine. India's national leaders and its top space officials are eager to accelerate cooperation with the United States. Nonetheless, space officials remain skeptical about the extent of cooperation the United States will ultimately agree to. At the time that ISRO's chairman signed the agreement with the United States, he noted that the U.S. track record of approving space-related exports to India was uneven.[26]

With the taboo on launch activities largely overcome, the principal impediment to U.S.-India space cooperation is commercial. Under present rules, India cannot launch U.S.-made satellites or satellites containing U.S. components. The problem is no longer a blanket prohibition, however, but a more limited concern for technology protection and the commercial conditions governing space and satellite services. The United States and India have negotiated—but not signed—a draft Technology Safeguards Agreement, which would resolve the first issue. Negotiations over a Commercial Space Launch Agreement have been held up, and a U.S. proposal to move ahead with noncommercial launch cooperation pending talks on these commercial issues seems to have stalled. The bureaucratic disputes that have delayed these discussions have echoes of the other high-tech issues discussed in this chapter, including Indian scientists' belief that the United States is still seeking to limit their space program and in general to "keep India down." On the U.S. side, the disputes are marked by a new concern: the possibility of commercial competition.

AFTER THE BREAKTHROUGH: NEW KINDS OF COOPERATION AND COMPETITION?

The nuclear and space cooperation agreements cleared away legal and policy barriers that had been in place for decades, and in the process they opened the door to a more vigorous U.S.-India partnership. The two countries now need to see what lies beyond that door. Three areas will be particularly important: the future shape of nonproliferation; both countries' expectations for future trade; and nongovernment science cooperation.

THE FUTURE SHAPE OF NONPROLIFERATION

The Bush administration hoped that the 2008 nuclear agreement would lead to India's more vigorous involvement in international nonproliferation efforts. But the global nonproliferation system will change significantly in the next decade. These changes may make both nonproliferation itself and U.S.-India cooperation either easier or more difficult to achieve.

The NPT remains the principal formal instrument for nonproliferation and the heart of its institutional structure. It was extended for 25 years in 1995 and is almost impossible to amend. It enjoys near-universal membership. However, the NPT is in trouble. One signatory, Iran, is pursuing a massive enrichment program in violation of an agreement with the IAEA and in defiance of a United Nations Security Council resolution. Another, North Korea, has withdrawn from the NPT and tested a weapon. India's weapons program enjoys a kind of de facto international recognition, and the other two non-signatories, Israel and Pakistan, have nuclear weapons. Under these circumstances, the NPT's authority has eroded and its members do not include some of the countries needed to form an effective anti-proliferation consensus.

The Bush administration's nonproliferation policy had been to prevent additional countries from acquiring nuclear weapons or sensitive, dual-use fuel cycle facilities (uranium enrichment or plutonium processing plants) capable of producing fuel for civil nuclear programs. It also aimed to prevent new countries from acquiring the fissile material needed to build nuclear weapons. In pursuing this policy, it treated different countries in very different ways. It sought to isolate Iran and end its potentially weapons-related enrichment program. It alternated between isolating North Korea and negotiating with it, with the objective of rolling back its weapons program. India's record of not transferring nuclear technology led the United States to conclude an agreement on civil nuclear cooperation, as we have seen. Pakistan's more troublesome record placed a similar deal beyond reach, but the United States in effect accepted that Pakistan would retain its nuclear weapons without losing its strategically important relationship with the United States. Under President Bush, Washington worked through the NPT-related institutions, but also began to develop informal mechanisms for cooperation that are not based on treaties, such as the Proliferation Security Initiative (PSI), which is discussed below.[27]

India, by contrast, sees its responsibility for nonproliferation basically as an obligation to control its own nuclear assets, respect safeguards, protect its nuclear installations and materials from theft or seizure, and prevent unauthorized exports. India does not want to see new nuclear weapons states in its neighborhood, but it has stayed generally aloof from international efforts aimed at these problems. As discussed in chapter 8, for example, India's criticism of Iran's nuclear program has been focused on Iran's violation of obligations it had voluntarily undertaken. India has been wary of new nonproliferation regimes, wanting to stay clear of the taint of NPT-related discrimination but also to avoid restrictions on its own nuclear program. Global nuclear disarmament remains at the heart of India's publicly stated policy on nonproliferation. As recently as March 2009, one of India's most senior diplomats made an impassioned plea for universal nuclear disarmament, arguing that an arrangement with the same kinds of intrusive powers as the Chemical Weapons Convention could be accepted only if it applied to everyone.[28] This policy is hotly contested, however. Many in the Indian strategic community and on the nationalist side of the Indian political system argue that India needs first and foremost to protect its own nuclear deterrent. Perhaps because its nuclear weapons are a recent phenomenon, in discussions of nuclear disarmament India has not yet focused on the kinds of steps that would be needed to move from a nuclear to a nonnuclear world—reducing numbers of weapons, embracing restraints on testing and fissile material production, and moving toward disarmament throughout the system.

The Obama administration plans to take a more active approach to nonproliferation. The approach endorsed by Barack Obama during his campaign emphasized negotiating and expanding international obligations. Obama supported the U.S.-India nuclear agreement and will implement it. As of early 2009, his team had not yet determined how fit this into the larger nonproliferation policy. Logically, it should lead to some important changes from the policy that prevailed before the Bush administration, most importantly some form of special status for India in the NSG and the other groups with which India aligns its export controls. Indeed, the process of fitting India in has begun. The NSG, in approving civil nuclear cooperation with India, stipulated that India should be "consulted" regarding future changes in the export control regime. This gives India an opportunity to influence the rules, an important step in ensuring its full participation in the system, but not the veto that full members of the NSG have. With time, India and the NPT-related institutions will need to develop mechanisms to overcome their legacy of mutual resentment.

Two treaties at the top of the multilateral arms control and disarmament agenda, a Fissile Material Cutoff Treaty and a Comprehensive Test Ban Treaty, would be key elements in a treaty-centered policy. In the 2005 statement launching its nuclear deal with the United States, India promised to help negotiate an FMCT, but real multilateral negotiations have not yet begun. India's insistence on a treaty that is "nondiscriminatory and verifiable" differed with the Bush administration's proposal, submitted in May 2006, which included no provisions for verification. The Obama administration will accept verification. There remain other extremely difficult negotiating issues, however.

The CTBT has a stormier history. As discussed above, it figured prominently in the Clinton administration's dialogue with India, and the Republican-controlled U.S. Senate voted it down 49–48 in 1999. The Indian government had taken strong exception to the draft that the U.S. Senate turned down, principally because India's participation was a prerequisite for the treaty to go into effect, a provision that India thought was designed to pressure it to join the treaty or make it look bad. The Bush administration opposed the treaty and made no effort to revive it.

Changed circumstances since the two treaties first appeared on the U.S.-India agenda would both facilitate and complicate an effort to bring India into a nonproliferation system centered on stronger treaty obligations. The biggest potential positive is President Obama's greater openness to negotiations that could eventually lead to nuclear disarmament.[29] The United States and the Soviet Union negotiated major reductions in their nuclear arsenals in an earlier era, but the five NPT-recognized nuclear weapons states have never taken seriously the obligation to work toward nuclear disarmament. If a serious initiative got under way, it would be a massive change in the nonproliferation landscape and could have a major impact on India (and many other non-weapons states). It would provide a great boost to the idea of a test ban treaty, but would also force a serious and unpredictable debate in India.

In other respects, the ten years since Strobe Talbott and Jaswant Singh started their dialogue on nonproliferation have made formal, treaty-based U.S.-India cooperation more difficult. In the negotiations on the U.S. nuclear deal, the Indian security establishment, backed up by the political leadership, sought above all to avoid legal restrictions on India's nuclear arsenal. The argument over the "right to test" illustrates the problem: India was prepared to offer, and to reiterate, a unilateral testing moratorium, but not to accept any formal embedding of that promise in a bilateral or multilateral instrument. This raises the bar for Indian participation in a future CTBT. The same argument applies to a future FMCT. The obligation to cease production of fissile material for nuclear weapons would be more burdensome to India, which is still building up its nuclear arsenal, than to countries whose weapons have been in existence and legally recognized for decades. If the current U.S.-India disagreement over verification in an FMCT is resolved, which is likely given Obama's support for a verifiable treaty, that will bring into the open this more fundamental Indian concern.

A different approach to reinvigorating the international nonproliferation effort would rely more heavily on informal or bilateral mechanisms that operate alongside existing NPT-related institutions. Standardization of export controls is the entry point, and provides a crucial linkage with the institutions through which export controls are coordinated. Intelligence cooperation can provide information vital to the nonproliferation effort, out of public view, either bilaterally or through some form of "nuclear interpol." Such efforts could be focused on the countries that are most likely to conduct nuclear exports. India's decision in the summer of 2008 to deny overflight to a North Korean aircraft bound for Iran is an example of this type of action.[30]

Nonproliferation-related exercises could become part of regular military-to-military contacts. Regular discussions on nuclear safety and security and, most importantly, on the potential weaknesses of existing systems could strengthen protection against unintended diversions of nuclear supplies.

Another proposal has been to expand the use of more "proliferation-proof" ways of producing fuel for civilian nuclear plants. Fuel leasing, it has been argued, would reduce the pressure on individual states to produce their own fuel. The IAEA has proposed the establishment of international fuel banks, with the same objective. India formally told the NSG that it "is interested in participating as a supplier nation," an undertaking it almost certainly would not have agreed to without having the nuclear deal close to completion.[31] A senior Indian official has suggested that India might also buy fuel from fuel banks.[32] But India considers fuel banks as a supplement to its own fuel cycle— not as a substitute.

The Proliferation Security Initiative or some successor arrangement like it could provide a framework for a multilateral approach that is not exclusively linked to the NPT. The Bush administration started the PSI as a cooperative arrangement with a limited purpose: to interrupt international shipments related to weapons of mass destruction or nuclear weapons programs. It does not require participants to be members of the NPT or related export control regimes. The United States has concluded reciprocal search agreements with a number of countries, including those that operate as the major "flags of convenience." Each member is free to respond according to its own law and policy. The PSI has deliberately avoided creating specific legal obligations.[33]

India kept the PSI at arm's length while the nuclear agreement was under debate, but observers inside and outside of government have argued that it should take another look. The PSI's loose and flexible design should be ideally suited to dealing with India's concern for maintaining its freedom of action. India has joined in the kind of effort envisaged by the PSI on a case-by-case basis. Before the PSI was created, India boarded a North Korean ship reported to be carrying missile parts to Pakistan. The question is how soon India will be ready to move beyond carefully vetted case-by-case cooperation to a presumption of participation in a larger international effort.

The difficulty of engaging India in nonproliferation work beyond securing its own assets raises a more fundamental question: what responsibility does India believe it has for the global nuclear environment? India is painfully aware that nuclear leakage could spread weapons technology through the already-troubled Middle East where its strategic interests are high. The response, from India's point of view, lies in nuclear disarmament—on which Indian opinion is divided—and in the nuclear deterrent. So far, at least, Indian leaders are unpersuaded that the multilateral nonproliferation system can help keep India and its neighborhood safe from nuclear proliferation. As noted earlier, they are also reluctant to take responsibility for the global nonproliferation system beyond maintaining the security of its own assets. On these two points, India's perspective clashes with that of the Bush administration and even more so with that of the Obama administration.

In short, the vision of India coming closer to the international "nonproliferation mainstream" is feasible only if the nonproliferation system is defined more broadly than the NPT-based institutions. With the nuclear deal in place, expanded bilateral and informal cooperation with the United States should come more easily. But India's advocates for nuclear self-reliance and strategic autonomy will remain skeptical about a formal, treaty-based system.

This discussion assumes that India maintains its voluntary moratorium on nuclear testing. The consequences of a fresh Indian test both for global nonproliferation and for U.S.-India relations would be severe; how serious would depend heavily on the circumstances. An Indian test without some precipitating change in international circumstances appears highly unlikely. Such an event would almost certainly provoke a termination of the U.S.-Indian nuclear agreement. However, if the current global taboo on testing broke down—if, for example, China or Pakistan resumed testing—the reaction both globally and in the United States could be quite different. The United States would certainly see such a development as a breakdown of the consensus on nonproliferation, with dangerous regional consequences. However, the response would need to go beyond India, and indeed beyond nonproliferation.

U.S. AND INDIAN EXPECTATIONS FOR FUTURE TRADE

The nuclear deal, expanded high-tech trade, and space cooperation have given both India and the United States expectations of great commercial and scientific benefits. Implementing these agreements and managing expectations for their impact will be a challenge for both.

Even before the nuclear agreement was completed, the U.S. nuclear industry had sent a series of trade missions to India, with an estimated $150 billion in new business in their sights. Now that the agreement is ready to be implemented, Russian and French suppliers are hot on the trail of the same business. The Indian government has sent the United States a "letter of intent" stating that it expects to buy at least 10,000 megawatts (MW) of nuclear power generating capacity from U.S. suppliers provided the cost of electricity is competitive. The same document undertook to resolve the issue of liability for foreign suppliers, something that major American companies considered to be a prerequisite for getting into the nuclear business in India.[34] Evaluating complex bids on enormous projects in India is slow, and everyone will be watching the outcome, ready to pounce on perceived shortcomings.

Indians will be watching to see how easy or difficult it is to do business in the newly open nuclear and space areas. They will be particularly vigilant in assessing their access to state-of-the-art technologies. The nuclear agreement includes two issues that go to the heart of India's concerns about U.S. reliability as a supplier of sensitive goods and technology. The first has to do with the security of fuel supplies to India's civilian nuclear plants. India believes that the United States gave it an unqualified assurance of fuel supply; the United States has made much more guarded statements about the circumstances in which this guarantee might operate. A problem would arise only if India withdrew from the safeguards requirements of the agreement or tested another nuclear device. Both sides entered the nuclear deal with the expectation and hope that these conditions would not come to pass. The real issue here goes beyond the nuclear agreement to the relationship between international agreements and U.S. domestic law. The U.S. courts have repeatedly upheld the authority of the Congress to overturn international commitments through subsequent ordinary legislation. The United States has often had to use energetic diplomacy to prevent discrepancies between its domestic law and international commitments from exploding. This has often created tension in U.S. international relations.

The second issue is reprocessing. The bilateral nuclear cooperation agreement granted India "advance consent" for reprocessing U.S.-supplied nuclear fuel, with the proviso that the reprocessing take place in a new facility to be built in the civilian sector, under perpetual safeguards. The negotiations to implement this pledge will be complex. At the same time, the Bush administration told the Congress that it would work toward further tightening the NSG members' policy on exports of reprocessing and enrichment equipment, restricting such exports to NPT parties, and the Obama administration has given no indication of willingness to loosen the rules on reprocessing. These commitments are not incompatible, but they demonstrate that the two governments face diametrically opposed pressures.

India will also be concerned about the longer-term future of its nuclear program. In negotiating with the United States, it protected its research projects for breeder reactors and thorium-based power generation, which its scientists believe could give India an important technical and commercial edge in nuclear power in the future. The ability to reprocess foreign-supplied fuel is especially important in this context, as reprocessing would supply plutonium that could be used in a thorium generator. Foreign suppliers would almost certainly insist on maintaining safeguards over their fuel through any possible reprocessing. India's judgment of the value of the U.S. civil nuclear agreement is based on the notion of "full nuclear cooperation," and the government and its domestic critics in India will be quick to cry foul if U.S restrictions on research or on reprocessing impede India's efforts to move in these directions.

Further down the road, India's commercial ambitions for its space program could put it in competition with some U.S. space services. Public expectations are not yet an issue here; there seems to be less public awareness of the details of India's space program than of its nuclear program. But both countries are already working hard to protect their respective industries' commercial opportunities, and the more India's space program grows, the more intense this effort will be. As in other aspects of trade relations, the price of success is new trade disputes.

NONGOVERNMENT SCIENCE COOPERATION

Nuclear and space activities are in the public sector in India, and they have a large public-sector presence in the United States. But outside these fields, the private sector is ever more important in U.S.-India science cooperation. A full description of the relationships that have already been created goes beyond the scope of this study. Both governments have supported scientific cooperation since the early days of India's independence, through a remarkable array of programs—

counterpart funds generated by U.S. food aid under PL-480; direct support from the U.S Department of Agriculture and the U.S. Agency for International Development; and a succession of agreements and consultative groups on scientific cooperation. USAID and the Indian Department of Science and Technology have sent private academic scientists on exchange programs. India is the largest single recipient of capacity-building grants through the Fogarty International Center of the National Institutes of Health.[35] More recently, as noted in chapter 3, India joined the International Thermonuclear Experimental Reactor, or ITER. India and the United States have signed a series of agreements to promote cooperative science and technology.

In both countries, the government directly or indirectly has a large role in financing scientific research. India-U.S. scientific ties will grow based largely on their own momentum. Government funding can accelerate that growth, and government policies outside the realm of science and technology can shape the environment so as to encourage or discourage this interaction. Of particular importance is the possibility of greater U.S. participation in higher education in India. Foreign universities face legal restrictions on their presence and ability to grant degrees in India. Legislation to ease these limits has been under consideration for years. This is a time of ferment in Indian higher education. Indian businesses are encouraging the government to liberalize, and Indian students and young professionals are flocking to the United States in ever-increasing numbers. Many of them come back to India with new skills and connections that have become one of the great strengths of the U.S.-India story. Linkages in the world of science and technology are likely to deepen the partnership between the peoples of India and the United States in much the same way that expanding trade and investment have done.

What makes the present phase of scientific cooperation different from earlier generations—and possibly even more promising—is the increasing role of Indians and Indian-Americans, not just in developing new ideas, but in bringing them to the marketplace. In biotechnology, nanotechnology, and other fields that are only just emerging, Indian and U.S. scientists and entrepreneurs are joined at the hip, creating economic connections even as they give birth to the scientific insights on which they are based. This is taking place in fields that are not subject to the kinds of controls that characterize nuclear development and space. These connections, like those generated by trade and investment and by student exchanges, will reshape the India-U.S. partnership over the next generation.

• • • • •

The common theme running through all of these questions is expectations. The nuclear agreement was a dramatic breakthrough. Both sides expect major progress to follow it, but their specific expectations differ widely. The United States made major changes in nonproliferation policy and a huge investment of political capital in order to get the nuclear cooperation agreement approved. While there is no specific quid pro quo, it expects India to give extra weight to U.S. concerns about proliferation and to give U.S. companies a reasonable shot at business in the nuclear and defense areas. The Indian government took a huge political risk in pushing the nuclear deal forward, and it expects to be fully accepted as a nuclear power and as a legitimate high-tech trading partner with the United States. It expects to be essentially free of bureaucratic obstacles to nuclear, high-tech, and space cooperation in the future, and it expects the United States to treat it like the "nuclear weapons states" acknowledged by the NPT (currently the United States, the United Kingdom, Russia, China, and France).

Reality is likely to fall short of both ideals. The United States is still a member of the NPT and wants NPT-like standards to govern the world's trade in these sensitive areas. The process of developing a less NPT-driven nonproliferation system that comfortably accommodates India will probably gain momentum, but it is still in its infancy. India is still attached to "strategic autonomy," is reluctant to break publicly with countries like Iran where it has other strategic interests in play, and is quick to perceive that it is being discriminated against. As was apparent during the debate on U.S. nuclear legislation in both 2006 and 2008, what Washington sees as clever legislative management tactics may appear duplicitous in Delhi, and vice versa. The disconnect between U.S. and Indian strategic hopes and styles of implementation will complicate the U.S.-India partnership in the future.

NOTES

1. At its foundation, the NSG included one non-NPT member—France. This, plus a somewhat more expansive definition of the items whose trade should be controlled, distinguished it from the Zangger Committee. When France joined the NPT, the NSG membership came to include only NPT members.

2. For a masterful account of these early years and of the development of India's bomb, see George Perkovich, *India's Nuclear Bomb: The Impact on Global Proliferation* (Berkeley: University of California Press, 1999).

3. "India...is now engaged in discussions with key interlocutors on a range of issues, including the CTBT. We are prepared to bring these discussions to a successful conclusion, so that the entry into force of the CTBT is not delayed beyond September, 1999....In announcing a [testing] moratorium, India has already accepted the basic obligation of the CTBT." Quoted in Strobe Talbott, *Engaging India: Diplomacy, Democracy and the Bomb* (Washington, D.C.: Brookings Institution Press, 2006), 126.

4. Talbott, *Engaging India: Diplomacy, Democracy and the Bomb*, especially pp. 146–147 and 227; author's interview with Strobe Talbott, October 28, 2008.

5. Remarks by Indian Ministry of External Affairs (MEA) official spokesman, May 13, 2005, http://www.indianembassy.org/press_release/2005/May/2.htm. Interestingly, India explained the legislation on the basis that it was needed to comply with United Nations Security Council Resolution 1540, which obliges all countries to take certain steps to prevent proliferation.

6. Statement by Prime Minister Atal Bihari Vajpayee, "Next Steps in Strategic Partnership with USA," New Delhi, January 13, 2004, http://www.indianembassy .org/pic/pm/vajpayee/2004/pm_jan_13_2003.htm; U.S. Department of Commerce, Bureau of Industry and Security, "Announcement on U.S.-India Next Steps in Strategic Partnership September 2004," http://www.bis.doc.gov/ news/2004/us-indianextstep.htm; U.S. Department of State, "United States and India Successfully Complete Next Steps in Strategic Partnership," Fact Sheet, July 18, 2005, http://www.state.gov/p/sca/rls/fs/2005/49721.htm.

7. Carlos Gutierrez, U.S. Secretary of Commerce, presentation to U.S.-India Business Council, Washington, D.C., June 12, 2008; David A. Sampson, Deputy Secretary of Commerce, speech to U.S.-India High Technology Cooperation Group, February 22, 2007, http://www.commerce.fov/NewsRoom/ DeputySecretarySpeeches/PROD01_002802.

8. The White House, Joint Statement between President George W. Bush and Prime Minister Manmohan Singh, July 18, 2005, http://www.whitehouse.gov/ news/releases/2005/07/print/20050718-6.html.

9. Interviews with Douglas Feith, former Under Secretary of Defense for Policy, September 6, 2006, and Philip Zelikow, former Counselor, Department of State, September 18, 2008; Robert G. Joseph, Under Secretary of State for Arms Control and International Security, Testimony before Senate Foreign Relations Committee Hearing on U.S.-India Civil Nuclear Cooperation Initiative, November 2, 2005.

10. John Stephenson, "Will the U.S.-India Civil Nuclear Cooperation Initiative Light India?" presentation for the Carnegie Endowment for International

Peace, June 5, 2007; World Nuclear Association, "Nuclear Power in India," September 2008, http://world-nuclear.org/info/inf53.html.

11. See, for example, "PM's N-Energy Argument Fails to Silence Critics," *Times of India,* June 17, 2008, http://timesofindia.indiatimes.com/India/ PMs_N-energy_argument_fails_to_silence_critics/rssarticleshow/3135117 .cms; author's interview with Nicholas Burns, June 23, 2008.

12. See, for example, Michael Krepon, "Faits Accomplis, Complicity and Nuclear Proliferation," Stimson Center, August 7, 2008, http://www.stimson.org/ pub.cfm?ID=654.

13. "Statement by External Affairs Minister of India Shri Pranab Mukherjee on the Civil Nuclear Initiative," September 5, 2008, http://meaindia.nic.in/ pressbriefing/2008/09/05pb01.htm.

14. Data on the Indian space program are drawn from the ISRO web site, http://www.isro.org/index.htm; Indian Space Research Organizations (ISRO), *Annual Report 2007/2008,* http://www.isro.org/rep2008/index.htm; and from "Indian Space Section," Web site of Bharat Rakshak, http://www.bharat-rakshak .com/SPACE/index.html.

15. G. Madhavan Nair, "Transforming India's Space Program," presentation to conference at the Center for Strategic and International Studies, Washington, D.C., January 30, 2008, http://www.csis.org/component/option,com_csis _events/task,view/id,1474/.

16. ISRO, *Annual Report 2007/2008,* http://www.isro.org/rep2008/index .htm.

17. D. S. Madhumathi, "ISRO Arm's Revenue Up at Rs. 940 Crore on Satellite Launches" *The Hindu,* August 31, 2008, http://www.thehindubusinessline .com/2008/08/31/stories/2008083150820500.htm.

18. V. S. Arunachalam, "Desire and Denial: The Nullification of Cryogenic Rocket Motor Technologies to India," http://www.eisenhowerinstitute.org/ themes/international/fos/arunarticle.dot .

19. Ibid.

20. Missile Technology Control Regime (MTCR), "MTCR Guidelines and the Equipment, Software and Technology Annex," http://www.mtcr.info/english/ guidelines.html.

21. Harsh V. Pant and Gopalaswamy Bharath, "India's Emerging Missile Capability: The Science and Politics of Agni-III," *Comparative Strategy* 27 (2008): 376–387.

22. Arunachalam, "Desire and Denial." The author was deputy assistant secretary of state for South Asia during most of this period.

23. Robert Ford, Senior Advisor, Office of Space and Advanced Technology, U.S. Department of State, presentation to conference on "U.S.-India Space Cooperation," CSIS, Washington, D.C., January 30, 2008; "India's Lunar Project—Chandrayaan I—To Be Remote Sensing Mission," *India-Defence,* December 16, 2007, http://www.india-defence.com/print/3650. .

24. Web site of National Oceanic and Atmospheric Administration (NOAA), http://www.international.noaa.gov/index.htm; Web site of International Char-

ter for Space and Major Disasters, http://www.disasterscharter.org/members/
isro_e.html.

25. ISRO, *Annual Report 2007*, http://www.isro.org/rep2007/International
%20Cooperation.htm.

26. G. Madhavan Nair, "Transforming India's Space Program," presentation
to conference on "U.S.-India Space Cooperation," CSIS, Washington, D.C.,
January 30, 2008, http://www.csis.org/component/option,com_csis_events/
task,view/id,1474/.

27. The White House, "National Strategy to Combat Weapons of Mass Destruction," December 2002.

28. Shyam Saran, Special Envoy of the Prime Minister for Nuclear Issues
and for Climate Change (presentation to conference on "The U.S.-India Nuclear Agreement: Expectations and Consequences," Brookings Institution,
Washington, D.C., March 23, 2009), http://brookings.edu/~/media/Files/
events/2009/0323_india/20090323_india.pdf.

29. Policy descriptions on Barack Obama Web site, http://origin.barackobama.
com/issues/foreign_policy/#nuclear; see also David Krieger, "Comparing the
Positions of Senators Obama and McCain on Nuclear Disarmament," Nuclear Age Peace Foundation, http://www.wagingpeace.org/articles/2008/07/16
_krieger_comparing_positions.php?print.

30. Glen Kessler, "U.S. Efforts Divert Iran-Bound Cargo: India Denied Passage to
N. Korean Jet," *Washington Post*, November 4, 2008, http://www.washingtonpost
.com/wp-dyn/content/article/2008/11/03/AR2008110302683.html.

31. "Report Pursuant to Section 104(c) of the Hyde Act Regarding Civil Nuclear Cooperation with India," report submitted to the House Foreign Affairs
Committee by President Bush on September 11, 2008, 12.

32. Saran, conference presentation, March 23, 2009 (see note 28).

33. President George W. Bush, Remarks on Weapons of Mass Destruction
Proliferation, National Defense University, Washington, D.C., February 11,
2004; Department of State, "The Proliferation Security Initiative," brochure
issued 2004; Mary Beth Nikitin, "Proliferation Security Initiative." Congressional Research Service, Washington, D.C., updated February 54, 2008, http://
www.fas.org/sgp/crs/nuke/RL34327.pdf; Wade Boese, "Proliferation Security
Initiative: A Piece of the Arms Control Puzzle," *Georgetown Journal of International Affairs* 6, no. 1 (Winter 2005): 61–70.

34. Siddharth Varadarajan, "No Deviation from Agreed Text in Implementing 123, Says India," *The Hindu*, October 12, 2008, http://www.hindu
.com/2008/10/12/stories/2008101260650800.htm; William Burns, Under
Secretary of State for Political Affairs, presentation to U.S.-India Business
Council, September 9, 2008.

35. For a summary of the major government forums for consultation and for
support of scientific research, see "India-U.S. Science and Technology Relations, Harnessing the Potential," Web site of the Embassy of India in Washington, D.C., http://www.indianembassy.org/indusrel/sci.htm, accessed October
14, 2008. For a fuller description of cooperation in one key part of the health

field, see Teresita Schaffer and Pramit Mitra, "Engaging India: The U.S. Role in India's Fight against HIV/AIDS," a report of the CSIS Task Force on HIV/AIDS, June 1, 2005, http://www.csis.org/component/option,com_csis_pubs/task,view/id,550/type,1/.

6

THE NEIGHBORHOOD
SOUTH AND CENTRAL ASIA

The preceding chapters have examined the tremendous strides the United States and India have made in building up the bilateral infrastructure for their relationship. Productive and dynamic bilateral ties are important, but to be truly strategic a partnership needs to fit into a regional or global context that is compelling for both participants. India and the United States have had more difficulty identifying common elements in their view of the world and deciding which ones lend themselves to a common approach. In assessing how far that effort has progressed and where it needs to go, we will start with India's immediate neighborhood, South and Central Asia. The chapters that follow will examine how the United States and India interact in dealing with East Asia, the Middle East, other global powers, and global institutions and issues.

Sitting between the regions of major U.S. military and political engagement in the Middle East and the Western Pacific, South Asia was a relatively low policy priority for the United States during the Cold War years. Central Asia was part of the Soviet Union, not the subject of separate policy. During several extended periods, U.S. engagement in South Asia was centered on Pakistan, which hoped the United States would serve as a counterweight to its difficult relations with India. Since 2001, however, the region has been near the top of the U.S. policy agenda. For the United States, there are two central issues: first, the closely linked problems of instability and militancy in Afghanistan and Pakistan, with their pressing short-term dangers; and second, the emerging partnership with India, a longer-term strategic opportunity. The major risk is that India and Pakistan could get into a war that might go nuclear. This is the first sustained period when the two rivals have each had major policy importance for the United States and have each had good relations with Washington.

For India, South Asia is the region where it has and is determined to maintain primacy. It has no real regional rival for size, military strength, or economic weight. Despite the view of Indian strategic thinkers that China represents their major strategic challenge, security threats emanating from South and Central Asia have an urgency that others lack. India's decades-long dispute with Pakistan is its central problem in this region. With its other immediate neighbors, India starts from a stronger base of friendship than with Pakistan, but suffers from the big neighbor–small neighbor problem familiar to Americans.

Afghanistan and Central Asia are not in India's shadow in the same way as its subcontinental neighbors, and their relations with Russia and, for Afghanistan, the United States are more important than their ties with India. But they are still neighbors, countries India believes are intimately bound up with its own security. In Afghanistan, India has for decades taken the classic "neighbor's neighbor" approach, maintaining close ties with all governments except the one run by the Taliban and causing predictable anxiety in Pakistan, positioned between the two. Throughout the region, India has traditionally been suspicious of close relations between its neighbors and large outside powers.

For a closer look at how the region dominated by India figures in U.S.-India relations, we will look first at Pakistan, then at the other South Asian neighbors, Afghanistan, and Central Asia. One common thread running through all these subregions is the impact of the U.S. intervention in Afghanistan and of instability in Pakistan.

SEPARATED AT BIRTH: PAKISTAN

The India-Pakistan dispute goes back to the partition of India and the birth of Pakistan. At its core, the dispute centers on identity. India is a multiethnic and multireligious state with a Muslim population as large as Pakistan's. This contrasts with Pakistan, established as a homeland for the Muslims of the subcontinent. More concretely, the dispute includes a military rivalry that led both countries to develop and test nuclear weapons, and it has severely inhibited most normal bilateral dealings, including trade, travel, and other economic ties. The best-known feature of the dispute is Kashmir, the one Muslim-majority state that did not become part of Pakistan, which has been the focus of two wars, one near-war, and decades of unsuccessful international diplomacy. For Pakistanis, Kashmir is the root of the India-Pakistan problem. Most of the enduring bilateral problems between these two neighbors are related in some form to the Kashmir dispute.

Pakistan has always seen India as an existential threat. The episode that crystallized this fear was India's intervention in what was then East Pakistan in 1971, cutting Pakistan in half and leading to the birth of an independent Bangladesh. From the time of partition, Pakistan's foreign and security policy was Indo-centric and was designed to reject an adverse regional power structure. Pakistan sought strong alliances with large outside powers who would compensate for India's larger size and more powerful military. It crafted its policies toward Afghanistan, the Middle East, and, more recently, Central Asia to prevent dominance by India and its friends. It developed nuclear weapons in order to neutralize both India's overwhelmingly larger conventional forces and the nuclear capability India demonstrated with its "peaceful nuclear explosion" in 1974.

Geography has repeatedly given Pakistan an importance to U.S. policy that it would not otherwise have had. In the 1950s, Pakistan was adjacent to the Central Asian "soft underbelly" of the Soviet Union. Pakistan's proximity to Afghanistan made it a critical U.S. partner when the Soviet army invaded in 1979, and again when a failed Afghan state played host to al-Qaeda at the time of 9/11.

U.S. policy has sought for decades to prevent and resolve conflict between India and Pakistan. In times of crisis, this has been the dominant U.S. objective, but during calmer periods, the United States focused more on its geopolitical interests in Pakistan and, in recent years, on its expanding partnership with India.

The United States and Pakistan, during their periods of close collaboration, were at least tacitly pursuing different objectives. The original 1954 alliance with Pakistan was part of the structure the United States created to counter the Communist threat. Pakistan's main purpose was to line up the United States with Pakistan and against India. In the 1980s, the United States sought to eject the Soviet army from Afghanistan. Pakistan accepted this purpose, but also saw in it the possibility of removing Indian influence from Afghanistan. More fundamentally, Pakistan once again sought to enlist the United States in its life-long struggle against India. This same objective figured importantly in President Musharraf's decision in 2001 to sign up for Bush's war on terror.[1] By that time, however, the U.S.-Indian rapprochement was well under way, and the revived relationship with Pakistan did not interrupt it.

During much of this time, U.S. involvement in Pakistan was more specific and focused than the more diffuse relationship with India. Especially during earlier periods of India-U.S. rapprochement, the United States struggled to balance its relationships with these discordant neighbors. This came to be known and criticized in India as "hyphenation." India increasingly bridled at having its ties with the United States restricted by what Pakistan was willing to put up with, and was galled by being linked with a country it considered of lesser power and importance. Since 2000, the United States has succeeded better in "de-hyphenating" its relationships with Pakistan and India, although the public and the governments in those countries assiduously keep track of the balance and comparative benefits in their respective ties with Washington.

Three recurring themes in U.S. policy toward Pakistan illustrate the complex interaction between U.S. and Indian policy and the continuing impact of the Pakistan factor on U.S.-India ties, despite "de-hyphenation." The first two, military supply to Pakistan and U.S. diplomacy toward the India-Pakistan dispute, have been recurring sources of tension in U.S.-India relations. The third, terrorism, is an area of strong agreement in principle, but the United States and India have different ideas about how to deal with Pakistan in this context.

U.S. MILITARY SUPPLY TO PAKISTAN

The United States has been a major arms supplier to Pakistan, especially during the periods of most intense foreign policy cooperation. In each case, the military supply relationship was part of a broader agreement: in the 1950s, Pakistan's alliance with the United States; in the 1980s, the aid package negotiated following the Soviet invasion of Afghanistan; and in the current period, the post-9/11 aid package. India made clear its unhappiness with each major arms purchase. In proposing arms sales to Congress, as is required by U.S. law, the United States always argued that Pakistan's purchases would stabilize—or at least not destabilize—regional relations. India argued that Pakistan had always used U.S.-supplied arms against India, but these arguments ultimately did not affect U.S. policy. The larger U.S. goals for relations with Pakistan were decisive.

The United States twice cut off military supply to Pakistan. In 1965, it took action against both Pakistan and India because the two countries were fighting a war with U.S.-supplied armaments that had been supplied to contain Communism. Pakistan was much more severely affected, because U.S. weaponry had a much larger place in its arms inventory, but in principle action was taken against both countries. The second cutoff was in 1990, when the United States ended all assistance to Pakistan because of its nuclear program. Interestingly, about a year before this cutoff, the United States had agreed to a sale of F-16 fighter aircraft to Pakistan; India objected, but with much less vehemence than in the past. The aid cutoff stopped all but a relatively small amount of humanitarian assistance. It ended all arms sales and many routine avenues for military-to-military contact between the United States and Pakistan for more than a decade.

By the time military sales to Pakistan resumed after 9/11, U.S. relations with India had been transformed, and the United States was developing a security relationship with India. Although Delhi was unhappy about the revival of U.S. military sales to Pakistan, U.S.-Pakistan relations had become a much smaller element in Delhi's ties with Washington. In 2005, the United States announced major milestones in its security relations with both countries in a single White House background briefing. The briefers said that the United States would license a major new F-16 sale to Pakistan. They also expressed the U.S. intention to "help India become a major power," and announced that the United States would allow U.S. aircraft producers to offer coproduction as part of their bids on an anticipated Indian tender for combat aircraft. The format was "hyphenated," but the content of the announcement suggested that the pattern of relations with both countries would move forward independently. U.S. arms sales to Pakistan will remain an uncomfortable subject for India, despite expanding Indian security ties with the United States. But the multifaceted nature of U.S. relations with India will continue to provide areas of cooperation to balance India's unhappiness with U.S. military relations with Pakistan.

U.S. DIPLOMACY TOWARD THE INDIA-PAKISTAN DISPUTE

Preventing conflict between India and Pakistan has always been an important U.S. policy objective, but the level of U.S. effort has varied considerably. Historically, Pakistan was eager to draw the United States in, believing that international involvement would raise the visibility of the Kashmir issue and improve the chances of settling it on Pakistan's terms. India is the status quo power, however, and controls the key parts of Kashmir. It accordingly tends to resist international involvement and for many years specifically objected to U.S. involvement, suspecting that the United States would tilt toward Pakistan.

The United States was deeply involved in mediation and facilitation efforts on Kashmir in the 1940s, 1950s, and early 1960s. These came to naught. Since then, major U.S. diplomatic initiatives have involved crisis management rather than long-term conflict resolution.

All three major U.S. diplomatic efforts since 1990 came about in response to situations triggered by the Kashmir dispute that the United States believed included a risk of hostilities. In 1990, President George H.W. Bush sent three senior officials headed by then-deputy national security adviser Robert Gates to India and Pakistan to press for more effective confidence-building measures in an effort to prevent a recurrence of the military buildup and brinksmanship that had taken place earlier that year. In 1999, after Pakistan's decision to send troops into the Kargil heights, in a remote part of Indian-held Kashmir, President Bill Clinton secured a Pakistani withdrawal, bringing an end to a near war. Once again, after the December 2001 bombing of the Indian parliament by apparent Islamic extremists, India mounted a massive military buildup along the borders, and President George W. Bush sent Deputy Secretary of State Richard Armitage to the region to secure Pakistani promises to prevent infiltration into Indian-administered Kashmir from Pakistan-controlled territory. In each case, the United States sought to cool immediate tensions and eliminate the risk of war. Sorting out the legal equities in Kashmir did not enter into these initiatives, and none of them included a serious U.S. effort to broker a long-term settlement. India was reasonably pleased with the results; for Pakistan, all three diplomatic efforts were a frustrating demonstration that its strategy of relying on outside help in its dispute with India was not working.

As of late 2008, the only diplomatic effort working toward an India-Pakistan settlement was a bilateral one between the two parties. India and Pakistan had maintained a border cease-fire and conducted a peace dialogue since January 2004, with the United States encouraging it from the sidelines rather than participating. This dialogue lasted longer than many previous ones and survived a number of bombings and other violent incidents, although it ultimately collapsed after the November 2008 attacks on Mumbai. It notched up several modest but useful confidence-building measures, but did not resolve more substantive issues. The most productive channel was a very discreet dialogue between high-level special envoys, which included candid discussions on Kashmir. The United States has repeatedly said that it would be willing to help the dialogue process if both countries wanted it to. India is unlikely to take up this offer.

From the perspective of U.S.-India relations, this relatively laid-back posture works well in the short term. Having both governments committed to dialogue has reduced the short-term risk of war, so U.S. policymakers feel no urgent need to enter the mine-strewn territory of India-Pakistan peacemaking, an exercise whose chances of early success would be poor. But, as we saw after Mumbai, this benign situation is always vulnerable to potential political instability in Pakistan and the Pakistani government's imperfect control of militant groups that might play a spoiler's role.

If serious fighting threatens in the future, the United States might find crisis management more difficult. India, eager to preserve its freedom of action, has been developing a military approach that minimizes the preparation time its army would need before taking action on the India-Pakistan border. Both India and Pakistan will draw on their experience with previous crisis management efforts to devise new ways of pressuring one another and the United States. In short, the irritant to U.S.-India relations that comes with an active U.S. diplomatic role on India-Pakistan peace has receded, but it would be back in full force if a full-blown crisis broke.

TERRORISM

The United States and India have differed over arms sales to Pakistan and U.S. diplomatic intervention. There are important but complicated policy overlaps, however, when it comes to terrorism and Pakistan's internal stability. India and the United States strongly agree in principle in their opposition to terrorism, and they also by and large agree that regional security is best served by preserving the stability of the Pakistani state. But they do not necessarily agree on what to do about either problem, and their disagreements generate mistrust. The importance and fragility of the U.S.-Pakistan relationship has impeded serious official discussions about Pakistan.

India, as noted in chapter 4, sees Pakistan as the heart of its terrorism problem. It believes that Pakistan, or organizations that operate from Pakistani territory, are involved not just in the insurgency in Kashmir but also in bombings and explosions in many other parts of India. The list of incidents is long and bloody. A Sikh separatist movement during the 1980s had at least indirect support from Pakistan. In 1993, a series of explosions aimed at economic targets in Mumbai did massive damage; a Muslim underworld figure accused of masterminding the attacks took refuge in Pakistan. After September 11, terrorist attacks by militant groups based in Pakistan hit high-profile targets in India, including especially the Indian parliament. Subsequent bombings have hit sites that included busy markets in New Delhi, a university meeting in Bangalore, the city of Varanasi, the suburban commuter train system in Mumbai, and a train on its way from India to Pakistan. In late November 2008, a spectacular simultaneous attack on some of Mumbai's best-known hotels and the main railway station went on for three days and left more than 170 people dead. In July 2008, India's national security adviser, M. K. Narayanan, publicly accused Pakistan's Inter-Services Intelligence (ISI) of responsibility for the bombing of India's embassy in Kabul, a charge that was apparently consistent with information available through U.S. intelligence sources.[2] Just as worrying, Indian security officials concluded that by mid-decade some Indian Muslims had been drawn into this kind of violence.

In the initial period after 9/11, India tried and failed to persuade the United States that terrorism in Kashmir was part of global terrorism and that it should impose antiterrorism sanctions on Pakistan. The United States walked a fine line, expressing outrage at violent incidents in India and designating several of the most prominent Pakistan-based militant groups as "foreign terrorist organizations."[3] The U.S. diplomatic campaign that followed the December 2001 attack on the Indian parliament pressed Pakistan hard to crack down on domestic extremist groups, but it stopped well short of designating Pakistan a "state sponsor of terrorism." The sanctions that flow from such a designation would have made the United States' security relationship with Pakistan untenable—and that was the top U.S. priority with Pakistan.

Over the next few years, the focus of U.S. terrorism concerns about Pakistan shifted to the Pakistan-Afghanistan border, with increasing evidence that Afghan insurgents were taking refuge on the Pakistani side. U.S. pressure on Pakistan ratcheted up. The U.S. director of national intelligence in January 2007 described Pakistan as a "major source of Islamic extremism."[4] A steady stream of visitors to Pakistan from both the U.S. Congress and the executive branch emphasized the urgency with which the United States regarded the terrorism threat. India's concerns on the same score also continued to rise. But the likelihood of common action by the United States and India is very low. U.S. military involvement in Afghanistan makes it imperative to harness Pakistan to a common strategy and, as we will see in the next section, limits India's role in that strategy.

SHARED INTEREST IN A STABLE PAKISTAN

India and the United States also share an interest in the stability and integrity of the Pakistani state. India's attitude toward President Musharraf, as with previous Pakistani military rulers, was initially very harsh, to the point of not wanting to do business with his government. Over the years, it softened, and by early 2007 Indian officials had concluded that the Musharraf government was probably the most favorable available option from India's perspective. In contrast to the unwelcome official comments Indian governments had previously made on domestic difficulties in Pakistan, the government in Delhi said little about the turmoil in Pakistan that preceded and followed the February 2008 elections, or on Musharraf's resignation later that year. The Indian government also made a point of inviting to India representatives of virtually all the major Pakistani political parties, in the hope of humanizing the relationship on both sides and taking some venom out of the public debate. As a result, India went largely unmentioned in Pakistan's 2008 election campaign.

Pakistanis have noted these signs of Indian support for a stable Pakistan, but many still believe that Indian intelligence services are looking for opportunities to destabilize them. In fact, India has good reasons not to seek additional trouble in Pakistan. The army controls Pakistan's nuclear weapons, and its ability to maintain that control is strongly in India's interest. India has long considered divided government and confused control in Pakistan to be its nightmare scenario. In these circumstances, India's interests and those of the United States will be reasonably well aligned at least for this aspect of Pakistan policy, though once again, this congruity is not likely to lead to any explicit policy coordination or even consultation.

The big issue for India and Pakistan in their dealings with the United States is not any of these specific questions, however. Rather, each country is watching carefully the overall weight and significance of the other's ties with Washington. For India, the revival of U.S.-Pakistan ties after 9/11 was a great disappointment. U.S. diplomatic intervention to ease tensions in 2002 left India pleased that the United States had been able to help reduce day-to-day infiltration, but acutely conscious that U.S. policy toward Pakistan was driven mainly by concern over the spread of violence from the Pakistan-Afghanistan border area. Indian policymakers believe there are severe limits to U.S. influence on Pakistan's behavior. India recognizes that it cannot control the basic shape of U.S.-Pakistan relations; it will live with the results, but it will be careful to preserve its freedom of action.

Pakistan, on the other hand, is deeply concerned about the emerging U.S.-India partnership and is easily caught off base when the Washington-Delhi connection is on public display. Both President Clinton's and President Bush's visits to Islamabad and Delhi are cases in point. In both cases, Pakistanis felt slighted by the hoopla attending the presidential visits to India, although the details of the visits had been well known for weeks. Pakistan looks at the U.S.-India nuclear deal and the prospect of significant U.S. arms sales to India and concludes that it has lost its preferred position in Washington. The contrast between expanding U.S. economic relations with India and the rather meager investment taking place in Pakistan accentuates this sense of grievance. These concerns, coupled with Pakistan's chronic insecurity, ensure that managing these twin relationships will remain a major challenge for the United States.

THE SMALLER NEIGHBORS

India's relations with its other South Asian neighbors do not have the same toxic history as do its ties with Pakistan. Bangladesh, Sri Lanka, and Nepal chafe, albeit less than Pakistan, at India's taking them for granted. India expects its other South Asian neighbors not to deviate too far from India's major foreign policy priorities, and it does not want their ties with outside powers to upstage India's prominent position. India has tried with considerable success to limit the role of outsiders, including the United States, in defense relationships and major infrastructure projects in which India sees military implications.

India's position has been strongest across its northern borders. Bhutan has long had a treaty obligation to take India's advice in defense and foreign affairs, and the treaty was only recently revised to reduce the scope of that obligation. In Nepal, India has been the dominant power, and on those few occasions when Nepal turned to China for road-building or military supply, India's response has been swift and harsh. The emergence of a Maoist-dominated government added another concern: Nepal's Maoists appeared to be making common cause with the so-called Naxalite insurgent movement in central India, across a porous and virtually unpatrollable border.

India's interest in Sri Lanka's ethnic conflict was driven by both strategic and domestic political considerations. India sought to ensure that Tamil rights were preserved along with Sri Lankan territorial integrity. India's decision in 1987 to broker an agreement that included the introduction of the Indian Peace Keeping Force misfired badly. The Tamil insurgents did not accept the agreement, the Indian peacekeepers lost 1,000 men and were in the end publicly expelled from Sri Lanka, and an operative of the Liberation Tigers of Tamil Eelam assassinated Rajiv Gandhi, then running for prime minister. The suspicions left over from this period of Indian activism have effectively prevented India from taking an active role in pursuit of its interests to the south, despite relatively friendly relations with the Sri Lankan government.

The relationship with Bangladesh has been the most mercurial. India midwifed the birth of Bangladesh as an independent country. Within a few years, India had become a lightning rod in Bangladeshi politics, the big neighbor all Bangladeshi politicians criticized. Bangladeshi governance deteriorated badly in the 1990s and beyond, and India with some justification saw Pakistan's hand in the increasingly active posture of a handful of Islamic extremists in Bangladesh and across its borders with India. Bangladesh is the clearest manifestation of a phenomenon that extends to all India's neighbors: acute sensitivity to any indication that Pakistan or its intelligence services are using neighboring countries' territory as a base for operations against India.

U.S. interests in all these countries have historically been modest. The United States has a major aid presence in Nepal and Bangladesh. It has never been a major player in negotiations to resolve Sri Lanka's ethnic conflict. Until about 2000, Indians were quite suspicious of U.S. relations with these countries. In deference to the sensibilities of India's neighbors, the United States took care not to appear too close to India on regional matters and to ensure that its relations with the rest of the region could stand on their own feet.

Unlike the rather thin consultations on Pakistan, U.S.-India discussions about these other South Asian countries deepened as ties between Delhi and Washington warmed. After the Nepalese king's institution of autocratic rule in February 2006, the United States let it be known that its response was carefully coordinated with both India and the United Kingdom. It has continued to work closely with India through the complex constitutional amendment process and the exit of the king. India's willingness to work with the Maoists who wound up as the largest political party in the constituent assembly overcame serious U.S. doubts about any role for the Maoists.

The U.S. response to the aborted Bangladeshi election in 2007 and the installation of an army-backed interim government followed a somewhat similar path. On that occasion, the United States took a more prominent position and was a bit quicker to call for a return to elected government. In Sri Lanka, consultations have been close, but there has been less inclination to develop a common plan of action, largely because of India's complicated history of involvement in the Sri Lankan conflict. These consultations revealed that Indian and U.S. policymakers had reasonably compatible views about the regional picture. This common interest was welcome in both capitals, but it did not prevent the inevitable accusations from the neighbors that the United States had simply "subcontracted" its policy to India.

STRATEGIC AMBIVALENCE ABOUT AFGHANISTAN

Afghanistan has been at the center of U.S. foreign policy since the attacks of September 11. India's long friendship with Afghanistan has special sensitivity for Pakistan, and consequently for the United States, because of Afghanistan's location on the other side of Pakistan. Except for the period of Taliban rule, Afghanistan has had difficult relations with Pakistan. The implosion of the Taliban government was a strategic benefit for India. In Pakistan, it was regarded as a strategic disaster. The accession of an Afghan government most of whose key personalities had close links with India accentuated Pakistan's worry.

The United States and India share important interests in Afghanistan, but U.S. deference to Pakistan's security concerns severely limits the degree to which they work together.

For the United States, Afghanistan is above all a battleground, a stubborn center of instability and Islamic extremism that radiate outward to the rest of its difficult neighborhood. Despite the fall of the Taliban and the initial enthusiasm of the Afghan people for a new political dawn, insurgency continues and the ultimate outcome for Afghanistan is far from clear. NATO's military campaign provided an opportunity for the organization to take on a new mission. The effect on the alliance has been contradictory. This operation provided a new focus for the alliance after the end of the Cold War, but the inconclusive results of the campaign have made it quite unpopular among many of the allies. Contributing nations have subjected troop contributions to a patchwork of restrictions or "caveats." One potential danger is that this undertaking might wind up diminishing the credibility and political impact of U.S. and NATO military strength.

India and the United States share one overriding interest in Afghanistan: restoring a viable, moderate government. Indian officials and strategic thinkers see a more stable governing structure in Afghanistan as essential to stem the export of violent Islamic extremism. Indian strategic thinkers are very conscious of Afghanistan's impact on the military and political credibility of the United States, and they clearly believe that preserving this credibility is important for India's security. They would welcome an increase in the size and effectiveness of the NATO contingent, which they see primarily as an extension of the U.S. presence. This welcoming attitude toward a U.S. military presence in India's neighborhood is a major change from India's traditional foreign policy. In 1979, for example, India's official reaction to the Soviet invasion of Afghanistan was to decry the prospect of greater U.S. involvement in and near Afghanistan.

Ironically, the future stability of Afghanistan is an interest India shares with Pakistan as well. India's other concerns in Afghanistan put it at odds with Pakistan, however. India wants to retain a significant role in Afghanistan, and it points out that India's educational institutions, traditional ties with many Afghan leaders, and incipient aid-giving capacity all make it a useful contributor to Afghan reconstruction. For Pakistan, any Indian role is anathema, an opportunity for India to meddle both in Afghanistan and across the border in Pakistan's most troubled provinces. The harsh Pakistani reaction when India established four consulates in Afghanistan in 2002 illustrates the problem. India would like to have direct land access to Afghanistan for trade as well as aid and reconstruction shipments. Pakistan has not been willing to allow Indian goods to transit, so the only avenue for land transit has been through Iran.

The United States has given priority to Pakistani sensitivities. It welcomes India's generous contribution to Afghan reconstruction—$750 million pledged in the first seven years after the fall of the Taliban—but has kept it at arms length on security.[5] For India, this "half a loaf" is not sufficient. It sees its own security interests affected by developments in Afghanistan and would like to establish a stronger and broader connection to the new government. The prospects for the United States and India coordinating their policies on anything beyond a strictly economic agenda appear remote as long as the U.S. effort in Afghanistan is heavily dependent on Pakistan's cooperation.

CENTRAL ASIA

In the rest of Central Asia, the United States and India have different strategic goals but the resulting policies are fairly compatible. The dominant power in the region is Russia, and the Central Asian countries carry the legacy of their years as Soviet republics. Their economies still depend on Russia, and most of their trade relationships are with Russia, displaying the "hub and spokes" pattern that prevailed during the Soviet years, rather than with each other. There are also important security ties with Russia. Most of the Central Asians are members of the Commonwealth of Independent States Collective Security Treaty (CST).

Since the end of the Soviet Union, a number of outside powers besides Russia have sought to strengthen their influence in Central Asia. China has probably been the most successful, promising major investments in the Kazakh oil sector and in Tajikistan's infrastructure and building up a very active network of regional networks through the Shanghai Cooperation Organization (SCO). Turkey and Iran have long-standing linguistic and cultural ties in Central Asia, but they have been less important players on the security and economic scene. India and Pakistan have each tried to stake out a major presence and to limit each other's influence.

For the United States, the key interest is the security and sustainable independence of the region. The United States would like to lessen the Central Asians' dependence on Moscow and to support their internal political and economic reforms. Washington also wants to preserve its security ties despite the closure of the U.S. facility in Uzbekistan in 2005 and the Kyrgyz parliament's decision to close down the U.S. air base at Manas in early 2009. The United States has overflight and refueling arrangements with Turkmenistan, Kazakhstan, and Tajikistan. These have been important for the U.S. and NATO missions in Afghanistan and represent the only alternative to routing logistic and air support through Pakistan. Finally, the United States wants to preserve access to Central Asian energy resources for the world market and for U.S. companies. Among the other outside powers active in Central Asia, Russia, China, and Iran are interested in limiting U.S. influence.

India also has energy and security interests, but different ones from those of the United States. Its security concerns derive from the region's geographic location, just beyond Afghanistan. India wants to establish itself as a significant player in Central Asia, to blunt Pakistan's influence, and to keep an eye on radical Islamic organizations. India has developed military ties in the region, primarily in Tajikistan, where a military airfield reconstruction project at Ayni is occasionally described as a "base" and may include a military access arrangement. India would clearly like to expand its involvement with the Central Asian military, for example, through training.

Central Asia's substantial energy resources represent India's most tangible economic interest in the area. At present, however, that interest is more potential than real, as geography and the turbulent politics of the region make reliable supply arrangements difficult. India's public-sector oil company, Oil and Natural Gas Corporation Videsh Ltd., has made major investments in production facilities especially in Kazakhstan, the energy giant of the region. There have apparently been swap arrangements involving Kazakh oil, but the only physical route, by pipeline to Ceyhan on the Mediterranean and thence by sea to India, is too long and expensive to be practical on a regular basis. A pipeline to India would need to cross the politically turbulent and geographically forbidding terrain of Afghanistan and Pakistan. Similarly, there is discussion about a gas pipeline from Turkmenistan, but Turkmenistan has not yet been willing to provide a long-term supply commitment, and transporting the gas to India would again involve crossing Afghanistan and Pakistan. The basic economics of electricity sales, taking advantage of surplus hydropower resources in Tajikistan and Kyrgyzstan, would be promising, but would require a major investment in dams as well as a solution to the transport problem.

Indian strategic thinkers and authors also cite the importance of restoring traditional trade and other economic links with Central Asia, which they hope will eventually cement India's role there. However, current trade is insignificant—just over $240 million in two-way trade with the whole region in 2007—and although investment has been going up, it still has not reached significant proportions.[6] The other missing ingredient for expanded trade is transportation infrastructure, in which India is poised to make major investments. Access through Iran, discussed in chapter 8, is critical. The roads India is working on could make a strategic difference to the trade possibilities for both Afghanistan and Central Asia. Trade from both areas with India would become easier: outside trade with Afghanistan would have multiple access routes; and the Central Asian countries would become less dependent on Russian trade routes.

India appears to have succeeded fairly well in outshining Pakistan's influence in Central Asia, especially since the turmoil in Afghanistan has become a major preoccupation for the Pakistanis. The United States has no interest in stoking this Indo-Pakistan rivalry, but it is not as deferential to Pakistan's sensitivities in Central Asia as it is in Afghanistan.

In what some people are calling the "new Great Game," India has an interesting position in Central Asia, somewhat at odds with China and sharply at odds with Pakistan, but with policies and goals that are more or less compatible with other outside powers interested in the region. India's interest in developing independent economic ties with Central Asia and its vigorous cultural relations harmonize well with the Central Asians' desire to broaden their international base of support, and they fit in well with U.S. interests in making the Central Asians' independence more sustainable. The interesting question is whether at some point India's policies will arouse opposition in Moscow, despite India's traditional ties with Russia. India and China eye each other with some suspicion. India sees Chinese influence in Central Asia as a device for potentially "encircling" India, and China has been quicker in lining up energy deals than India.

REGIONAL ARCHITECTURE

Regional institutions have played a very modest role in South and Central Asia. The South Asian Association for Regional Cooperation (SAARC), launched in 1985, consists of India, its six subcontinental neighbors (Pakistan, Nepal, Bhutan, Bangladesh, Sri Lanka, and Maldives), and now Afghanistan. It has always been a weak organization. India is skeptical of its value and does not want it to become a venue where the seven smaller members can gang up on India. Largely at India's insistence, the SAARC charter precludes any discussion of bilateral problems, and the group's annual summits must be attended by all heads of government. For many years, SAARC's main accomplishment was to provide an opportunity for India and Pakistan to do quiet business in between formal meetings. More recently, the organization has been the umbrella under which several of its members undertook trade liberalization, including partial free trade agreements between India and two of its neighbors. The members have agreed in principle to move toward a free trade area. This suggests that if India and Pakistan found the basis for moving ahead on economic relations, SAARC might be a setting for developing more constructive regional relations. The admission of the United States together with Russia and China as observers in 2006 was another indication of India's greater willingness to recognize the interests of other countries in its neighborhood.

The region's other grouping, the Shanghai Cooperation Organization, has a more anti-American cast. Formally launched in 2001, it includes China, Russia, Kazakhstan, Kyrgyzstan, Tajikistan, and Uzbekistan. Observers admitted in 2004 and 2005 include Mongolia, India, Pakistan, and Iran. Its purposes include cooperation on economics and foreign policy, and its founding documents include a convention on combating separatism, terrorism, and extremism. The SCO called for the "expulsion of foreign bases" in 2005, a transparent reference to the U.S. presence in Central Asia. India has attended its meetings at a relatively low level. At present, unlike SAARC, the SCO seems to be largely an arena for Russia and China to compete for local influence.

LOOKING AHEAD

Three features make U.S.-India interaction in South Asia sharply different from U.S.-India interaction in other parts of the world. First, the two countries still often work at cross-purposes in South Asia. The United States' alliances with Pakistan were never explicitly aimed against India—indeed, the United States took great care to make clear that they had different targets—but Pakistan used them as part of its defense posture against India, and India regarded them in the same light. The United States went along with this up to a point. The military equipment it supplied to Pakistan was in many cases useful only in the context of possible hostilities with India (e.g., F-16 aircraft). In Afghanistan, the United States today remains quite deferential to Pakistani sensitivities about India's role. The United States traditionally tried to avoid acknowledging India's primacy in the region, out of respect for the smaller countries' concerns about their large neighbor. Since 2001, U.S. and Indian policies in the region have become more compatible, although the sensitivities of Pakistan and the smaller South Asian countries will continue to be a factor.

The second unique feature of this region is India's dominance. India has a major political, economic, and security stake in each of its neighboring countries and in Afghanistan. The United States is far away; it is an important export destination for Bangladesh, Nepal, and Sri Lanka, but in other respects it has less day-to-day impact than India does. This feature makes the new practice of U.S.-India policy coordination on the smaller South Asian countries noteworthy, because it suggests a degree of mutual confidence between India and the United States that was not there even a decade ago.

This situation could change, however, if the U.S. and NATO military forces departed from Afghanistan leaving a rickety government behind. That would raise serious questions in the minds of India's leaders about whether the United States intended to remain a major factor in South Asian events. India would work hard to achieve the level of influence it believes is its due. One consequence would almost certainly be an increase in India-Pakistan tensions.

Finally, this region is strongly influenced by the India-Pakistan dispute. The risk of conflict could rise with little warning. India's ties in this region have a profound impact on its ambitions for a larger global role and on the kind of global relationship it can create with the United States. India's relations with China and with the Muslim world, its ambitions for a permanent seat on the UN Security Council, and more generally its ability to brand itself as a world power are to some degree inhibited by the decades-long face-off with Pakistan.

This suggests that both India and the United States may at some point need to reconsider their relatively passive approach to India-

Pakistan diplomacy. For India, the prevailing view for some years has been that the present situation is preferable to "making concessions." India finds the prospect of working with an outside power distasteful, and it suspects that the United States would favor Pakistan. This view does not fully take into account the fact that preserving regional peace and stability tops U.S. interests. As a result, the United States in practice favors maintaining the territorial status quo, as India does.

For the United States, an overloaded foreign policy agenda discourages policymakers from undertaking a new and difficult task, and the sorry fate of earlier India-Pakistan agendas reinforces this caution. But once the new government is in place in Delhi, both countries need to take a sober look at the costs of allowing the current drift to continue. The answer might or might not include a major U.S. diplomatic initiative, but hopefully India would look on its peacemaking efforts with Pakistan with greater urgency.

NOTES

1. See, for example, Musharraf's speech explaining his decision to the Pakistani people and citing in particular "the sacred cause of Kashmir" as one of his reasons for joining the U.S. campaign. President Pervez Musharraf, "Address to the People of Pakistan," September 19, 2001, http://www.americanrhetoric.com/speeches/pakistanpresident.htm.

2. "ISI Involved in Kabul Attack, Says Narayanan," *The Hindu*, July 13, 2008, http://www.hindu.com/2008/07/13/stories/2008071359580800.htm.

3. "Foreign Terrorist Organizations," Fact Sheet, Office of the Coordinator for Counterterrorism, December 30, 2004, http://www.state.gov/s/ct/rls/fs/2004/40945.htm. The designations took place between 2003 and September 2008.

4. John Negroponte, Director of National Intelligence, "Annual Threat Assessment of the Director of National Intelligence," testimony before the Senate Select Committee on Intelligence, January 11, 2007, http://intelligence.senate.gov/070111/negroponte.pdf.

5. Richard Boucher, remarks at conference on "Bridging Strategic Asia," CSIS, Washington, D.C., June 28, 2007.

6. Ministry of Commerce, Government of India, "Export Import Data Bank," http://commerce.nic.in/eidb/irgncomq.asp.

7

LOOKING EAST
INDIA AND EAST ASIA

In May 1998, India's nuclear tests shook the foundations of the country's external relations and jolted its ties to its east in Asia. India explained its tests by noting the strategic threat that it faced from China. The Chinese reacted sharply. Two months later, the Indian foreign minister, Jaswant Singh, attended the annual ASEAN Regional Forum (ARF) meeting in Manila, and his nuclear brief got a chilly reception from his Southeast Asian counterparts. A particularly painful part of the meeting must have been his participation in the after-dinner songs and skits that have become a standard ASEAN ritual. No one, least of all him, enjoyed his light verse about the nuclear test, which he no doubt found out of keeping with the dignity of India's foreign minister and his own somber style.[1]

Fast forward a decade, and the change is dramatic. East Asia has emerged as a major focus of India's diplomacy and its external economic relations. China is India's largest source of imports. India's military forces have conducted exercises with Japan, China, and several Southeast Asian countries; most remarkably, India and ASEAN have negotiated a free trade area.

Indian and U.S. interests in East Asia are similar. India's profile there is lower, and the U.S. profile higher, than in India's immediate neighborhood. Asia's strategic importance for both partners is tremendous. Their environment will be fundamentally shaped by the rise of China and by India's and China's interaction with Japan and the United States. It is therefore useful to ask to what extent India and the United States share a common vision of the world beyond India's immediate neighborhood, how the shared elements of that vision affect their partnership, and how they deal with differences.

For Indian policymakers, East Asia is the land of opportunity, the site of some of India's most successful foreign policy gains, both in major power relationships such as those with China and Japan and in expanding economic relations. For more than a decade, Indian strategic thinkers have described all of Southeast Asia, rather than only the subcontinent and its surrounding waters, as falling inside India's strategic environment. India's "Look East" policy was first articulated in 1992, and it became a significant element in Indian policy about five years later. Indian leaders now visit East Asia often, and their visits have a higher profile, as witnessed in Manmohan Singh's attendance at the ASEAN Summit in Manila in January 2007 and in his summit meetings in Japan in 2006 and in China in 2008. Economic ties with the region are also growing. In 2006–2007, 29 percent of India's foreign trade was with Asia, up from 24 percent in 2000.[2]

The U.S. focus on East Asia goes back to the early days of U.S. independence. The long-standing U.S. presence in the Western Pacific, the Opening of Japan, the colonial and postcolonial relationship with the Philippines, the postwar occupation of Japan and the alliance that grew out of it, the legacy of the Korean War, and the sensitive relationship with Taiwan make the United States an Asian power. For reasons of both bureaucratic organization and past regional dynamics, however, the United States put India and East Asia in different mental and policy categories. The U.S. military, as we have seen, puts ties with India within the responsibility of the commander in chief, U.S. Pacific Command (CINCPAC), but most U.S. civilian government agencies assign responsibility for India to different officials and different bureaus from East Asia. As a result, U.S. policy was slow to respond when India began working to insert itself into the larger Asian milieu, and mechanisms for comparing notes about Indian and U.S. interests in this larger environment have been difficult to develop. Japan's economic heft passed India's in the 1950s, and its alliance with the United States had a policy importance that dwarfed ties with India. China from the late 1960s onward was acknowledged as a great power whose nuclear weapons were accepted under the Non-Proliferation Treaty. By the 1990s, China was also an economic powerhouse, which gave it yet another claim to priority in relations with the United States. The structure of U.S. relationships in East Asia therefore left little room for exploring where India fit in, especially in an earlier period when India's own attention was elsewhere.

On China, Japan, and Southeast Asia, India's interests today are close to those that drive U.S. foreign policy, despite the very different historical baggage India and the United States bring to the table. Both India and the United States see Asia as essential to the world's and their own peace and prosperity. Both hope and expect that Asia will evolve toward a balance of power rather than a single dominant force, and both have taken care to engage with all major Asian powers.

This overlap in interests ought to allow India and the United States to develop a broad pattern of cooperation. With a few exceptions, however, this cooperation remains mainly tacit. The overlap in Indian and U.S. interests would also suggest that the United States would benefit from India's greater integration into the larger Asian community. In practice, however, the United States has been ambivalent about regional institutions centered on East Asia, and cool toward India's efforts to join them. And India does not have a clear idea about how it sees the United States' role in East Asia, nor about how East Asia relates to the India-U.S. partnership. This chapter will look in turn at China, Japan, Southeast Asia, and the issue of regional architecture for East and South Asia.

CHINA'S RISE, AND INDIA'S

For both India and the United States, China's expanding power is the most important development in East Asia. Both partners stress engagement with China; both also see China as a major strategic challenge, requiring an unusually high degree of subtlety and sophistication in their diplomacy. Partly because neither country wants to be seen as part of an anti-China alliance or to feed Chinese concerns about "encirclement," official contacts between India and the United States have not devoted much time to in-depth discussion of China. As a result, one of the most important areas of policy convergence is left largely unstated at the official level, and the differences between Indian and U.S. policies and perceptions are rarely explored.

Indian policy toward China has gone through several metamorphoses in the past half-century. The heyday of good feeling summarized by the Hindi slogan "Hindi-Chini bhai-bhai," or "Indians and Chinese are brothers," gave way to intense suspicion especially after

China bested India in the 1962 war in the high Himalayas, and then to a less active posture still dominated by Indian suspicion of China's ties with Pakistan, followed by a period of revived political and economic engagement. As China has become more powerful economically and militarily, Indians have increasingly come to look on China as the standard against which India's own international role and international acceptance should be measured. It is a lopsided relationship: China is more important to India than the reverse. Since about 2000, India's economic success and greater international profile have increased its importance to China without ending the asymmetry.

For many years, the most visible bilateral issue was their border dispute. In 1993, the two sides signed an agreement to reduce tensions on the border and respect the Line of Actual Control between Chinese-held and Indian-held territory in the Himalayan region. In 1996, they agreed to start serious border talks. That agreement led to a partial exchange of maps in 2000, the first in nearly 40 years, and to discussions on border management issues. The unspoken assumption behind these moves was that if there was a solution, each side would keep what it already controlled, an arrangement that would require each to give up some of its claims. Neither was in a hurry, and both were determined not to let the dispute cause serious problems. Multiple meetings have occurred, but actual border negotiations have yet to take place.

With rare exceptions, this tacit commitment to restraint has worked. The border is generally peaceful, and border trade arrangements have expanded, most recently by adding a border trade point in Sikkim. The few instances in which Chinese officials have publicly reasserted their old claims, as happened in 2006, caused consternation in India. Both countries are taking careful note of each other's activities in the region, including China's upgrading of infrastructure and India's expansion of an air base and the modest increase in the size of its forces. But the border issue, despite being unresolved, is no longer the signature issue for India-China relations.

The other political bone of contention, the Dalai Lama's presence in India, has enjoyed a similar tacit agreement not to upset the current policy balance. India formally recognized the Tibet Autonomous Region as part of China in 2003. India is still home to the Dalai Lama and his supporters, and it goes to some lengths to avoid embarrassing demonstrations during high-level Chinese visits. China is willing to live with this situation. Protests in India during the movement of

the Olympic Torch toward Beijing in 2008 occasioned some unpleas-
antness between Beijing and New Delhi, but fundamentally, India and
China agree to disagree on this issue, usually without incident.

The issues at the top of the current bilateral agenda are economics,
energy, and strategic competition, including China's ambitions in South
Asia and the Indian Ocean. Both countries emphasize the positive aspects of their relationship, but in practice, these coexist with a continuing rivalry. China does not see India as an obstacle to its "peaceful rise,"
though it is not eager to see India's influence increase in the region.
Indian strategic thinkers see China as an important economic relationship and a vital element in the multipolar region and world they hope
for. They also see China as a potential barrier to India's global ambitions, a view that was reinforced by China's last-minute lobbying at the
Nuclear Suppliers' Group against the U.S.-India nuclear agreement.

On the economic side, two-way trade has grown nearly sixfold since
2002. India would like to redress the adverse structure of trade. India's
exports to China are dominated by primary products, with iron ore the
dominant commodity and ores, slag, and ash composing more than
half of those exports. China, by contrast, exports primarily manufactured goods. By 2002, India's trade had slipped into deficit with China.
Like the rest of the relationship, trade is asymmetrical. India accounts
for less than 2 percent of China's trade, whereas China is India's top
merchandise trade partner.[3] But despite these shadows, the expansion
of India-China economic ties practically guarantees that India will
continue to look on China as a vital economic partner, and that their
competitions and disagreements will be tempered by engagement.

Investment has expanded more slowly and cautiously. Indian government figures show only $4 million in investments from China be-
tween 1991 and 2008.[4] The two countries signed a Bilateral Export
Promotion Agreement in November 2006, pledging to work toward $5
billion per year in two-way investment flows. India has excluded Chinese investment from some sensitive areas, especially ports. As India's
major corporations become global, they will inevitably seek a presence
in the Chinese market. The same may also be true, perhaps with a lag,
of Chinese companies. If this exchange of investments materializes, it
will serve as another stabilizer for India-China relations.[5]

Expanding trade has a political dimension as well. High-level commitments to double trade in five years, like the one China's president
Hu Jintao made during his 2006 trip to Delhi, underscore both the

importance of India's economic expansion and the fact that the Chinese government, unlike its U.S. counterpart, is sufficiently involved in the economy to be able to influence directly the volume and composition of trade.

In the energy field, the two countries are mainly competitors, as was spelled out in greater detail in chapter 4. Their mutual dependence on a global energy market is likely to limit the effects of their competition more than declarations of Asian solidarity or of cooperation.

China's relations with India's neighbors are a source of resentment and some anxiety. The biggest issue is Pakistan, which has a close relationship with China going back nearly half a century. China has long been a major military supplier to Pakistan and contributed importantly to Pakistan's development of nuclear weapons. India sees the Chinese-funded port at Gwadar, on the Pakistani coast near the Iranian border, as a future strategic threat. Chinese policy has become more nuanced in recent years. It has shifted from explicit endorsement of Pakistan's position on Kashmir to an even-handed stance, and in 1999, China pressed Pakistan to end its incursion into the Indian-controlled part of Kashmir. But despite these signs of caution, and despite the improvements in India-China relations, China still seems to want to keep open the option to use Pakistan as a strategic check on India. China's close relations with India's other neighbors—Nepal, Bangladesh, and Sri Lanka—look to New Delhi like a potential challenge to Indian primacy in the subcontinent.

India watches with particular unease Chinese involvement in and around the Indian Ocean. Indian strategic writers, citing Chinese journals, have noted China's expansive naval doctrine and its aims to go beyond the current "green water" fleet to a "blue water" fleet that reaches the second island chain beyond China's coast by 2020. The dispute over Chinese construction on Mischief Reef, in the disputed Spratly Islands in the South China Sea, is regarded as a harbinger of things to come, with China biding its time and becoming more overtly aggressive when its near-term domestic objectives have been met.[6] India sees Chinese military ties to Burma as another part of China's "string of pearls" in the waters around India, along with China's interest in a port on the southern coast of Sri Lanka at Hambantota. Not surprisingly, the Indian navy is more suspicious than other parts of the Indian government about Chinese maritime intentions. Naval officials recognize that China, like India, has a vital interest in protecting the

Indian Ocean sea-lanes that transport much of its energy supply. But they believe that within the next decade or two, China will also have ambitions to project its power into this area, potentially impinging on India's position.

More generally, India sees China's military modernization efforts as the foundation of a future effort to increase China's footprint in India's strategic neighborhood. The areas that have been a particular focus for China's military upgrades, strategic nuclear forces, surface-to-surface missiles, space warfare, and navy are all elements in long-range power projection, and hence strengthen New Delhi's concerns.

U.S. interests vis-à-vis China have strong similarities to India's. Neither the United States nor India wants to see a single power dominate Asia. Both have a substantial economic stake in China, and both want to ensure that China's and India's massive energy needs are met without disrupting international energy markets.

The predominant U.S. analysis of China's military modernization is more benign than India's, however. It starts from the premise that a significant military upgrade is a natural and inevitable consequence of China's economic development. With some exceptions, U.S. observers do not believe that China aims at a long-term presence in the Indian Ocean in the next decade or two. They find the concerns of the Indian security establishment exaggerated.

U.S. and Indian policy responses to this major challenge have both similarities and differences. For both, engagement is the heart of their diplomatic approach. U.S. policy stresses strong relations with the other major Asian powers, Japan and more recently India. Indian policy is moving in that direction, with a growing relationship with Japan. A major U.S. goal is to have China become, as then-deputy secretary of state Robert Zoellick put it, "a responsible stakeholder" in the international community.[7] The one major element in U.S. policy that is largely absent from India's has to do with Taiwan. For the United States, averting conflict over Taiwan is central to relations with China and to the peace of East Asia. India has largely sidestepped the Taiwan issue, although it established a nonofficial mission there in 1995. Indian trade with Taiwan is modest ($2.6 billion in 2006–2007).[8]

India's basic strategy for expanding its international role despite China's head start is twofold: to tend its own power base, strengthening its military and especially its economy; and to develop a well-rounded set of relationships with the rest of Asia. Indian strategists see this as the best pathway to emerging as an alternative center of power. India has no interest in forming alliances, formal or informal, against China. Such a move would undercut the engagement that has been mutually beneficial to both countries and would probably alienate India's other friends in Asia, none of which wants to pick a fight with China.

Indian policy represents a kind of double hedge against being taken for granted by either the United States or China. India and China share a desire to see the region and the world become more multipolar. They also share a strict concept of sovereignty and noninterference in other countries' internal affairs, which they apply to the operation of multilateral organizations. For India, the fact that there are international issues on which it works with China and in opposition to the United States represents an example of foreign policy independence, politically useful to Indian governments in spite of the strong political consensus behind today's close relationship with Washington. At the same time, Indian leaders understand that China is watching their growing ties with the United States, and they hope that the U.S. connection will expand India's margin for maneuver vis-à-vis China.

DISCOVERING JAPAN

Japan has for half a century been the primary U.S. ally and partner in the Western Pacific and the centerpiece of U.S. security policy in Asia. It is also the principal U.S. economic partner in Asia, although China's trade passed Japan's in 2006. Japan and the United States have had a harmonious partnership on global affairs as well as on security issues, and Japan is the only country whose bid for a permanent seat on the UN Security Council the United States has consistently and openly backed. The United States and Japan have certainly had their differences on international issues, in particular on China. But these issues were always worked out bilaterally and were not allowed to get in the way of the fundamental alliance relationship, based on a common view that the United States needed to remain a major member of the East Asian community.

India's relationship with Japan, by contrast, was very limited for half a century, but has been expanding since the late 1990s. It was initially dominated by economic aid. Japan has been India's largest donor since 1986, and India has been Japan's largest aid recipient since 2003, accounting for 20–27 percent of Japan's development assistance. Trade and investment, very limited for many years, began to pick up after

2002, although both are still well below what one would expect given the size of Japan's economy and the rapidity of India's economic growth. Two-way trade in 2006–2007 was just $7.5 billion, about 25 percent of India's trade with China. India's exports are dominated by primary products (e.g., iron ore) and low-level manufactures (e.g., gems and jewelry). Japan runs a substantial trade surplus. Direct investment in India from Japan was similarly modest, about 6 percent of total inbound investment and one-third of the U.S. level. If India's growth continues strong and Japan's economy revives, both trade and investment are likely to expand more rapidly.[9]

The new dimension of India's emerging ties with Japan is political. For a half-century after India's independence, Japan's preoccupation with its immediate East Asian neighborhood, its unfamiliarity and discomfort with South Asian politics, and the very different Cold War policies of both Japan and India left their political ties very thin. India's nuclear explosions in 1974 and 1998 reinforced Japan's lack of interest in a closer relationship. But India's heightened concern for maritime security in its extended Asian neighborhood, its more active international economic relationships, and its interest in participating in a multicornered Asian power structure all brought Japan into sharper focus.

Prime Minister Manmohan Singh's visit to Japan in December 2006 showcased the change in both India's approach and Japan's response. In his speech to the Japanese Diet, Singh gave pride of place to the economic relationship, not surprisingly in view of his standing as one of India's best-known economists. The decision to launch negotiations for a Comprehensive Economic Partnership Agreement indicated that both countries felt the time was right to bring their economic interaction up to par. Singh gave public recognition to the contribution of Japanese aid over the years, including its funding of the Delhi metro system, a highly successful project that India would like to replicate with other Japanese-funded infrastructure projects. But Singh's visit also underscored two themes that are new to India-Japan relations, but very much in line with India's new role in Asia: energy and regional security.[10]

Both India and Japan are major energy consumers and importers. The documents that set forth the structure of India-Japan cooperation, notably the "Joint Statement towards India-Japan Strategic and Global Partnership," include concrete proposals for India-Japan cooperation on energy efficiency, clean energy, and approaches to the international energy market. Such plans are also standard fare in Indian agreements with other countries, including the United States, and implementation sometimes lags. But this is another piece of evidence that energy looms large in India's foreign policy, as well as in India's and Japan's view of regional security.

Their common agenda on regional security starts with defense cooperation, on which the two countries signed a joint declaration when then-defense minister Pranab Mukherjee visited Tokyo in May 2006. Both countries' strategic environment includes Southeast Asia and the Strait of Malacca. Indian naval ships have visited Japan, and in April 2007 they conducted a trilateral naval exercise including U.S. ships. Both countries have pointed to their work on tsunami relief in 2005 as a critical point in building the experience of collaboration in the defense field, broadly interpreted.

The "elephant in the room," once again, is China. Both Japan and India are watching China's evolution carefully, and they have calibrated their public statements and actions to avoid triggering a hostile Chinese reaction. A good illustration of their cautious approach is the proposed four-way consultations among India, Japan, Australia, and the United States, which came up during Singh's visit to Tokyo. There is a broad consensus that such consultations are appropriate and necessary, but that they should be kept informal in light of Chinese sensitivities.

India's expanding relationship with Japan is tacitly connected with its emerging partnership with the United States. Senior Indian officials have commented that India's defense ties with Japan received a boost from its growing security relationship with the United States.[11] Prime Minister Singh suggested as much when he noted, in an interview in the *Yomiuri Shimbun* just before he visited Tokyo, that Indo-Japanese bilateral ties are "rooted in similar perceptions about the evolving environment in our region."[12] Those "similar perceptions" have important parallels with those of the United States. However, Japan and India have different habits for dealing with international controversies. Japan is comfortable staying close to the U.S. position where possible; India tends to sit on the fence, concerned that coming down on the same side as the United States may impair its strategic autonomy. This Indian practice will become more difficult to sustain as India becomes a more important international actor.

SOUTHEAST ASIA

India's ties with Southeast Asia do not have the same strategic impact as its ties with China and Japan, but deepening economic ties and expanded political dialogue reflect the same trend toward growing Indian involvement in East Asia. India has strong cultural ties with the region, and there are substantial ethnic Indian populations in Malaysia, Indonesia, and Singapore. The principal driver in relations with Southeast Asia, however, is economic. India's exports to ASEAN member countries grew sixfold, increasing from 6 percent to 10 percent of India's total exports between 2001 and 2007.[13] The most active Indian relationship is with Singapore, which accounts for close to half of India's trade with the ASEAN countries. Singaporean firms are active investors in India, and the Singaporean government has provided technical assistance to three of the new Special Economic Zones being set up in India.

Singapore is also the most active partner when it comes to political and military relations. Singapore has become an important center of strategic thinking about India's role in the Indian Ocean and Asia, with a small but impressive group of Indian academics working in Singaporean universities and think tanks on a long-term basis. From Singapore's perspective, India offers an expanding market and an opportunity to balance strong economic and political ties with China. India is also deepening its military ties with the other Southeast Asian countries, especially Malaysia, with which it has embarked on a training program for air force pilots.

The one significant policy disagreement between the United States and India in this region concerns Burma. Following the military takeover of the Burmese government, India initially supported restoring democracy. In the early 1990s, as Pakistan and China became more active in Burma, and especially with Burma's development of military ties with China, India decided to engage with Burma for strategic reasons. It invited Burma's military ruler to visit Delhi in 2004, undertook to finance a port at Sittwe, in northwestern Burma, and in 2007 pledged sales of tanks, artillery, and a military helicopter.

This change in Indian policy seems to have had mixed results. The most significant benefit for India was Burma's help in cracking down on sanctuaries used by rebels from India's troubled northeastern state of Nagaland. India reciprocated with attacking Burmese rebel bases in Mizoram.[14] India became Burma's principal export market within a decade after the new engagement policy got started.[15] But, as we have seen, the other hoped-for benefit, a new reliable source of gas supplies, did not work out. China apparently remains the preferred customer.

U.S. policy toward Burma, by contrast, has been driven by the democracy issue. Until recently, Burma was the world's largest producer of illegal heroin, but heroin production has now largely shifted to Afghanistan. U.S. security and economic interests in Burma are relatively modest, so there is no significant counterweight to the democracy issue. India's priorities are far from those of the United States, and for India, there is a clear strategic agenda at work.

REGIONAL ARCHITECTURE

Southeast Asia is the principal entry point for India's interest in joining Asia-wide regional institutions. Since the early 1990s, India has seen these institutions as attractive additional forums to establish its presence on the larger Asian circuit. Three themes run through the discussion of regional organizations: India's interest in closer integration with East Asia; China's role (including its reluctance to facilitate Indian integration); and the question of U.S. participation in regional institutions, an issue on which India has ambivalent views.

India and China have launched competing initiatives for regional development in Southeast Asia: China's Kunming initiative and India's Mekong-Ganga Cooperation Plan. The membership in both includes several countries in the Mekong River basin. Both include proposals for major infrastructure development that would link Southeast Asia with India by road. Both plans embody a vision of South and Southeast Asia as a vibrant region whose integration will bring growing prosperity. India has been pushing yet another organization that pursues this same vision but includes more substantial membership from the eastern side of the subcontinent: BIMST–EC (Bangladesh, India, Myanmar, Sri Lanka, Thailand–Economic Cooperation). From India's perspective, these initiatives and organizations are all tools for accelerating economic development to India's east without being dependent on China. That may explain India's reluctance to associate China too closely with its initiatives, or to become identified with China's.

ASEAN has become the most vigorous regional organization in East Asia, and it is the nucleus for a web of dialogues and institutions that connect ASEAN's members with nonmember countries from Asia as well as with important outside powers. ASEAN's links with China and Northeast Asia are stronger than its ties with India, but India is becoming a more active participant in these forums. India became a sectoral dialogue partner of ASEAN in 1992 and a full dialogue partner in 1995. India and the ASEAN countries signed a Framework Agreement on Comprehensive Economic Cooperation in 2003, and in August 2008 completed negotiations on a free trade area. Manmohan Singh, more than his predecessor, saw a trade agreement as a way to accelerate India's integration into the Asian economy and to spread the benefits of India's growing economy around the country.

In 1996, India joined the ASEAN Regional Forum, the only Southeast Asia-centered forum specifically dedicated to security cooperation. India has been an active participant. In August 2007, the Indian defense minister proposed a package of training and cooperation measures on maritime security for ARF members, including modules on anti-piracy, search and rescue, anti-smuggling, and narcotics control. He also offered to conduct a regular training program on UN peacekeeping for ARF members. In making these proposals, India was playing to its strengths, but also emphasizing the maritime security and counterterrorism themes that have been so important in its overall approach to the Indian Ocean and East Asia.[16]

But India has not had an easy time moving into the East Asian "clubs." It started late. India was uninvolved in East Asia during the 1970s and 1980s, when the region was beginning its dynamic economic rise. As a result, Indian and East Asian officials have not developed the habits of consultation and camaraderie that exist within Southeast Asia. India's relatively late adoption of market-oriented policies has made it look like a poor performer in the arena where Southeast Asia shone. But China has also tried to hold India back. One Indian who is a close observer of India-China relations has noted that India and China have different views of Asian regional organizations. India sees South Asia as its home turf, but also sees itself as a legitimate player in Asia-wide organizations. China, by contrast, seems to prefer to work with distinct subregions, with China as an active participant in all of them but India belonging only to South Asia.[17]

India's entry into the East Asian Summit (EAS) illustrates this phenomenon. The EAS membership includes ASEAN countries plus an additional six countries. Before the group's inaugural meeting, in

December 2005, China went to some effort to discourage the admission of India, as well as of Australia and New Zealand. The effort failed, and ASEAN members also fended off a Chinese effort to delink EAS meetings from their ASEAN "home base." This experience suggests, however, that India needs to work harder if it wishes to establish a higher Asian profile.

The United States has been deeply involved in both economic and security issues in East Asia for decades. But there is some ambivalence in the region about its role in East Asian institutions. Among the ASEAN-led institutions, the United States has been invited to join only one, the ARF. The requirements for membership in the EAS include signing the Treaty of Amity and Cooperation in Southeast Asia, which the United States had been unwilling to do because of concerns about how certain of its provisions would fit in with U.S. defense obligations. Several U.S. allies, including the UK, France, and Australia, have now signed. The Obama administration's decision to start the signature and ratification process has been well received in the region and will help keep the United States engaged in Southeast Asia.[18]

The United States has emphasized the Asia Pacific Economic Cooperation forum, which includes not only the East Asian countries but also Australia, New Zealand, Canada, Mexico, and several Pacific-coast countries in Latin America. India is immediately adjacent to the APEC area, but its application was not accepted in 1997, and APEC then declared a ten-year moratorium on new members. At the 2007 meeting the moratorium had ended, but the question of India's membership was sidelined.

The United States has been cool toward Indian membership. APEC has an ambitious program for trade liberalization, including a stated commitment to a regionwide free trade area. Despite India's market-opening moves, its trade regime is more restrictive than that of many APEC members, so Indian participation appears to Washington as a drag on progress in an institution that has in any case already had trouble achieving its goals. Moreover, India's hard line in the Doha Round of international trade negotiations raised U.S. doubts about the kind of role India would play in regional multilateral organizations. On the other hand, India has negotiated a free trade area with ASEAN, so there is a case to be made that a closer association with the APEC members would reinforce the voices calling for economic reform in India.

LOOKING AHEAD

The U.S. role in East Asia has enhanced the opportunities that India is trying to take advantage of in the region. As discussed above, strong U.S. ties with Japan have reinforced those that India is building, and something of the same dynamic is at work in Singapore. Japan, China, and India all need their relations with the United States at least as much as they do with each other. This tends to put a brake on their disputes with one another. Brahma Chellaney, one of India's most nationalistic security analysts, who is generally mistrustful of both U.S. and Chinese intentions toward India, argues that this makes the United States a critical player in the East Asian environment, preventing China from "containing" India at a time when India's goal needs to be the single-minded pursuit of expanded national power.[19]

The region will be pushed in different directions in the coming decade. On the one hand, the center of gravity in U.S. foreign policy has shifted toward Asia. The same is true of India. This is likely to lead to deepening U.S. engagement with the countries of the region, further expanding trade and investment ties, and an intensification of the common interests that the United States already shares with India.

The fallout from the global financial crisis may create contrary pressures, however. Since about 2003, the United States has been a major factor for economic growth in the world, well below China's and India's growth as a percentage of GDP but dwarfing them in absolute terms. In 2009 and perhaps beyond, global economic growth will come primarily from the more dynamic emerging economies. Even assuming a reasonably rapid recovery, the large Asian economies, including both China and India, will have a bigger footprint in the world. The United States may have to work hard to retain the level of influence it has in East Asia. India's future decisions on how closely to work with the United States at the Asian regional level will reflect both its own success in integrating into the region and the effectiveness of U.S. diplomacy in the intervening years.

This book argues that one of the critical strategic goals for the United States in developing a serious partnership with India is to create a benign and peaceful balance of power in the region from India through Japan. That goal requires a regional policy to underpin it. Given the changes already taking place in the region and in the world, a strategic dialogue with India about the security and prosperity of the greater Asian region needs to be an urgent priority.

NOTES

1. Strobe Talbott, *Engaging India: Diplomacy, Democracy and the Bomb* (Washington, D.C.: Brookings Institution Press, 2004), 112–114.

2. Ministry of Commerce and Industry, Department of Commerce, Government of India, "Export Import Data Bank," http://commerce.nic.in/eidb/Default.asp.

3. Ibid.

4. Ministry of Commerce and Industry, Department of Industrial Policy and Promotion, "Statement on Country-Wise FDI Inflows," *Fact Sheet on FDI Inflows from August 1991 to March 2008,* http://www.dipp.nic.in/fdi_statistics/india_fdi_March2008.pdf.

5. Department of Commerce, Government of India, "India Welcomes Chinese Investment, Says Kamal Nath," press release, November 23, 2006, http://commerce.nic.in/pressrelease/pressrelease_detail.asp?id=1848.

6. See, for example, Swaran Singh, "The Indian Ocean in China's Maritime Strategy," *Stockholm Journal of East Asian Studies* 15 (2005): 61–73; also Vijay Sakhuja, "Maritime Power of People's Republic of China: The Economic Dimension," *Strategic Analysis*, Institute for Defense Studies and Analysis, New Delhi, February 2001.

7. Robert Zoellick, Deputy Secretary of State, "Whither China: From Membership to Responsibility?" (address to National Committee on U.S.-China Relations, New York, September 21, 2005).

8. Ministry of Commerce and Industry, "Export Import Data Bank," http://commerce.nic.in/eidb/iecnt.asp.

9. Report of the India-Japan Joint Study Group, New Delhi and Tokyo, June 2006, p. 28, para 2.8, Table 3, and p. 56, http://www.mofa.go.jp/region/asia-paci/india/report0606.pdf; Ministry of Commerce and Industry, "Export Import Data Bank," http://commerce.nic.in/eidb/iecntq.asp.

10. "Joint Statement towards India-Japan Strategic and Global Partnership," Tokyo, December 15, 2006, http://meaindia.nic.in/declarestatement/2006/12/15js01.htm.

11. Author's conversations with senior Indian officials, January 2007.

12. Cited in B. Raman, "India and Japan: Democracy as a Strategic Weapon," South Asia Analysis Group, Paper 2064, December 17, 2006, http://www.southasiaanalysis.org/%5Cpapers21%5Cpaper2064.html.

13. Ministry of Commerce and Industry, "Export Import Data Bank," http://commerce.nic.in/eidb/ergnq.asp.

14. Author's interview with G. Parthasarathy, former Indian Ambassador in Burma, February 2008.

15. M. A. McAteer, "India and the Junta: Business over Democracy," *Burma Issues* 15, no. 7 (July 2005): 5–7, http://www.burmaissues.org/En/Newsletter/BINews2005-07.pdf.

16. P. S. Suryanarayana, "India's Offer on Maritime Security," *The Hindu* (Chennai, India), August 3, 2007, http://www.thehindu/2007/08/03/stories/2007080362110100.htm.

17. Dipankar Banjerjee, presentation at the Center for Strategic and International Studies, Washington, D.C., June 5, 2008, http://www.csis.org/media/csis/events/080701_summary_india-china_talk.pdf.

18. Hillary Clinton, Secretary of State, remarks with ASEAN Secretary General Dr. Surin Pitsuwan, Jakarta, February 18, 2009, http://www.state.gov/secretary/rm/2009a/02/119422.htm

19. Brahma Chellaney, *Asian Juggernaut: The Rise of China, India and Japan* (New Delhi: HarperCollins, 2006), 212–224.

8

THE MIDDLE EAST
ISRAEL, THE GULF, AND IRAN

Two events illustrate the old and new trends that coexist somewhat uncomfortably in India's Middle East policy. India's launching of two Israeli satellites on one of its rockets in January 2008 represented a technological and political milestone, associating Israel publicly with India's most sophisticated high-tech program. The launch took place less than 20 years after the two countries established diplomatic relations. At the same time, India's somewhat mercurial support for the proposed gas pipeline from Iran through Pakistan into northern India that has been under negotiation for some years illustrates both the enhanced importance of energy in India's foreign policy and its continuing commitment to strategic autonomy. The United States has publicly opposed the project, and India's ties with Iran represent one of its sharpest foreign policy disagreements with the United States.

In the 1950s and 1960s, under Jawaharlal Nehru's foreign policy, nonaligned solidarity with the Arab countries was the driving force in India's approach to the Middle East. Egypt was the key partner. Nehru and Gamal Abdel Nasser had close personal ties and were both leaders in the Non-Aligned Movement. The Arab-Israeli problem was the principal focus of India's regional attention, with India tilting more or less automatically toward the Arab viewpoint. Then as now, policy toward the Middle East had two objectives that hit closer to home: countering Pakistan's influence and reassuring India's large Muslim population.

Today, the Middle East accounts for two-thirds of India's oil imports, and energy is the key dimension with all India's interlocutors except Israel. India deals separately with four distinct parts of the region, each with its own policy drivers. Its relations with Israel are warm and have a vitally important security edge, with Israel emerging as India's second-largest military supplier. India's policies toward the Arab states of the Persian Gulf are built around oil supply and Indian expatriate labor and financial flows, and maintaining the security of the oil-rich region is a high priority. Iran is the most complex relationship, combining energy supply with strategic considerations such as access to Central Asia and Afghanistan. India does not want Iran to develop nuclear weapons, but it also does not wish to get caught up in the containment policy practiced by the United States. India has traditionally had close relations with Iraq and is pulled in different directions on Iraq policy.

Indian and U.S. policies in this region are marked by contradictions as well as common interests. India's defense and intelligence links with Israel line up well with U.S. interests, as do its economic and security interests in the Arab countries of the Persian Gulf. India has serious misgivings about U.S. policy toward the Israeli-Palestinian dispute and Iraq, leading India to keep its distance from the United States across the Middle East. Iran has been the subject of sharp disagreement between Washington and Delhi, with high emotion making it hard for India and the United States to relate to each other's strategic compulsions. This chapter will review each of these major subregions in turn, starting with the ones where Indian and U.S. policies are most compatible, Israel and India's major Arab oil suppliers, and going on to the more contentious issues of Iran and Iraq.

ISRAEL AND THE PALESTINIANS

In 1992, only three years after it had voted for a United Nations General Assembly resolution condemning Zionism as a form of racism, India established formal diplomatic relations with Israel. This was not the first contact between the two countries, but the establishment of formal ties started a new era. It also eliminated a major disconnect between U.S. and Indian foreign policy.

The implicit bond between Israel and India—the fact that both countries had hostile relations with Muslim neighbors—boosted their relationship, although on the Indian side little was officially articulated in public. Within weeks, there was a flowering of active and vigorous connections involving security, science, and trade, and visits by cabinet-level officials from both countries became increasingly frequent.

By far the most important connection was security. Defense and intelligence consultations began almost immediately after the establishment of diplomatic ties. A counterterrorism dialogue started in 2000, even before 9/11 put the issue on the world's front page. Both countries saw Islamic extremism as a serious danger. From India's perspective, this dialogue remains an important vehicle for keeping track of extremist activity in the Middle East, including operations near vitally important sea-lanes. Training has been part of the defense relationship, including some Special Forces training in counterinsurgency.

Defense sales also started in 2000, when Israel announced that it was lifting a self-imposed ban on military exports to India, and these sales have assumed major importance for both countries. From the start, the accent was on high technology. One of the early sales, in 2004, was the Phalcon aerial early warning radar, a system Israel had ultimately decided not to sell to China after strenuous U.S. objections. The United States did not object to the sale to India, an action that was interpreted at the time as a major signal of the new U.S.-India relationship. The first one arrived in India in January 2009, and was to be mounted on a Russian-built aircraft.[1]

By 2005, Israel had become India's second-largest foreign supplier of military equipment after Russia. Indian government figures cited in the press show $1.5 billion in sales contracts in 2006, more than one-third of Israel's reported arms contracts in that year.[2] Equipment supplied from Israel includes surface-to-air missiles, unmanned aerial vehicles, sophisticated sensors, artillery pieces, and specialized equipment for counterinsurgency purposes. Because of the close ties between the Israeli and the U.S. defense industries, many of the items Israel sells include components that are subject to U.S. licensing requirements. As Indo-U.S. ties have improved, so has U.S. willingness to license Israeli sales to India.

Scientific collaboration has been another satisfying area of Indo-Israeli relations. Some of this cooperation has been in the defense field, such as joint work on a new-generation Barak shipborne surface-to-air missile with extended range. Other scientific work, while formally civilian, has been in fields where advanced research is subject to export controls or similar defense-related restrictions. India signed an agreement on space cooperation with Israel in 2002. India's main contribution is launch services, where India has advantages of both cost and geographic location. Israel's satellite construction is more sophisticated, and India hopes to benefit from that.

Trade has grown rapidly. Civilian commerce had been $855 billion per year in 2001 and had nearly tripled, to $2.2 billion, by 2005.[3] Information technology and related services were recognized early on as a priority area, and cooperation agreements were signed between the industry associations in both countries.

The Israel-India friendship has little impact on either country's policies beyond their bilateral ties, however. India has made a point of condemning terrorist actions, including the Hamas kidnapping of an Israeli soldier that started the Israel-Lebanon war in the summer of 2006. But this is the exception. In international discussions of the Middle East peace process, and especially at the United Nations, India's position still tends to be pro-Palestinian. It is strongly critical of Israeli settlements, and it is careful to keep in close touch with countries like Syria that might be willing to help counter Pakistani resolutions on Kashmir in the Organization of the Islamic Conference, OIC. India has participated in the larger international conferences on the Middle East, and one of its most senior retired diplomats represented India at the Annapolis conference to revive the Israeli-Palestinian peace process in December 2007. But India has not sought a significant role in Middle East diplomacy. Israel has taken little interest in India's regional disputes and does not appear to have made an issue of India's ties with Iran. Neither India nor Israel, in other words, expects the other to stick its neck out with regard to its relations with its neighbors.

An interesting sidelight to the Israel-India relationship is the increasing importance India attaches to the American Jewish community. From the late 1990s onward, India has maintained regular contact with the major U.S. Jewish organizations. The Indian Embassy has arranged joint business events in the United States featuring both Indian and Israeli commercial delegations, and it is not unusual in today's Washington to receive invitations to Capitol Hill receptions jointly featuring prominent U.S. Jewish groups, Indian-American groups, and visitors from India. Some of the major U.S. Jewish organizations, such as the American Jewish Committee, have added staff to provide their members with a regular flow of information on developments in India and U.S.-India relations, something they would not have considered relevant in earlier years. Indian and Indian-American lobbyists see the American Jewish community as an instructive role model. They also believe that highlighting India's close ties with it and with Israel is useful in building up their ties with the United States, especially with the U.S. Congress.

THE ARAB SIDE OF THE GULF: AN ECONOMIC LIFELINE

India's ties to the Arab riparians of the Persian Gulf, by contrast, are dominated by economics and are influenced to a lesser degree by regional security issues. Centuries-old trading ties are now a vital link in India's economic security.

The economic ties start with energy. The countries of the Gulf Cooperation Council[4] (GCC) supply more than one-third of India's oil imports and are its only regularly contracted source of gas imports.[5] India's primary investments in the Gulf are also in the energy field. The state-owned Oil and Natural Gas Corporation has focused mainly on exploration, and the more downstream-oriented Reliance Industries has invested in both exploration and refining. These investments fit into the Indian strategy, discussed in greater depth in chapter 3, of diversifying energy suppliers and trying to build up a long-term presence in energy-producing areas. Energy trade works in both directions. Refined oil has become India's largest export, and the UAE is one of the country's top two markets. India hopes to expand imports of Gulf oil to its refinery and to gain business building more refineries in the Gulf.[6]

India also encourages investment in its energy sector from the Gulf countries. It has sought investments in LNG terminals, for example, to support expanding use and importation of natural gas. Oman Oil Company is investing, in partnership with the public sector Bharat Petroleum Corporation (BPCL), in a 6-million-ton per year refinery at Bina, in Madhya Pradesh (in central India).

Economic linkages are also growing outside the energy sector. Much of this trade is driven by investments. India has been fairly successful in expanding its markets in the Gulf, including negotiations toward a free trade area with the GCC. Interestingly, the big holdup has been

India's reluctance to abolish duties on oil imports, a significant source of revenue for the Indian government.

India has also tried to encourage non-oil investment between India and the Gulf. In February 2004, India hosted the first ever GCC–India Industrial Conference to discuss trade, mutual investment, transfers of technology, and greater industrial cooperation. The conference produced the Framework Agreement on Economic Cooperation that, among other things, committed the two sides to eventually reaching a comprehensive free trade agreement. The participants also agreed to set up a $50 million holding company to assist small and medium-sized enterprises in developing joint ventures and trade between India and the Gulf countries.

An estimated 4 million to 5 million Indian expatriates live and work in the Gulf. Overall, remittances to India doubled between 1999–2000 and 2005–2006. Remittances from the Gulf in 2005–2006 came to $6 billion, or 24 percent of financial remittances. This makes the Gulf the second-largest source of remittances to India, after North America. The regional impact of these financial flows is in some cases even more dramatic than the national impact. Remittances from the Gulf are well above those from North America in Kerala, a state highly dependent on remittances, and nearly equal to North America in the major cities of Mumbai and Chennai. More than half of these flows are devoted to family maintenance, so the Indian population that depends on India's economic presence in the Gulf is several times the size of the Indian expatriate population that lives there.[7]

The Gulf countries have small indigenous populations, and imported labor makes up a majority of the labor force in the UAE. The Indian communities in the Gulf include skilled professionals in such fields as medicine, nursing, information technology, engineering, accounting, education, and a thriving commercial and banking sector, as well as construction and maintenance labor. One of the attractions of the Indian workforce to prospective employers is that, as outsiders, they are generally aloof from local political passions.

The importance of energy in India's economic prospects and its foreign policy has made security interests an important driver in its relations with the Arab countries along the Persian Gulf. Like the United States, India considers the safety of the Bab el Mandeb Strait and the Strait of Hormuz, the two critical "choke points" that feed into the Arabian Sea, essential to its security. This has made the Gulf an increasingly important focus for India's military, especially the navy. India's plans for building up the navy's power projection capacity aim at giving India the assets and relationships it needs to protect its interests, including both the integrity of the oil trade and the interests of India's expatriates and investors. It is noteworthy that the first overseas visit by the newly appointed naval chief, Admiral Sureesh Mehta, was to Abu Dhabi in February 2007. Indian naval vessels have visited Bahrain and Qatar as well as the United Arab Emirates in recent years, and the commanding admiral of India's Western Fleet proposed joint exercises with Qatar during an August 2007 port call. The Indian Coast Guard has visited the UAE as well. Officers from Qatar and the UAE have been trained in India.

The most important and diverse Indian bilateral relationship in this region is with the UAE. It accounts for about one-third of India's expatriate population in the Gulf (1.4 million) and a similar percentage of remittances ($2 billion). It supplies just under 7 percent of India's oil imports, making it India's sixth-largest energy supplier; and it purchases about 18 percent of India's refined oil exports. It accounts for most of India's non-oil trade in the region, much of it in all likelihood entrepôt trade. Energy accounts for only half India's imports from the UAE and about 25 percent of its exports.[8] Some 40 Indian firms have offices there, many of them using Abu Dhabi as their regional headquarters. On the defense side, the relationship with the UAE involves regular Navy staff talks and appears to be more sophisticated than with the other Gulf countries. Visitors to the UAE are struck by the high visibility of the South Asian expatriates. The most useful languages in the bazaars of Dubai, for example, are Hindi and Urdu rather than Arabic.

Saudi Arabia is India's largest oil supplier, providing 25 percent of its oil imports. King Abdullah was the chief guest at India's Republic Day celebrations in 2006, a major honor. Saudi Arabia is also home to 1.4 million Indian expatriates, many of them blue-collar workers. However, Saudi Arabia does not have the same centuries-old trading links with India as the smaller countries on the Gulf coast do, nor the cultural rapport that goes with them. This reflects the more inward-looking Saudi society, the important role of the royal family, and the larger Saudi population. Saudi Arabia's status as the homeland of Islam's holiest shrines makes India more of an outsider.

As is the case in other places on its western periphery, one of India's interests in the Gulf is to ensure that Pakistan does not upstage it. Pakistan's presence in the Gulf is smaller than India's, and the 2 to 3 million Pakistani expatriates are not very different in overall composition from their Indian counterparts.[9] The Gulf dominates Pakistan's vitally important financial remittances, accounting for $2.06 billion in FY 2005-2006, or nearly half of Pakistan's total worker remittances.[10] India's economic footprint is larger, both in terms of oil imports and in terms of trade and investment.

Pakistan has cultivated close ties over the years with several of the Gulf ruling families, especially in Saudi Arabia and in certain components of the UAE. Several sheikhs from the UAE have residences in Pakistan and enjoy hunting trips in the Pakistani outdoors. Saudi Arabia, Kuwait, and the UAE have been major aid donors to Pakistan over the years, through government funds and through the personal generosity of their rulers. When Pakistan faced economic crisis in the second half of 2008, it turned to Saudi Arabia and the UAE for help, and apparently was given concessional terms of payment for its oil imports. Pakistan also has extensive military ties with the Gulf, especially with the UAE and Saudi Arabia. The UAE and Pakistan have a military pact dating back to 1992 that allows Pakistani soldiers to serve in the UAE army.[11] These connections and the bond of Islam give Pakistan a strong position in Saudi Arabia. India has succeeded in preventing the Pakistani connection from turning the Gulf into a hostile region, however, and its commercial presence is becoming increasingly important as both oil industry ties and non-oil investment expand.

IRAN: SYMBOL AND REALITY

In contrast with Israel and the Arab countries of the Gulf, where Indian and U.S. interests have much in common, certain of India's interests in Iran are sharply at variance with those of the United States. India's view of Iran, more than any other country of the Middle East, is driven not just by energy but by geopolitics, specifically by India's drive to expand its influence in Central Asia. India shares with the United States one of the latter's overriding interests—that Iran not acquire nuclear weapons—but differs with the United States on what to do about it. Despite India's preoccupation with terrorism, it does not see Iran as a factor in its own terrorism worries.

Iran has a symbolic and emotional importance in both India and the United States that makes these differences hard to manage. In the United States, policymakers and politicians still have sharp memories of the 1979 hostage crisis and regard Iran's flamboyant hostility to Israel and its promotion of terrorism as intensely threatening. The Bush administration took a very hard line on Iran, but, with the exception of its opposition to the proposed Iran-Pakistan-India gas pipeline, it accepted the Indian government's explanations that its ties with Iran did not undercut Washington's strategic requirements. The Obama administration has reached out to Iran, and as of early 2009 had not tried to change India's policy toward Iran. However, for others, especially in the U.S. Congress, it is almost impossible to understand how India can claim to be friendly toward the United States while continuing to do normal business with Iran. As India's relationship with the United States has developed, Iran has emerged on the Delhi political scene as the primary symbol of India's independent foreign policy not subservient to Washington.

Iran's primary importance to India stems from energy supply. Iran is India's fourth-largest source of imported oil, supplying 10 percent of its imports.[12] Both public-sector (ONGC) and private-sector (Reliance and Essar) Indian energy companies have been active in Iran's energy sector, in exploration and planned refinery construction.[13]

Iran is also a major potential source of gas imports. India's principal public-sector gas company, the Gas Authority of India Ltd., signed a 30-year memorandum of understanding with the National Iranian Gas Export Corporation in 2005, providing for the import of up to 7.5 million tons per year of LNG. This agreement has never been implemented because Iran lacks the infrastructure for liquefaction. At about the same time, the state-owned Indian Oil Corporation reached agreement with the Iranian oil and gas developer Petropars to develop a gas block in the South Pars field.[14]

The other way to get gas from Iran to India would be by pipeline. Discussion of possible pipelines goes back at least a decade and a half and includes both overland and undersea options. At this writing, the only one under active consideration is a 2,775-kilometer land pipeline passing through Pakistan. The proposal has been controversial in India primarily because of widespread concern about the reliability of importing a strategic commodity through Pakistan. Since India and Pakistan began their long-term peace dialogue in 2004, the Pakistani government has made clear that it was willing to move ahead on the pipeline without waiting for prior progress on Kashmir. This has made the project more attractive to India.

The Indian security establishment remains skeptical about the pipeline, however. Pakistan's stated willingness to allow the pipeline to move forward without linking it to an elusive Kashmir settlement reduces but does not eliminate the political risks that India faces, which would need to be addressed in the financial arrangements governing the pipeline. Negotiations have been beset by speed bumps, with preliminary agreements on price and transit fees being upset by changes in Iranian positions and negotiating tactics. Security problems in Pakistan, including both the insurgency in Balochistan (through which the pipeline would have to pass) and extremist violence in many parts of the country, coupled with the weakness of the Pakistan government after early 2007, add to India's skepticism. The Indian government's stance reflects this ambivalence. It supports the pipeline publicly, but has periodically stayed away from key negotiating sessions (such as a series of price negotiations in 2007).

Many analysts believe that these difficulties will ultimately make the pipeline project impossible. However, the importance that India attaches to diversifying energy sources means that no government of India will want to disavow the project. And Iran's position as a symbol of Indian strategic autonomy makes it all the more important for India to maintain its formal support for the project, in spite of—and perhaps partly because of—strong U.S. opposition.

The other major factor in India's policy toward Iran is India's strategic posture in Central Asia. As was discussed in chapter 6, India has traditionally had close ties with Afghanistan, based in part on their difficulties with Pakistan. It has sought to maintain a strong enough presence in Afghanistan and Central Asia to prevent them from becoming "Pakistan's hinterland." Iran, unlike Pakistan, has allowed Indian transit over land to both places. India's involvement in expanding Iran's port at Chahbahar is intended to consolidate India's links to the areas north of Iran. Energy is a factor here too: India would like to be able to import oil and gas from the Central Asian and Caspian countries, which have limited transport options for exporting their energy resources. India sees Iran as an important potential route for opening up this additional source of energy to the thirsty Indian economy. Iran's troubled relations with Pakistan make it a particularly useful connection for India.

India's other dealings with Iran are basically intended to reinforce India's primary interests in energy and its regional posture. In 2003, Iran's president Mohammad Khatemi came to India as the guest of honor at India's Republic Day celebrations. India signed a declaration establishing a "strategic dialogue" with Iran and creating a framework for bilateral cooperation. As often happens with such documents, the declaration paints in bold hues a relationship encompassing economic and defense cooperation; but outside the energy field, the reality is quite modest. Non-oil trade is about $2 billion dollars a year.

Defense ties are perhaps the best example of a relationship India wants to maintain for reasons of both symbolism and strategy, without giving it a great deal of substance. Iran has expressed interest in a long list of things India might supply, including ambitious equipment purchases and upgrades. Most of these have remained unfulfilled. There are regular contacts between the Iranian and Indian militaries, and in 2003 and 2006 the two navies carried out what were variously described as "exercises" and "port calls." The technical sophistication involved appears to be minimal, but the timing, especially in 2006, was an embarrassment to U.S.-India relations, coming at practically the same time as President Bush's visit to India. India has allowed Iranian officers to participate in certain training courses that are also open to officers of many other nations. All these activities reinforce India's view of strategic autonomy and play well in Indian politics.

India and the United States are both concerned about the implications of possible nuclear weapons in Iran. India's formal position was spelled out in a statement by Prime Minister Singh to the Indian parliament on February 17, 2006, that Iran had the legal right, under the NPT, to "develop peaceful uses of nuclear energy consistent with its international commitments and obligations." But Iran must, he said, abide by those obligations, including its promise to suspend enrichment and reprocessing. Beneath this carefully crafted statement, it is clear that the Indian government does not want to see any more of its neighbors develop nuclear weapons. Singh's statement to the parliament referred in barely veiled terms to Pakistan's apparent role in helping Iran acquire sensitive technologies.[15]

This is an important point of strategic convergence, but the Indian and U.S. governments do not agree on what to do about it. India twice voted with the United States and other IAEA members against Iran's nuclear program, including one vote to refer Iran to the United Nations Security Council. That vote generated a storm of political controversy in India, with political opponents of the government lambasting the government's willingness to "subordinate" Indian foreign policy to the United States. India's reference point is that Iran is bound by the obligations it has undertaken, including those in the Non-Proliferation Treaty. India's votes at the IAEA were justified domestically on that basis. But India is extremely reluctant to be caught up in an international campaign, and both its other strategic interests in Iran and the domestic symbolism of its Iranian connections intensify this instinct. India's willingness to participate in U.S. anti-nuclear efforts on a more energetic basis will hinge on whether Iran can be shown to have violated its international obligations.

Iran likewise tends to see relations with India in geopolitical terms in ways that reinforce India's tendency to see Iran as an emblem of foreign policy autonomy. Today's Iranian government considers itself a major regional power in much the same way that the Shah once did. Its only truly worthy regional partner is India, with Russia and China over the horizon. Pakistan lacks the stature to be a worthy partner (and in any event is too Sunni-dominated and too close to Saudi Arabia); and Iranian and Pakistani interests in Afghanistan have frequently been at odds. Whatever nuclear transfers may have come from Pakistan in the past, the Iranians probably doubt that they will continue under present circumstances. By contrast, India is an important market, buying an estimated 7.5 percent of Iran's oil exports. It is also a potential source of investment in energy infrastructure. And India's preoccupation with strategic autonomy gives Iran the hope of using India to thwart U.S. strategic plans and relationships in the region.

Differences in both analysis and policy on Iran are likely to remain an irritant in U.S.-India relations for some time. There have been many conversations on Iran at the senior government level, but there has been little dialogue in the sense of a genuine exchange of views. As a result, U.S. officials do not understand well India's interests in Iran outside the energy field. More frustratingly, U.S. opposition is one of the attractions of a strong relationship with Iran for India's left-of-center politicians: even those who support India's ties with the United States are determined to maintain some areas of policy where New Delhi and Washington clash.

IRAQ: A DARK FUTURE?

In the past, Iraq was one of India's closest friends in the Middle East. It was a secular country, a major oil supplier, and had a reliably difficult relationship with Pakistan. Iraq was the site of some of India's early efforts to acquire an upstream stake in oil exploration and production. The two Gulf wars between Iraq and the United States posed a problem for Indian policy-makers: on the one hand, their economic interests and the end of the Cold War were pushing them toward closer ties with the United States and the West; on the other, they had major political and economic interests at stake in Iraq. This explains India's last-ditch effort to find some kind of accommodation between Iraq and the mainstream of the international community after Iraq's invasion of Kuwait in 1990. This was not simply an exercise in non-aligned triangulation: it was an effort to reconcile important conflicting interests.

By the time of the U.S. intervention in Iraq in 2003, ties with the United States had become a pillar of Indian foreign policy. India's economic interests in Iraq were still strong. Bilateral trade under the oil-for-food program was estimated at $1 billion, and the state-owned ONGC had signed agreements for exploration in Iraq's southern oil fields.[16] Opinion both inside the government and in the foreign policy-watching public was strongly opposed to the invasion that seemed increasingly inevitable. Iraq's credentials as a secular Muslim country burnished its image in India. The Indian government did its best to steer clear of the controversy, however, because it had no interest in stirring up hostility in the U.S. government at a time when prospects otherwise seemed so promising.

Shortly after the invasion gave way to the occupation, the United States invited India to participate in the stabilization of Iraq by sending a division to participate in post-conflict operations. That would have made India the third largest troop contributor on the Iraqi scene. The United States sent a senior delegation headed by Assistant Secretary of Defense Peter Rodman to India to discuss the prospects. India agonized over the request for several weeks, a development that was in itself remarkable. In an earlier era, India would not have been asked, and if asked, it would have given an immediate "no."

India's answer, given July 14, 2003, was indeed a negative, but the way it was crafted showed how far India had moved in the direction of tending its ties with the United States. The official response was that India could not send troops without a UN mandate. The United States argued that the Security Council's invitation to countries to contribute troops to keeping the peace in Iraq amounted to the same thing, but ultimately, this argument did not prevail—the mission to Iraq, in the words of one U.S. participant, was "a bridge too far."[17] The decision was preceded by a debate in both houses of parliament, and each house unanimously passed a resolution expressing its opposition to the intervention in Iraq. The phrasing of the resolutions was carefully crafted to avoid gratuitously offending the U.S. government. Prime Minister Vajpayee publicly took credit for having chosen a Hindi word that criticized the U.S. intervention without condemning it. Two months later, the Indian prime minister explained to the U.S. president that the unsettled situation with Pakistan made it impossible for India to spare any additional troops. In the end, the United States proved quite understanding about India's unwillingness to participate. An Indian division would surely have benefited U.S.-India security relations, but its absence did not damage them.

As Iraq created a new government, India reestablished economic ties to Iraq. India pledged $20 million in rehabilitation and reconstruction funds in answer to the UN secretary general's appeal, and contributed an additional $10 million to UN and World Bank trust funds for Iraqi reconstruction.[18] Iraq remained a major oil supplier, accounting for close to 9 percent of India's oil imports in 2004/5.[19] Two Indian oil companies, the public sector ONGC and the private Reliance, remained active in Iraq's oil sector after the U.S. intervention.[20] India's expatriate population in Iraq, once substantial, has dwindled to almost nothing; in response to the high levels of violence, the Indian government in 2005 banned labor brokers from hiring people for Iraq.[21]

At a more strategic level, India's attitude toward Iraq is divided. India has no interest in getting involved in that increasingly controversial undertaking, and most of India's strategic thinkers inside and outside of government have concluded that the aftermath of the U.S. intervention was likely to be many years of violence and instability. But the strategic community looks on this prospect with foreboding. Unsettled conditions so close to major oil transportation routes and to India's west coast are worrisome. Perhaps more importantly, Indians see the possibility of a U.S. reverse in Iraq as a dangerous thing in and of itself, likely to reinforce existing tendencies toward extremism in the Muslim world. And they are deeply concerned about the effects of a U.S. failure in Iraq on Afghanistan and by extension on Pakistan, areas where India's strategic interests are even more directly engaged. This menacing outlook has strengthened India's determination to develop a security presence and good relations in and around the Persian Gulf, including Iran. It does not seem to have had much impact, however, on the way India structured its security relations or its strategic conversation with the United States. And the United States, preoccupied with its short term problems in Iraq, has no great interest in starting a long conversation with India, given India's clear disinclination to get involved. In other words, an area of major strategic interest to both countries, in which their interests were not really in conflict, has basically been left on the sidelines of this emerging partnership.

LOOKING AHEAD

Both the turbulence of the region and the world's growing appetite for energy will make the Middle East even more important to both Indian and U.S. foreign policy in the coming decade. Even under the most optimistic assumptions, the Israel-Palestinian conflict will continue to simmer, and will remain vulnerable to reverses and sabotage by spoilers. The internal conflict in Iraq is likely to remain a feature of the landscape for the better part of the next decade, and Iran's concept of its role in the region will make it a revisionist power even if current diplomatic efforts to curb its nuclear program are successful.

On the energy side, international projections consistently hold that the Middle East will remain the world's major source of energy, and that carbon-based energy will remain central to the world's economy for at least another two decades. India and China are the fastest-growing markets for internationally traded energy. India is likely to increase its dependence on Middle Eastern energy. The IEA expects India to account for at least 20 percent of Middle Eastern gas exports by 2030.

If India's economy continues to grow and its military continues to increase its presence and intensify its security relationships beyond South Asia, the countries around the Persian Gulf will be a major focus for Indian policy attention. India's interests straddle both of the region's sharpest internal cleavages: between Israel and its Arab neighbors, and between Iran and the Arab countries across the Gulf. Thus far, India and Israel have been quite willing to accommodate each other's different approaches on Palestine-Israel problems, and India's effort to maintain a serious relationship with Iran has not provoked much of a reaction from Israel. In the Persian Gulf, the Arab-Iranian rivalry has not had much impact on India's efforts to maintain ties with both sides. As time goes on, and especially if the situation in Iraq remains unsettled and Iran remains active there, India may find it more complicated to service its ties with both sides.

The convergence between Indian and U.S. interests in this region is likely to increase with the passage of time, except on Iran. That would argue for a more serious and sophisticated bilateral strategic dialogue covering the Middle East—both the areas where the United States and India agree and those where the two countries disagree. Limited discussions have taken place at the operational level, especially in defense channels. The U.S. delegation to high level defense talks with India has normally included a briefer from Central Command, whose area of responsibility starts with Pakistan and extends Westward including the entire Persian Gulf region. India, which is within the area of responsibility of the U.S. Pacific Command, asked in 2005 to be allowed to establish regular liaison relations with Central Command as well. The United States said that India needed first to establish a resident liaison with the Pacific Command, but as of the end of 2007, India had not responded to the Pacific Command's invitation.

But turning these staff-level contacts into a strategic dialogue may be even more difficult than in East Asia. In the Middle East, the interests that diverge between the United States and India are much more contentious and emotional. The United States will be reluctant to focus the discussion too much on Pakistan, with which the Central Command has important responsibilities. Finally, an effective dialogue will require the United States to sort out its mixed feelings about India's commitment to strategic autonomy.

One Indian official has argued that the future evolution of U.S. policy toward Iran will be the primary determinant of how the United States and India relate to each other in the Middle East. If the United States succeeds in developing a more substantive dialogue with Iran, as the Obama administration has made clear it wants to do, and especially if Washington and Tehran are able to work toward similar goals, perhaps in Afghanistan, this will change the way India looks at U.S. policy.[22] On the other hand, the development of nuclear weapons in Iran, coupled with a U.S. military response, could threaten the foundations of the U.S.-India relationship by polarizing the region and India's role in it.

NOTES

1. "India's First Phalcon AWACS System Arrives Ahead of Schedule," domain-b.com, January 15, 2009, http://www.domain-b.com/aero/mil_avi/mil _aircraft/20090115_awacs.html.

2. Doug Tsuruoka, "India's Major Tech Needs Are Often Met by Israel," *Investor's Business Daily*, January 26, 2007, http://www.globalsecurity.org/org/ news/2007/070126-india-tech-needs.htm.

3. Ministry of Commerce and Industry, Department of Commerce, Government of India, "Export Import Data Bank," http://commerce.nic.in/eidb/ Icntcom.asp.

4. The members of the Gulf Cooperation Council are Saudi Arabia, Oman, Qatar, United Arab Emirates, Kuwait, and Bahrain.

5. "Report of the Expert Committee on Integrated Energy Policy," Government of India Planning Commission, August 2006, http://planningcommission .nic.in/reports/genrep/rep_intengy.pdf, 59.

6. Indian government trade statistics are subject to much misinterpretation. Indian Ministry of Commerce figures at http://commerce.nic.in/eidb/Default. asp show two-way trade in excess of $20 billion between India and the GCC countries; however, a closer inspection of the figures shows that this number includes substantial energy trade, which is incorporated in the figures in some years but not in others.

7. Reserve Bank of India, "Invisibles in India's Balance of Payments," bulletin, November 2006, http://rbidocs.rbi.org.in/rdocs/Bulletin/PDFs/74250. pdf.

8. Ministry of Commerce and Industry, "Export Import Data Bank," http:// commerce.nic.in/eidb/Default.asp.

9. Talal Malik, "India-Pakistan Trade with Gulf Hits $36 Billion," *Arabian Business.com*, August 14, 2007, http://www.arabianbusiness.com/index .php?option=com_content&view=article&id=497795.

10. State Bank of Pakistan, "Country-wise Workers' Remittances," 2007, http://www.sbp.org.pk/ecodata/Homeremit_arch.xls.

11. "Defence Deal with UAE Being Agreed Today," *PakistaniDefence.com*, July 13, 2006, http://pakistanidefenceforum.com/index.php?showtopic=57005.

12. Government of India Planning Commission, *Report of the Expert Committee on Integrated Energy Policy*, August 2006, p. 59, http://planningcommission .nic.in/reports/genrep/rep_intengy.pdf.

13. Bethany Danyluk, Juli A. MacDonald, and Ryan Tuggle, *Energy Futures in Asia: Perspectives on India's Energy Security Strategy and Policies"*(report prepared by Booz Allen Hamilton for Director, Net Assessment, Office of the Secretary of Defense, June 2007), 4–12 to 4–21.

14. Geoffrey Kemp, "The East Moves West," *The National Interest*, no. 84 (Summer 2006).

15. Manmohan Singh, "PM's Suo Motu Statement on Iran," February 17, 2006, http://pmindia.nic.in/lspeech.asp?id=279.

16. Siddharth Srivastava, "Indian Firms Fight Back for $10 Bn Iraq 'Prize,'" *Asia Times Online,_*December 13, 2003, http://www.atimes.com/atimes/South_Asia/EL13Df05.html.

17. Author's conversation with Peter Rodman, December 14, 2007.

18. E. Ahamed, Minister of State for External Affairs, response to parliamentary question, March 1, 2006, http://meaindia.nic.in/parliament/ls/2006/03/01ls07.html.

19. Government of India Planning Commission, *Report of the Expert Committee on Integrated Energy Policy*, p. 59.http://planningcommission.nic.in/reports/genrep/rep_intengy.pdf.

20. "OVLQualifies for Oil, Gas Contracts in Iraq," *Economic Times,* April 14, 2008,http://economictimes.indiatimes.com/News/News_By_Industry/OVL_qualifies_for_oil_gas_contracts_in_Iraq/articleshow/2951068.cms.

21. E. Ahamed, Minister of State for External Affairs, response to parliamentary question, November 30, 2005, http://meaindia.nic.in/parliament/ls/2005/11/30ls18.htm.

22. Author's interview with Indian official, October 2008.

9

THE OTHER GLOBAL POWERS

India's vision of itself as one of the poles in a multipolar world power structure rests on the notion of between five and eight key powers: the United States, China, Russia, Europe, and India, and possibly Japan, Brazil, and South Africa. All have substantial population and considerable economic and/or military power. Only the first four have permanent representation in the United Nations Security Council. Among the last four, only Japan appears in all the other small groups that run international institutions.

We have already examined India's relations with China and Japan in chapter 7. In this chapter, we will look at India's bilateral relationships with the remaining countries that enjoy some form of global status. By far the most substantive, and the most consequential for the emerging partnership with the United States, is the relationship with Russia, which has deep roots in the Cold War years. Military supply is its most important dimension. Both countries also share an attraction to multipolarity. India's ties with Europe have great economic importance but have little impact on the strategic outlook in either place. Those with Brazil and South Africa are thin by comparison, but they embody India's hope that the major developing countries, with India itself in the lead, will emerge in the medium to long term as more important centers of world power.

RUSSIA: OLD FRIEND, UNCERTAIN FUTURE

During the long years of the Cold War, Russia was India's most steadfast international partner and easiest international friend. Nehru believed that Russia's experience modernizing and "socializing" a peasant economy was more relevant to India's experience than the industrialization of Europe and North America. Pakistan's decision to join two of the U.S. anti-Soviet alliances in the 1950s pushed India toward a strategic relationship with the USSR, and Soviet willingness to accept India's position on Kashmir cemented that relationship. Soviet diplomatic support in the international arena was reliable and welcome. A substantial economic relationship followed, including aid, trade, and what were initially fairly generous barter and countertrade arrangements, making it possible for India to obtain more from the Soviet Union than its meager foreign exchange reserves would have permitted. Most importantly, the Soviets provided generous and inexpensive military supply.

Following the collapse of the Soviet Union and the sharp decline in the Russian economy, Moscow was in no position to play the same role in India's world as it had in the past. By the time the Russian economy had begun to recover and the Putin government started to play a more active international role, India had established a major relationship with the United States.

Russia's economic revival and growing international assertiveness, however, revived the interest of Indian strategic thinkers and policymakers. The strongest element in today's India-Russia relationship is defense trade, with energy supply as an attractive possibility. The two countries share some important perspectives about the global environment, notably their preference for a more multipolar global power structure. For Russia, the attraction is de-emphasizing the role of the United States; for India, multipolarity offers a way of enhancing its own status. Both countries seem to see their relationship as both coexisting and competing with their ties to the United States.

Military supply is likely to remain the most important element in Indo-Russian bilateral ties. Russia is India's largest supplier of imported military hardware, though Israel has moved up fast. Analysts with close ties to the Indian government estimate India's annual military imports from Russia at $2 billion.[1] The importance to India goes beyond volume. Far earlier than any other supplier, Russia was willing to allow India to coproduce major end items, a vital feature for an Indian defense establishment determined to improve its industrial capability and become self-sufficient. In addition to the many systems purchased in the past, India has signed contracts for procurement and production of

140 Sukhoi Su-30 fighter aircraft and for several hundred T-90 tanks. A Russian joint venture with India's Defense Research and Development Organization, part of the prime minister's office, is developing missiles for sale to the Indian armed forces, and is expected to set up a manufacturing facility in southern India. There are also plans for joint development of a multirole transport aircraft and a fifth-generation fighter aircraft. Another attraction of Russian military supply is that Indians are now able to mount high-tech electronics from the West (principally the United States and Israel) on less expensive Russian platforms.[2]

For Russia, Indian procurement has been a crucially important source of foreign exchange during the lean years after the end of the Soviet Union. India and China together accounted for some 60 percent of Russia's defense export revenues in 2006.[3] But India and Russia have gone through a jarring adjustment from their Soviet-era arms supply relationship. Although Russia's equipment is less expensive than roughly comparable Western items, India no longer has access to the easy long-term credits it enjoyed in earlier years. And Russia no longer has a protected market, as India goes out to European, Israeli, and U.S. suppliers in search of state-of-the-art equipment. This has led to some testy exchanges, as occurred in November 2007 when the Russian authorities tried to impose a massive cost increase on the already-concluded contract for the purchase and refurbishment of the aircraft carrier *Admiral Gorshkov*. Russia is bidding alongside competitors from Europe and the United States for a contract for 126 multirole combat aircraft. The Russian leadership is trying to make the contract a symbol of the bilateral relationship—and so are the United States and other contenders.

Indian security and foreign policy analysts describe Russia as a major potential energy supplier. India's public-sector oil company, OVL, has invested in exploration and production facilities as far afield as Sakhalin in keeping with its effort to improve India's energy security by strengthening its upstream position. However, apart from the occasional swap deal, there is little trade taking place now, principally because the means of transporting oil and gas to the Indian market are lacking. Moreover, Russia currently has insufficient natural gas to service its existing domestic demand and its contracts in Europe, for which the transportation infrastructure already exists. Servicing the Indian market is attractive in principle but a lower priority in practice.[4]

Perhaps Russia's most interesting potential contribution to expanding Indian energy supply is the talk of possible Russian financing for the construction of the proposed Iran-Pakistan-India gas pipeline. The pipeline project is fraught with commercial and political complications, but if Russian investment were to help bring it about, that would represent a significant contribution both to gas supply and to Russia's position as an arbiter of energy matters in the subcontinent.[5]

India's economic relationship with Russia outside the defense trade and energy fields is modest. Two-way trade was $3.3 billion in 2006–2007, below the level in the last years of the Soviet Union.[6] Both governments regularly express their determination to increase trade, and when Prime Minister Manmohan Singh visited Moscow in December 2007, he signed an agreement to increase trade to $10 billion by 2010. But trading with Russia is still complicated for the Indian private sector. Only in 2005 did Indian banks establish branches in Russia, and a Russian bank was not authorized in India until 2007.

Indo-Soviet trade in Soviet days was dominated by the state on both sides. The residue of the special barter arrangements from that era arrangements is still a factor in economic ties between the two countries. In late 2007, India and Russia reached agreement on a schedule for servicing $1 billion that India still owed in Soviet-era rupee-ruble debt. Funds generated by the Indian government under this agreement will be used, among other things, to finance Russian participation in the joint venture slated to produce a multirole military transport aircraft. This type of arrangement may create investment that otherwise would not exist, but it does not necessarily create lasting economic ties.

Russia has been a leader in high-tech and nuclear cooperation with India. As we saw in chapter 5, India-Russia space cooperation goes back to the early years, and, unlike cooperation with the United States, was not restricted by export controls. Russian nuclear cooperation too has been less restricted than that of the United States. Russia signed an agreement to build two nuclear reactors at Kudankulum in southern India in 1988, and promised another four reactors in 2000. More recently, when Prime Minister Singh visited Moscow in November 2007, he was expected to sign an agreement for fuel supply to these reactors. In the end, no agreement was signed. Both parties agreed that they needed to wait for the Nuclear Suppliers' Group to authorize civilian nuclear trade with India, and the NSG's consideration of the issue was held up by the complications attending the

U.S.-India nuclear agreement. Once the NSG had authorized civilian nuclear trade with India, however, Russia was one of the first countries to sign an agreement.

Beyond these specific bilateral issues, India looks on Russia as a country that shares its interest in a multipolar global power structure with a larger recognized role for India. Russia has long accepted India's sovereignty in Kashmir, and it continues to support India internationally in its dispute with Pakistan. Russia has made some effort to strengthen its ties with Pakistan in an effort to avoid being the only major power with a one-sided policy in the subcontinent. India pushed hard and apparently successfully, however, to prevent Russian arms sales to Pakistan.

India and Russia, as we have seen, share an interest in keeping Central Asia stable and in preventing the emergence of Islamic governments there. More generally, both countries are very concerned about Islamic extremism, and both resist international intervention to protect human rights. India has supported Russia in its troubles in Chechnya, and it made no public comment on its intervention in Georgia in the summer of 2008. But India does not share Russia's primary interest in Central Asia, which is to retain Russian political and economic primacy through its central position in the region's transportation and infrastructure. For all India's warm feelings about Russia and preference for Russian over Pakistani or Chinese influence, India's own quest for a position of significance in Central Asia relies to some degree on nurturing the Central Asian countries' economic independence from Russia. India's interest in obtaining oil and gas from Central Asia also conflicts with Russia's "hub and spoke" approach to its economic ties in the region: pipelines capable of bringing oil and gas to India would lead away from Russia, thus reducing the economic dependence on Russia that has been a primary goal of Russian policy.

Since 2005, India, Russia, and China have engaged in a series of formal foreign minister-level meetings, an effort to develop a triangular relationship among Asian powers that excludes the United States and Japan. "Triangulation" of this sort exerts a powerful gravitational pull in all three countries. The list of potential areas for cooperation sounds impressive: defense and security dialogues, coordination on United Nations and other international affairs, energy, transport infrastructure, health, information technology, and biotechnology. But the actual joint activity coming out of these meetings appears to be quite thin. Both Russia and India are developing closer ties with China but nonetheless have reason to be wary of it. Neither wants China to dominate Asia. For its part, China has no great interest in enhancing India's international stature or helping it to gain a permanent seat on the United Nations Security Council. While all three have differences with the United States in a number of policy areas, including Iran and Central Asia, they have no interest in raising the temperature of those disagreements with Washington. And with respect to Central Asia, China has no interest in facilitating a major Indian role, which would without question be largely an anti-Pakistan one. The communiqué that followed the three-way meeting in Harbin in October 2007 retreats into platitudes, suggesting that this triangle has not developed a strategic meeting of the minds.[7]

In short, apart from military supply, the Indo-Russian relationship appears to offer more hope than substance. The hope is not insignificant, however, especially when one considers the importance Indians attach to strategic autonomy and the impact of Russia's more fractious relationship with the United States.

Seen from Moscow's perspective, Russia's top foreign policy priorities are to consolidate Russian primacy in its immediate neighborhood—the former Soviet Union and Eastern Europe—and to reestablish itself as a recognized global power. India plays a useful but secondary role in this endeavor. India's attachment to strategic autonomy (especially from the United States) and its long history of close ties with the Soviet Union make it a comfortable partner. India's size and growing role in Asia give it some value as a counterweight to China, with which Russia maintains a relationship of both friendship and rivalry. India's energy investments have not developed to the point where they threaten Russia's control over energy resources and transport routes from and through Central Asia. Russia can make common cause with India in trying to keep down Chinese and Islamic influence in Central Asia. Neither Russia nor India would like to see Iran develop nuclear weapons, but neither is interested in participating in an international pressure campaign against Iran.[8]

In the early days after the end of the Cold War, the United States looked on the India-Russia relationship with something approaching benign disinterest. Its own ties with Russia were friendly, and the rivalry of the Cold War years had vanished. A decade and a half later, U.S. ties with Russia are more troubled. A more assertive Russia has locked horns with the United States over U.S. missile defenses in Europe and over its own efforts to maintain primacy in the "near abroad." As India looks for ways to balance a strong partnership with the United States with demonstrations of strategic autonomy, India and Russia are likely to use each other as counterweights to a "unipolar" U.S. posture in the world. Russia will push hard to maintain its military supply position in India; India and Russia will on occasion emphasize common positions that diverge from those of the United States, such as on Iran; and they will seek out opportunities to demonstrate that multipolarity is alive and well. This growing multipolar choreography has not yet required any strategic choices on India's part, and it has posed no real threat to U.S.-Indian cooperation.

In a sense, India's relations with Russia represent the antithesis of its ties with the United States. U.S.-India ties are strongest in the economic area and just beginning in military supply. While they are based on a growing convergence of interests in East Asia and to a lesser extent the Middle East, they still involve divergent views of how the world should be organized and a relatively thin but growing strategic dialogue. With Russia, on the other hand, India has a meager economic relationship, huge military supply, some convergence of interests in India's neighborhood (in this case, Central Asia), but an easy dialogue on how the world is organized and considerable confidence, going back to Soviet times, that each country knows how the other approaches the strategic issues that both care about.

EUROPE: ECONOMICS TRUMPS POLITICS

The driver in India's relations with Europe is unquestionably economics. The EU, taken as a group, is by far India's largest trading partner, with two-way trade amounting to $56 billion in 2006.[9] Investment has grown from $3.7 billion in 2006 to $16.1 billion in 2007.[10] Within Europe, the UK receives by far the largest share of Indian investment, including both direct investment and local companies that have been purchased by major Indian business houses (the purchase of British Steel/Corus by Tata in 2006 is a case in point). India is the third-largest investor in Britain. European partners are increasingly important in India's network of scientific relationships around the world.[11]

The scale and strategic importance of the political and security relationship with the EU falls well short of this economic profile. India has a strategic dialogue with the EU, which generates what one observer referred to as "frequent but essentially formalistic" discussions.[12] At the political level, India seeks support for a larger role in the world, including a permanent seat on the United Nations Security Council. This is not within the competence of the EU, however, and the two member states that currently have permanent Security Council seats will be wary of any formula that puts their own seats at risk. The EU, on the other hand, wants to encourage India to streamline its regulatory environment for investment and strengthen its participation in international discussions on democracy and human rights, issues that India tends to look on as intrusive.

In practice, India's relations are stronger with a handful of EU member states than with the union as a group. Serious political discussions take place mainly at the level of individual states; military supply discussions are with member states; and one observer with ample experience in the field has argued that even major trade issues for which the EU has competence are usually worked out in national capitals rather than in Brussels. The strongest and most complex ties are with Britain and France. The largest trade ties are with Germany, whose trade with India came to $20 billion in 2006–2007.[13]

India has had a mercurial relationship with the UK since independence, but always an important one. The economic underpinnings are strong: a major trade and investment relationship as well as substantial aid flow. India is the largest recipient of British development assistance, with $434.8 million in 2006–2007 and $496.47 in 2007–2008.[14] The imperial legacy created resentment, but also bonds of affection and tradition, ranging from cricket to university education. These remain strong, although the number of Indian students in the United States now exceeds the number in Britain by a factor of five. Most importantly, the one-million-strong Indian community in Britain creates multiple linkages, affecting immigration policy, financial flows, law enforcement in both countries, and antiterrorism operations.[15]

These are issues of great importance to both countries. India has ready recognition in Britain, with both the government and the public, as a country that matters, a status it has had to struggle for in many other capitals. In part because of its long history in South Asia, the UK has taken a far greater interest in regional political and security issues than any other European country. But the strategic importance of the UK in India's worldview has to a significant extent been eclipsed by the partnership with the United States.

The other interesting relationship is with France. Indians have long admired France's independent streak and the way it pursued a foreign policy at variance with that of the United States in spite of its membership in NATO. French attachment to multipolarity and willingness to sell advanced military equipment strengthened India's interest and has led to the creation of a structure of formal dialogues and working groups more elaborate than those with most other countries. India has looked to France for support both in civil nuclear cooperation and in its quest for a permanent seat on the UN Security Council.

It is not clear how far the French are prepared to go in either of those efforts, however. One former Indian ambassador to France warns against unrealistic expectations, pointing out that France's willingness to support India depends entirely on whether France's own interests in nuclear commerce and in retaining its permanent Security Council seat are protected. The relationship remains a useful but fairly limited one, imbued with emotional resonance on geopolitical issues, but with limited foreign policy weight.[16]

The relationships with Europe have relatively little impact on India's partnership with the United States. The United States and Europe compete commercially in the Indian market. Almost all the countries of the EU are allied with the United States and share with it central security interests. Politically, the European countries and the United States consult frequently about India and more generally about South Asia. Their policies are generally similar, and they make some effort to work together during times of crisis on the subcontinent. Britain is the only European country that has played a major diplomatic role, however. The similarities between U.S. and Indian interests in Asian security also extend in some measure to the larger EU countries, but partnership with the United States is a far more significant element in Indian foreign policy.

THE GLOBAL SOUTH

India's current foreign policy puts much greater emphasis on relations with major powers, but it still makes room for its traditional ambition of leading the world's developing countries into a larger global role. In the first three decades after India's independence, India pursued its "north-south" goals through the Non-Aligned Movement and other large groups of developing countries. Today, India's presence in major developing countries outside its own neighborhood takes more tangible forms: trade, investment, and occasionally aid. The economic weight of these relationships is still modest, but it is beginning to lead to new kinds of political cooperation. And these relationships now have an additional global dimension: in much of the "global south," and especially in Africa, China is trying to establish itself as a preferred partner, so India also appears in competition with China. India's most important ties are with Brazil and South Africa.

Brazil and India are both giant countries with major influence in their immediate region and impressive economic potential. The Goldman Sachs study on the BRIC countries (Brazil, Russia, India, and China) included both in the group whose economic heft and influence is likely to grow significantly in the next decade.[17] Hardeep Puri, former Indian ambassador to Brazil, writing in a volume commissioned by the Indian Ministry of External Affairs, puts the accent on three themes in India-Brazil relations: economic potential; a shared developmental vision that suffuses the two countries' cooperation; and their common desire to break into the big leagues of global governance.[18]

The economic relationship is easiest to define. Trade between Brazil and India grew sixfold between 2000 and 2007, but was still quite modest, at $2.5 billion or less than 1 percent of each country's total trade. Comparable trade partners for India are Malaysia and Bangladesh. Investment has both grown and diversified in the past decade, with Indian drug companies manufacturing both bulk drugs and finished formulations in Brazil, and strong Brazilian interest in India's market for infrastructure development and passenger aircraft. The accent, however, is on potential. Indian observers see the possibility of a rapid further increase in both trade and investment, especially if the currently inadequate transport facilities between the two countries can be improved. State-owned oil companies from both countries are investing in each other. Indians see Brazil as an increasingly important supplier of the commodities India needs to provide food and energy security, including both fossil fuels and biofuels.[19]

The same sense of new possibilities suffuses the political relationship. Brazilian president Inacio Lula da Silva has visited India twice since 2004, including one appearance at India's Republic Day, its most prestigious slot for a visiting foreign leader. India and Brazil both seek a larger role in global affairs. Both are now regular guests at the annual meetings of world leaders at the G-8, and they have joined forces in trying to gain permanent seats on the United Nations Security

Council. They have also sought high-profile roles in global trade negotiations, most recently in the Doha Round. This last was a traditional
partnership: for at least the past three decades, India and Brazil have
positioned themselves as leaders of the developing countries in trade
negotiations. It was also an odd one, because on agricultural trade, the
make or break issue for the Doha Round, their interests are opposed.
Brazil, a major agricultural exporter, needs to open other countries'
markets; India's primary goal was to preserve the right to cut off agricultural imports if they were hurting its farmers. The Brazilian government faced pressure from its business community to distance itself
from India's hard-line stance.

India's approach to Africa shows even more strongly the impact of
India's more global approach to foreign policy. South Africa is by far
the most important political relationship here. India's historical connections with South Africa add a unique dimension. Mahatma Gandhi
first made his mark as a fighter for social and racial justice as a young
lawyer in South Africa before returning to India to take up his iconic
role in the freedom struggle. There is a substantial Indian community
in South Africa, and India maintained a steadfastly anti-apartheid position during the long years of white rule in South Africa.

In today's world, South Africa shares all the attractions of the India-
Brazil connection: South Africa is a large country; economic ties are
relatively substantial and have the potential for growing; India's corporate sector has discovered South Africa as a venue for investment; and
India and South Africa share a desire to become global decisionmakers
on a larger scale and to acquire permanent seats on the UN Security
Council. In 2003, India, Brazil, and South Africa inaugurated a three-
way grouping, the IBSA Dialogue Forum, that meets regularly at the
ministerial level and tries to present a common front in multilateral
economic settings.

In Africa, India has gone beyond its ties with the largest country and
begun to develop a regional approach that embodies India's changed
"personality" on the world stage. India's voracious appetite for oil and
a security policy that treats the Indian Ocean as India's security zone
gives Africa enhanced strategic significance for India. At the same
time, India's private sector has begun investing in Africa, with particularly significant contributions in pharmaceuticals, primarily through
the provision of reasonably priced generic antiretroviral drugs to treat
the HIV/AIDS epidemic in the continent, and in telecommunications,

where India's Bharti Airtel is negotiating to purchase a controlling share in South Africa's Mobile Telephone Networks. Overall, trade with sub-Saharan Africa reached close to $26 billion in 2007–2008, approximately half of it petroleum-related.[20]

India has also emerged as a donor of aid and export credits to Africa. The amounts of aid are still modest; the lines of credit for exports, which totaled $750 million as of early 2007, will be more significant if they are fully utilized. But beyond their economic weight and the boost they will provide to the Indian private sector, these programs are beginning to reposition India as a country that can contribute to other countries' development rather than simply as a user of development funds. Africans have also benefited considerably from India's training programs, especially those in medical and management skills.[21]

These new overtures to the major players in the developing world are important as a "branding exercise" even beyond their strict economic or strategic significance. The glittering 14-nation Africa Summit hosted by India in April 2008 demonstrates how relations with Africa form part of the global position India is cultivating. However, India is playing catch-up both in Africa and in Brazil. China is working hard in both places and is better able to put significant governmental resources on the table. India and China are not in direct competition on regional issues, but in a larger sense India is trying to achieve the global status China already has.

Given India's and China's focus on energy as a driver for their foreign policy beyond their immediate region, their approach to Africa and Latin America raises another issue. Both India and China appear to be bent on acquiring captive energy resources. As has already been noted, this is unlikely to be a winning strategy for developing long-term energy security.

There is a strong multilateral flavor to the relationships India is building up in Latin America and Africa, and even to some degree in Europe. As we will see in the next chapter, this has both advantages and disadvantages for India's relationship with the United States. Some of India's multilateral initiatives come in areas where the United States and India regularly clash, such as India's campaign on agricultural trade and its position in the UN General Assembly. At the same time, India, Brazil, and South Africa are countries whose involvement will be essential in tackling some of the major global issues facing the world. India's emerging ties with these other large developing countries could lay the groundwork for developing new channels of cooperation for such vital issues as HIV/AIDS and climate change.

NOTES

1. Atish Sinha and Madhup Mohta, eds., *Indian Foreign Policy: Challenges and Opportunities* (New Delhi: Academic Foundation, 2007), 736.

2. "Russia's Defense Industry: Phoenix from the Ashes," *Strategic Comments* 13, no. 8 (London: International Institute of Strategic Studies, 2007).

3. Ibid.

4. Bethany Danyluk, Juli A. MacDonald, and Ryan Tuggle, *Energy Futures in Asia: Perspectives on India's Energy Security Strategy and Policies* (report prepared by Booz Allen Hamilton for Director, Net Assessment, Office of the Secretary of Defense, June 2007), 5–8; Anuradha Chenoy, "India and Russia," in Sinha and Mohta, *Indian Foreign Policy: Challenges and Opportunities*, 736–738.

5. See, for example, "Gazprom Confirms Interest in IPI Gas Pipeline," *Reuters*, May 5, 2007, http://www.expressindia.com/news/fullstory.php?newsid =86016.

6. Ministry of Commerce and Industry, Department of Commerce, Government of India, "Export Import Data Bank," http://commerce.nic.in/eidb/ Default.asp.

7. "The development of China, Russia and India is a major contribution to peace and development of the region and the world and is beneficial to the process of global multipolarity. The three countries have chosen their respective development paths in accordance with their domestic situation and past experience." Quoted in M. K. Bhadrakumar, "A Velvet Divorce in China," *Asian Times*, December 14, 2007, http://www.atimes.com/atimes/printN.html.

8. Andrew C. Kuchins, *Alternative Futures for Russia to 2017* (Washington, D.C.: CSIS, November 2007); N. S. Sisodia and C. U. Bhaskar, eds., *Emerging India: Security and Foreign Policy Perspectives* (New Delhi: Institute for Defense Studies and Analyses, 2005), 165–170.

9. Ministry of Commerce and Industry, "Export Import Data Bank," http:// commerce.nic.in/eidb/Default.asp.

10. "EU Investment in India Surges Past China," *EUBusiness*, May 19, 2008, http://www.eubusiness.com/news-eu/1211195822.7/.

11. Ministry of Commerce and Industry, "Export Import Data Bank," http:// commerce.nic.in/eidb/default.asp; Krishna V. Rajan, "India and the United Kingdom," in Sinha and Mohta, *Indian Foreign Policy: Challenges and Opportunities*, 743–766.

12. Dilip Lahiri, "India and France," in Sinha and Mohta, *Indian Foreign Policy: Challenges and Opportunities*, 727.

13. Ministry of Commerce and Industry, "Export Import Data Bank," http:// commerce.nic.in/eidb/Default.asp.

14. Department for International Development, "DFID India", April 2008, http://www.dfid.gov.uk/pubs/files/india-factsheet.pdf.

15. "The UK Population, By Ethnic Group," UK Census, Office for National Statistics, April 2001, http://www.statistics.gov.uk/statbase/Expodata/ Spreadsheets/D6588.xls.

16. Lahiri, "India and France," 711–728.

17. Tushar Poddar and Evelyn Yi, *BRICs and Beyond* (New York: Goldman Sachs, 2007), http://www2.goldmansachs.com/ideas/brics/BRICs-and -Beyond.html. The acronym BRIC, standing for Brazil, Russia, India, and China, was coined by Goldman Sachs in 2001.

18. Hardeep Puri, "India and Brazil: A New Dynamic," in Sinha and Mohta, *Indian Foreign Policy: Challenges and Opportunities*, 839.

19. Ministry of Commerce and Industry, "Export Import Data Bank," http:// commerce.nic.in/eidb/iecnt.asp.

20. Ministry of Commerce and Industry, "Export Import Data Bank," http:// commerce.nic.in/eidb/Default.asp.

21. Gurjit Singh, "India and Africa: A Response to African Institutionalization in the 21st Century," in Sinha and Mohta, *Indian Foreign Policy: Challenges and Opportunities*, 500.

10

GLOBAL GOVERNANCE

Two snapshots convey the flavor of India's pursuit of a larger role in the councils that run the world. The first dates from India's accession to the United Nations Security Council in January 1991, just as the Soviet Union was coming apart and the end of the Cold War was in sight. The first major issue to come before the council was the package of resolutions that would end the first Iraq war. Harried Indian diplomats, faced with draft resolutions being pressed on them with great insistence by their American counterparts, spoke of their need to "find the nonaligned consensus." Whatever decision India made was bound to alienate a constituency it cared about. This moment captured, for Indian officials, both the advantages and the drawbacks of participating in the world's decisionmaking. The Indian ambassador to the United States, Abid Hussein, expressed considerable frustration in a conversation at the time with the author: "Do you realize that we will have to do this for *two years*?"

Seventeen years later, in November 2008, Prime Minister Manmohan Singh and his top economic advisers attended the G-20 Summit on Financial Markets and the World Economy in Washington. Speaking with evident satisfaction to reporters on his flight home, he noted how serious the discussions had been and how he and India were being taken seriously at this gathering convened to address a major global crisis. He recognized that the institutional and financial reform processes had barely begun, and he foresaw India's continuing participation in both.

During a time of dramatic improvement in relations between the United States and India, multilateral settings have produced some of their most difficult encounters but have also created some of the most effective means for the countries to advance interests they share. The frustration is most acute in the United Nations, although there are some signs of policy convergence below the surface. In the World Trade Organization, as we have already seen, the two countries largely work at cross-purposes. In both formal and informal international financial institutions, on the other hand, the United States has already been working to expand the representation and role of emerging market countries like India. The global financial crisis that started in the summer of 2008 may accelerate that process. In the International Energy Agency, the United States has been pushing for an expanded Indian role as part of a broader effort to bring financial institutions and consultation mechanisms into line with global realities.

In assessing how the United States and India deal with global problems, this chapter will first review how they work in these institutional settings. It will then explore how they approach climate change, an issue that is handled in a looser institutional structure and that spans both international and domestic politics. These issues, especially when taken together with the nonproliferation issues discussed in chapter 5 and the questions of global financial management that preoccupy all governments following the 2008 economic meltdown, raise a question that will be central for the U.S.-India partnership down the road: How do the two countries perceive their responsibilities for global leadership?

GLOBAL INSTITUTIONS:
BREAKING THE GLASS CEILING?

In global institutions, the United States is the "status quo power," with a privileged position in the United Nations and the international financial institutions. The United States helped found these institutions, but discomfort with multilateral restraints on U.S. sovereign action has deep roots in U.S. politics. India wants to expand its role and status, and Indian policy has at times embraced great ambitions for global governance, such as Rajiv Gandhi's proposal for global nuclear disarmament. But in other contexts, India, like the United States, mistrusts global governance and global institutions, seeing them as an intrusion into its sovereign decisionmaking.

India has a great deal to offer international institutions: well-trained technical staff, a skilled diplomatic service with English-language skills honed for drafting and persuasion, and a strong sense of India's natural leadership role. India's role has been surprisingly selective, however. It has given clear priority to two groups of institutional forums: the United Nations, the first and most prestigious of the global institutions; and the economic institutions (the International Monetary Fund, World Bank, Asian Development Bank, and World Trade Organization), whose work is closely linked to the economic expansion that fueled India's expanding global role. A look at the senior staffs and executive councils of these institutions reinforces the point: India consistently fields a board member at the three international lending institutions to which it belongs, along with an impressive array of senior staff. In the World Health Organization and other technical institutions, India's contribution seems to be less consistent and more dependent on the personal qualities and interests of its representatives.

INDIA AND THE UNITED NATIONS

India regularly assigns top diplomats to the United Nations, and it is involved in practically everything the organization does. Its long-term goal is a permanent seat on the Security Council. It also seeks to keep its leadership credentials in the developing country club strong, and to avoid establishing precedents or norms that India might find distasteful or costly in the future.

India has not been on the Security Council since 1992, so its activities in New York center on the UN General Assembly and the committees that include all General Assembly members. From the U.S. perspective, the voting numbers tell a dismal story. India voted with the United States 14.7 percent of the time in 2007, compared with 18 percent for all countries. On votes the United States considered "important," India and the United States voted together 52 percent of the time if one includes consensus votes, and zero percent without consensus votes. All these figures represent a significant drop since 2002. To put this in perspective, India's voting record is not unusual. Other countries that maintain good bilateral relations with the United States, such as Pakistan and Egypt, had even lower levels of voting coincidence with the United States (11 percent and 6.3 percent respectively).[1]

Behind this pattern of voting against each other, there are some signs of change. On a string of issues that regularly come up for discussion in the General Assembly and its committees, Indian diplomats and strategic thinkers acknowledge that their interests have grown closer to those of the United States. India and the United States have similar concerns on small arms trade, land mines, and cluster munitions. India's voting coincidence with the United States on disarmament issues is twice as high as it is across the board. With respect to humanitarian operations, Indian policy is pulled in different directions. On the one hand, it has capabilities that few of its neighbors can match, as illustrated by its participation in tsunami relief in 2004–2005. This makes it cautious about resolutions that could be financially costly in the future, a concern the United States faces regularly. India has deep misgivings about humanitarian interventions against the wishes of the host government. Depending on the country involved, this may or may not align Indian concerns with those of the United States. In discussions on the United Nations' development operations, India finds itself closer to the United States than to the Western Europeans or Canada, with their focus on orienting assistance toward the social sectors. But in the General Assembly and its UN-wide committees, India is wary of attracting too much attention when its policy interests diverge from the NAM consensus. Its diplomats prefer to work behind the scenes to avoid bruising the sensibilities of their NAM partners, including countries regularly at odds with the United States like Sudan and Cuba. Votes in the General Assembly are in part a way of punching the NAM ticket.

This frequent discordance in the General Assembly, however, matters relatively little to either country; both seem to have discounted it in advance. Much more important are their solid and practical collaboration on peacekeeping operations and the structure of and deliberations in the Security Council.

India and the United States both recognize peacekeeping as a unique contribution of the United Nations to world peace, and both see India as an essential participant. India has been involved in peacekeeping operations since the mid-1950s. Today, it is one of three major contributors of personnel, together with Pakistan and Bangladesh. Each of them contributes 8,000–10,000 troops and police, or 11–13 percent of the United Nations' total peacekeepers. India maintains a training facility for United Nations peacekeepers and has sent peacekeeping training missions to other contributor countries. It has trained troops, police, and other specialized personnel. India has offered to designate one brigade for a UN Standby Arrangement. Its troops are skilled, well-trained, and disciplined. Senior Indian military officers have served as military advisers to the United Nations Secretary General. India and the United States have regular consultations on peacekeeping. India looks on its peacekeeping role with considerable pride, and sees in it an opportunity both to do good and to enhance its status.[2]

India's main argument for a permanent Security Council seat is that the council's permanent membership no longer reflects global realities, and that its size, growing economy, and regional and global prominence merit a place at the high table. Its last serious effort took place in 2005, when India joined forces with Japan, Germany, and Brazil (the "G-4"). At least seven different proposals have been circulated that would expand the Security Council, with different powers for the new members and different arrangements of permanent or longer-term members. The General Assembly resolution sponsored by the G-4 would have increased the size of the Security Council from 15 to 25, including the four sponsors and two unnamed African countries as new permanent members, at least initially without a veto. This resolution failed to get the necessary two-thirds vote in the General Assembly, so it never went through the more difficult tests of Security Council passage and actual election of new members.[3]

Expanding the council would involve changing the United Nations charter, and therefore requires the assent (or at least the non-veto) of all the current permanent members. Three permanent members, Russia, France and the UK, have endorsed India's bid for membership, but none of them appears ready to move a concrete proposal forward. China is for practical purposes opposed. The United States thus far has supported only Japan's interest in a permanent seat. It is not actively opposed to India's, but it has little interest in a larger council. Any proposal to expand the Security Council attracts opposition from regional rivals (in India's case, primarily Pakistan) or from countries more interested in advancing their own claims.

Recognizing that the moment was not propitious for a permanent seat, India began campaigning in 2008 for a nonpermanent seat that is scheduled to open up in 2011. The start of its campaign coincided roughly with the election of an Indian diplomat as Secretary-General of the Commonwealth, and the techniques that worked in the Commonwealth are being brought to bear in the United Nations. If this succeeds, as seems likely, India's votes on a range of international issues will shape the global response but may also irritate its international partners.

The results are likely to be stressful at least as often as they are helpful to U.S.-India relations. The United States cares far more about Security Council decisions than about most General Assembly votes. On peacekeeping, as we have seen, India and the United States have an established cooperative relationship, though peacekeeping decisions are powerfully influenced by the politics of the particular conflicts involved. On any issue that touches India-Pakistan relations or Kashmir, or that could be cited as a precedent in that context, India will stoutly resist any consequential UN role. On these issues, India's policy is decidedly realistic. On other questions, India will be looking for cover and trying to avoid a public break with Russia and China. India and the United States faced the same challenge in working together on the Security Council in 1991–1992. The intervening years may have given both countries some ideas about how to manage their different political requirements, but they have not eliminated the basic tension between Indian and U.S. aims for the Security Council.

INDIA AND THE MULTILATERAL ECONOMIC INSTITUTIONS
In the United Nations, relatively few of the issues being decided directly involve India's core interests. In the multilateral economic institutions, many decisions have a concrete impact on India. These institutions, as a result, are looked on in Delhi more as an extension of India's economic policymaking than as places to pursue a vision of global governance.

This is clearly the case with the World Trade Organization, as we saw in chapter 2. Trade negotiations go to the heart of India's politics. The WTO is primarily a forum for negotiations among member countries rather than a technical organization run by an expert secretariat. India's participation is carried out almost entirely by accredited representatives of the government—the commerce minister and negotiators drawn from India's civil service—rather than by Indian nationals on the international staff. This reinforces the political, rather than technical, character of WTO decisions. From the U.S. perspective, dealing with India in the WTO is more difficult than in the other economic organizations.

The international financial institutions—the World Bank, International Monetary Fund (IMF), and Asian Development Bank (ADB)—

are generally less contentious. All three are run by boards of directors of 20–24 members. The five largest shareholders appoint a director each, and the others elect directors, most of them representing more than one country, every two years. India always has a director on all three boards, representing itself and three of its smaller neighbors. Voting in all three institutions is weighted based chiefly on the size of a country's contribution, which in turn is related to the size of its GDP. As a result, India has a relatively small vote share.

India's consistent, long-term presence on the boards provides an opportunity to shape the policies of all three institutions over the longer term. In practice, the effectiveness of the Indian voice depends on the people appointed as executive directors. Another source of long-term influence are the Indian experts on the permanent staff of all three institutions. For example, one of India's most distinguished economists and senior officials, Montek Singh Ahluwalia, served for three years as the first director of the IMF's Independent Evaluation Office and set the standard for the way the Fund assesses its own programs.

The World Bank and Asian Development Bank are important sources of development funding, so India's representatives are responsible for bringing in resources. However, for India, as for other very large developing countries, official aid represents a relatively small share of its economy. Its priorities go beyond securing adequate funding and include climate change, financing adaptation strategies for clean energy generation, and avoiding excessively tight conditionality on development programs.[4] On this last point, India has been predictably at odds with the U.S. preference for results-based assistance. But in general, India and the United States have far fewer clashes in the development banks than in the WTO.

India last approached the International Monetary Fund for resources in 1991. Since then, it has tried to manage its economy so as to avoid the conditionality and limitations that go with IMF financing. India's participation in IMF deliberations has focused more on the institution's structure and global role.

In recent years, the United States has been pushing for expansion of the IMF's resources, a sharpening of its focus on exchange rate surveillance and openness to international analysis, and reform of its governance arrangements. In particular, the United States has called for "increas[ing] the shares of under-represented countries and cut[ting] the weight of over-represented nations." In practice this means expanding the vote share and role of India and the other emerging markets and reducing those of the European countries. The United States was prepared to forego the quota increase that this formula would normally have provided, but would retain a share large enough to block action in the board under the Fund's weighted voting system.[5]

On most of these points, the U.S. and Indian positions are quite similar. India was slow to engage in IMF negotiations over quota realignment in 2006, but by 2008 it was fully involved. The same issue was under discussion in the World Bank as well, and India made clear that increasing the "voice and participation" of developing countries was a priority. India's finance minister made a point of calling for the Fund to play a more vigorous role in responding to the global financial crisis and the spike in food and fuel prices during the summer of 2008, including expanding its financing capacity and updating its "financial toolkit."[6]

It is not just the governing structures of the World Bank and the IMF that need to adapt to changing world realities. As noted in chapter 3, India, despite being the world's second-fastest growing energy market, is not a member of the premier energy consumer countries' group, the International Energy Agency. Moreover, much of the world's high-level economic business is done in a series of more or less informal groups of countries, the most exclusive of which is the G-8, or group of eight major economies, whose meetings India and a few other countries have attended as guests. Recent experience suggests that these groups badly need to update their membership structure, and this could provide a useful setting for U.S.-Indian cooperation.

The story of the IEA starts with the Organization for Economic Cooperation and Development (OECD), which has consisted principally of highly industrialized countries but which has expanded its membership in the past few years to add South Korea and Mexico. In 2007, India was invited, along with China and three other developing countries, to participate in an "enhanced engagement" process, as a way of assessing whether eventual membership would be desirable. As part of this process, India has been an active participant in six OECD bodies and attended the 2008 ministerial meeting. The United States has encouraged this process and has suggested that India should seriously consider moving toward full membership.

India's experience with the OECD has been positive thus far. The OECD is the world's premier developed-country "club," however. Moving toward membership would pit India's interest in being seen as a great power against its identity as a leader of the world's poorer countries. Beyond that, OECD members are expected to abide by some 160 OECD codes of conduct on the management of a market economy. Especially important among these are rules governing private investment. While India has made major moves toward market-oriented policies, it is not ready yet for the full OECD list.

The IEA would be of much greater immediate interest. The United States has been exploring some arrangement that might make full IEA participation possible without OECD membership. The benefits to the global energy dialogue are obvious. Such an arrangement would also change the quality of India's policy dialogue with the United States and other OECD members. The major obstacles to changing the membership structure of either the OECD or the IEA are both organizations' traditionally dominant European members. India would represent a huge addition to either institution, especially if it were joined by China, as has been suggested for the IEA in particular.

India is not a member of the group of eight major economies, the G-8, but its participation in their annual summit meetings has become one of the high points on the Indian prime minister's travel schedule, and a constructive international engagement. The group started in the 1970s as an informal annual gathering of heads of state or government, with the smallest possible circle of advisers in attendance, to review the global economy. Over the years, the size of national delegations has grown, the agenda has expanded to include political issues, and the process has become more bureaucratic. Russia was invited to join after the Soviet Union broke apart. Although the G-8 does not have its own headquarters or staff like other international organizations, it has become institutionalized to a large extent.

India is one of five countries, together with China, Brazil, South Africa, and Mexico, whose leaders have been guests at the G-8 every year since 2005. G-8 deliberations take place behind closed doors, and by tradition relatively few details leak out. The participation of India and the other guests has avoided the controversy that dogs deliberations at the United Nations, for example. From the U.S. perspective, this is a huge plus. For India, joining this type of leadership dialogue on the international economy is a big attraction. India is very conscious of its current junior status, but is evidently prepared to begin that way with the hope of eventually expanding that role.

India has a strong interest in the G-8's economic agenda, especially climate change, which has been an important focus since the early 1980s. (The next section of this chapter will examine this issue more closely.) The G-8 has come closer than other forums to setting the stage for a decision on the difficult question of commitments to reduce greenhouse gases. Among the issues discussed at the G-8, this one has received the greatest attention in India.

After the 2007 meeting of the G-8 in Heiligendamm, Germany, the group established a two-year dialogue including its eight members and the five "outreach countries." The dialogue focused on major themes that affect the global economy, including innovation, investment, development assistance, and energy efficiency. This format was apparently intended to make the "outreach countries" integral to the discussion, with the possibility that the two groups might eventually merge at some point in the future. India has been an active participant in this process, providing the cochairs for two groups, on innovation (with France) and energy efficiency (with Canada).[7]

Observers outside the G-8 member governments have put forth several proposals for giving the G-8 a larger role in global governance. One proposal would de-emphasize the G-8 in favor of a loose network of somewhat larger issue-specific discussions including the current G-8 members and a varying number of other countries, focusing on specific issues such as climate change and energy. Others propose adding members—China and India, or all of the "outreach 5" plus three more Muslim-majority countries—and using the resulting group to "pre-negotiate" global issues that would eventually come up for decision in some other setting.[8] The common thread in these proposals is that all retain the predominantly consultative rather than decision-making character of the organization.

With the world in the grip of a financial crisis, President Bush invited the leaders of 20 countries to Washington in November 2008. With this gathering, the slow process described above—moving gradually to expand emerging markets' voices in the international lending institutions and thinking about bringing the larger ones into other economic forums—seems to have speeded up. When the G-20 met again in April 2009, with President Obama representing the United States, it made specific decisions expanding the membership in some key financial groups and tripling the resources of the IMF. The G-20 is an informal group, initially created in 1999 to bring together finance ministers and central bank governors, roughly half from industrialized and half from emerging market countries, without the structured voting or secretariat that one finds in formal institutions. The group had met from time to time over the preceding decade, but never at the head-of-government level. These two meetings catapulted it to higher international importance.

India fielded a team that was exceptionally expert on the subject at hand, starting with Prime Minister Manmohan Singh. In contrast to the listening brief India's representatives have generally carried at the G-8, Singh made a substantive intervention at the G-20. He urged stronger surveillance of the global financial system by the IMF and a renewed call for inclusiveness. He called for expanding the voice of emerging market countries in the IMF and for bringing emerging markets into two associations of regulators and central bankers from more than 20 industrialized countries that have a low public profile, the Basel Committee on Banking Supervision and the Financial Stability Forum (FSF).[9]

The official reactions of both India and the United States to the G-20 meeting expressed considerable satisfaction at the quality and results of the meeting. The meeting's closing communiqué was primarily an expression of principles, but it included a number of action items, and the key points in Manmohan Singh's intervention were reflected in it. It was a constructive first step toward coordinating international policies and creating more effective means for eventual collective action.

In the G-8, G-20, and OECD committees, India and the United States have joined in debates on some of the world's most difficult issues with a degree of candor and without acrimony. Part of the reason for this success, as contrasted with debates within the United Nations and the World Trade Organization, has to do with the style and format of the forums themselves. Most of these gatherings explore ideas or enunciate principles, and few make binding decisions. They are relatively small groups whose deliberations take place behind closed doors. Developed and developing countries are both present, but not in a structure that casts them as blocs. The issues that they deal with do not have the same political resonance as, for example, trade negotiations. The relatively small size of the organizations is important in another respect: India's participation marks it as an insider whose views are important. Especially at a time of financial crisis, participating in creating what is sometimes billed as the "next Bretton Woods" is a responsibility that seems to have brought out the most constructive side of India's leaders.

In looking for a future model for U.S.-India interaction on issues of global concern, these characteristics are worth replicating. They do not eliminate differences of national interest. Nor do they provide a mechanism for bringing private financial institutions or businesses into the discussion, a step that will eventually be essential, as private financial flows generally dwarf those provided by governments and international organizations. Informal groups cannot replace actions that need to be taken by formal institutions, whose membership structures still need to be updated. But this type of gathering provides a constructive setting for addressing global issues. And these groups have a track record of solid cooperation, without triggering the emotive responses that have so often discouraged U.S.-India interaction on the international scene.

CLIMATE CHANGE: LONG-TERM BENEFITS, SHORT-TERM COSTS

In the United Nations and the international economic institutions, India and the United States are working as members of institutions with a wide range of concerns. As international interest groups get better at using the extraordinary communications capacity of the Internet, a growing number of issues may be handled in a less linear, messier fashion, with the formal processes of international organizations co-existing and competing with dramatic public campaigns and domestic political lobbying. Climate change is a good example of how India and the United States operate in this more free-form model for global decisionmaking, which their governments cannot control.

Climate change is truly a global problem, in which individual countries depend on the collective effect of all countries' actions. The cost of inaction will be felt in the long term, but the costs of action are palpable right away, and taking action requires massive financial resources. Climate change will affect countries differently, based on their wealth, geographic location, opportunity cost, and ability to implement and finance alternative ways of powering their economies.

In recent years, India and the United States have participated in several international forums that address climate change, most recently the 13th Conference of Parties of the United Nations Framework Convention on Climate Change (UNFCCC) in Bali in December 2007. They have taken different positions, especially on the actions expected of developing and developed countries to address the problem. But their differences have caused barely a ripple on the surface of U.S.-India relations. Fundamentally, both have been trying to avoid binding commitments. Looking ahead, however, as the United States begins to take climate change more seriously, the stage is set for a high-octane disagreement between the two governments, requiring new creativity and flexibility. In both countries, the debate will take place outside as well as inside government, with civil society organizations generally pushing for a more aggressive policy and businesses resisting environmental constraints or commitments. The future of the climate change debate, in other words, will engage not just the two governments, but their publics as well.

Climate change poses a real danger to India. The effects predicted by both international and Indian government analysts feed directly into some of the country's security managers' biggest concerns: population movements and disputes over basic resources with India's equally desperate neighbors.

The National Action Plan on Climate Change,[10] the Indian government's basic policy framework, paints a sobering picture of what lies ahead if present trends continue. It draws heavily on the 2007 report of the Intergovernmental Panel on Climate Change (IPCC).[11] Likely effects include a surface temperature rise over the next century of 2.5–4 degrees Celsius under its more optimistic scenario, and 3–5 degrees under the more pessimistic one. Each degree of increase in temperature would cut India's wheat production by 4–5 million metric tons. This could lead to crop losses as high as 41 percent for wheat and 32 percent for rice. The temperature increase would severely affect India's forests, with more than 60 percent changing in type. In much of India, the rise in temperature would make malaria transmission possible year-round, with potentially severe health effects.

The action plan estimates that climate change will stress India's water supply, already a major political and economic issue throughout the subcontinent. The melting of Himalayan glaciers would increase water flows in the medium term, aggravating the expected intensification of the summer monsoon. In the longer term, it would reduce the availability of fresh water. The most vulnerable parts of India would be the coastal regions. Seven million Indians now live in areas that would be flooded if sea levels rise by one meter. Inundation would be even more severe in neighboring Bangladesh, where 35 percent of the country would be flooded, resulting in a near-certain influx of people into eastern India. The impact of these environmental changes would fall most heavily on the agricultural and health sectors, and especially on India's poor.[12]

To curb carbon emissions, India would need to make major changes in its energy strategy. Depending on how its new policies were structured and whether India received financial support for the change, this process could reduce GDP growth by up to 1.4 percent per year over 20 years. Both politically and economically, this process would be more manageable if reductions in emissions were spread out over time and encouraged by tradable emission quotas.[13]

The Indian government and private organizations are trying to develop realistic policies to moderate the growth in greenhouse gas emissions. The amount of energy used in India per unit of GDP has been falling for a couple of decades, as noted earlier. India's environmental legislation has set standards for air pollution in cities. These have been enforced by court rulings in public interest lawsuits. In 2002, for instance, after years of courtroom battles, the courts gave Delhi one month to complete the long-delayed conversion of common carrier transit from gasoline and diesel to compressed natural gas. The deadline was eventually extended by three months to provide time to establish the filling stations to service Delhi's large fleet of taxis, three-wheelers, and buses.

The National Action Plan on Climate Change sketches out the broad outlines of a long-term approach to moderating emissions. Seeking to encourage an "inclusive and sustainable development strategy, sensitive to climate change," it outlines eight new "national missions" devoted to different aspects of the problem, such as use of solar energy, energy efficiency, sustainable habitat, conservation of water, sustaining the Himalayan ecosystem, and promoting afforestation and sustainable agriculture. India is understandably reluctant to make significant sacrifices in short-term growth. The kinds of policies that will eventually be required to make India's economy "greener" reach into many aspects of life and complicate the already daunting task of raising the standard of living in a rapidly growing but still poor economy. As with the urban air quality standards, implementation will be an even bigger challenge.

Against this background of slow-moving and difficult policy change, India has participated actively in the international debate on climate change. Besides participating in the UNFCCC, India has signed several international agreements, including the Kyoto Protocol.[14] Climate change has been a major theme at G-8 meetings, at the 2007 East Asian Summit, and at a July 2008 meeting of the environment ministers of SAARC. The prime minister appointed India's just-retired top diplomat, former foreign secretary Shyam Saran, as his special envoy on climate change. Both Saran and the minister of science and technology, Kapil Sibal, have made climate change a frequent theme in their public discussions, both domestic and international.

In all these forums, India argues that responding to climate change is vital for the future of the world, but that it is primarily the responsibility of the developed countries. India above all resists any binding commitments on reduction of greenhouse gases. It argues that it had little part in the cumulative impact of carbon emissions over the past 200 years. Its per capita emissions are tiny compared to the developed countries (1.5 tons per year in 2000, or 6 percent of U.S. levels).[15] The Indian government has tried to show a more general willingness to participate in international efforts to prevent climate change through broad undertakings, such as Prime Minister Manmohan Singh's 2007 pledge that India's per capita greenhouse gas emissions will never exceed those of the developed countries.[16] It has undertaken to increase its forest cover from 28 to 33 percent of the country's area.[17] The first pledge is certainly achievable, given the massive difference between India's emissions and those of the developed world. The feasibility of increasing India's forest cover is less clear. Underlying India's position is a key watchword drawn from the UNFCCC and other international agreements: "common but differentiated responsibilities," or a distinct set of responsibilities for India compared to the richer countries.

These positions put India at odds with the United States, which was pushing in international forums to have the "major developing countries," including India, accept some degree of discipline on their emissions if the developed countries are to accept limits. This reflects the political reality that an international agreement in which countries as large as India and China undertake no obligations will have great trouble getting assent in the U.S. Congress. It also reflects concern that a system in which developing countries are free of environmental requirements will encourage investment flight and job loss. The absence of any binding commitment for the developing or "non-Annex I" countries in the Kyoto Protocol was the principal reason that it was so spectacularly unpopular in the U.S. Congress, even under an administration that actively sought international agreement on climate change.

But in practice, this difference of position mattered little. The Bush administration was trying to avoid obligations rather than to take action; so was India. This extended as well to the Bush administration's domestic policies. The administration resisted increasing the automotive fuel economy standards in the United States until December 2007, and it interpreted environmental regulations so as to require the least possible action on the part of U.S. industry.

As a result, the international results were modest, which in practice suited both governments. The road map agreed to at the 2007 Bali Conference of Parties of the UNFCCC sets forth general principles to guide the negotiation of environmental "rules of the road" following the end of the Kyoto convention in 2012. It calls for "enhanced national/international action on mitigation of climate change," including "consideration of measurable and verifiable commitments" and "nationally appropriate mitigation actions" by developing countries. It also calls for enhanced action on adaptation to those aspects of climate change that can no longer be prevented, for technology transfer, and for appropriate financing mechanisms.[18] This decision tiptoes up to the edge of international action, but the actual negotiation remains to be done.

The Obama administration is taking a different tack. The energy/ environment nexus is one of the three areas where it seeks major policy change as an urgent priority. The decision to allow the State of California to impose tighter emissions standards on vehicles—reversing a Bush administration decision—will push the domestic economy toward a stronger position on limiting emissions. Having started by putting the United States' own house in order, the administration has made clear that it wants to move toward serious international agreements on climate change, and that it wants all major countries to participate. This will inevitably become a new source of Indian-U.S. friction. Moreover, trends in greenhouse gas emissions will accentuate this friction. China has now passed the United States as the world's largest national source of greenhouse gas emissions, and emissions of carbon dioxide are growing more than twice as fast in China and India as in the United States.[19]

As the international debate has focused on setting ground rules for national control of emissions, the major multilateral institutions have paid somewhat less attention to the techniques that could be used to facilitate the adoption of practical strategies for control of greenhouse gases. There have been general references to the need for enhanced financing, especially for developing countries, and to strengthening technical cooperation.[20] The Asia Pacific Partnership on Clean Development and Climate has focused on studying and propagating "best practices" in different industrial sectors.[21] As the United States takes a more active stance on climate change, the international debate may shift away from blanket accusations about who is neglecting the future of the planet, but will probably focus more pointedly on the resources needed to mitigate climate change.

Climate change is not simply the responsibility of officials and government-to-government institutions. National and international NGOs play a prominent role. Two of the most prominent figures in the international debate on climate change are the 2007 Nobel Peace Prize winners, former U.S. vice president Al Gore and Dr. R. K. Pachauri, chairman of the IPCC and head of one of India's most successful think tanks. Neither holds an official position, and both have been critical of their own governments. Both are forceful advocates for financing for developed countries' green policies. Both command a ready audience at home and around the world.

Private business too is involved in the climate change debate. U.S. businesses that see emissions control as costly and burdensome have made their concerns known in the U.S. government and the Congress. The same is no doubt true in India. In both countries, some major businesses advertise themselves as "green." Internationally, businesses that believe they are leaders in environmentally friendly technology are trying to use this as an advantage. Japan, for example, has been urging that the international norms for emissions controls be broadened to include sectoral caps, based in part on some of their businesses' success in developing energy efficiency and emissions "best practices."[22]

Behind the activities of civil society organizations and businesses lies public opinion, which seems more sympathetic than governments toward policies to prevent climate change. In a November 2005 survey of the Indian public, 69 percent of respondents agreed that "all countries have a responsibility to make some efforts to limit their emissions," compared with only 26 percent who held that "less-developed countries like India should not be expected to limit their emissions."[23] A 2008 poll in the United States showed large majorities of both political parties in favor of controlling emissions, and relatively few differences between the political parties with respect to specific methods of controlling emissions.[24]

The India-U.S. dialogue on climate change, in other words, will play out in a kind of free-for-all, with government policies on both sides being pushed by non-governmental actors, both domestic and international, who are also players in shaping international commitments. Actions that affect climate change will also include standard-setting by private business or professional organizations, corporate policies on norms for domestic and worldwide investment, and the raucous democratic debate in both countries. This enormous list of players will sometimes help create harmony, but probably more often aggravate tensions. Nongovernment actors in both countries will be sympathetic to the Indian argument that the developed countries need to mobilize the resources for addressing climate change, but they will also push India to take action if the resources are found. India and the United States are working toward both a partnership between governments and one between countries. On climate change, both kinds of ties will be engaged.

LOOKING AHEAD

India and the United States will also work together in a host of other institutions and on many other issues. The World Health Organization, UNAIDS, the public-private partnership of the Global Fund for AIDS, Tuberculosis and Malaria, and universities in both countries will shape the international health environment; technical organizations like the World Meteorological Organization, the International Telecommunications Union, the World Postal Union, and the World Intellectual Property Organization are standard-setters in their particular spheres; and the list goes on. Each of these groups provides an opportunity for India to showcase its talent. Especially in the case of the health organizations, India has a chance to position itself as a country that is helping poorer and less-capable countries to live a better life.

The conventional wisdom is that the United States and India can work together bilaterally but not multilaterally. The reality is more encouraging. Indian involvement in some informal multilateral organizations has worked well both from India's perspective and from that of the United States. This suggests that U.S. efforts to adapt the membership and governance of most of the major international economic institutions to the world's changing economic structure are wise. The process has moved slowly in the formal institutions, complicated by the fact that there is one region of the world—Europe—whose influence stands to suffer disproportionately if India joins the "leadership groups."

This adjustment process needs to accelerate. India is sure to seek a more important role in the major organizations discussed in this chapter. There will undoubtedly be a push in the next decade to challenge the monopoly the United States and Western Europe now have on the top positions at the World Bank and the IMF. At some point, India will field a candidate for one of those jobs. India's willingness to put more resources into the international institutions may be an essential ingredient in such an effort, and if India's economy remains strong, it may decide to increase its quota in the IMF and gain a larger share of the weighted voting. The recent statement by Montek Ahluwalia, chairman of India's Planning Commission, that India would in principle be willing to buy $10 billion worth of IMF bonds should the fund decide to issue them, is an indication that India may be edging closer to this view.[25] How a larger Indian role affects the U.S.-India partnership depends on how India decides to use it.

Behind all these aspects of global governance lies a bigger question: what do the United States and India want to achieve on the global scene? The United States is accustomed to the burdens of leadership and recognizes its responsibility for dealing with many global problems. India, by contrast, may understate its influence on key global issues—finance and trade, for example—and hence its responsibility for the way the world manages them. Its goals include both status and policy. At the moment, both India and the United States are somewhat ambivalent about strong global governance. Both are sometimes more concerned about avoiding constraints on their own behavior than about establishing global norms that place agreed-upon constraints on all participants.

Over the next decade, this may change. The financial crisis has confronted both countries with an urgent need for international coordination, which will inevitably lead to some level of policy restraint in the financial area. For the United States, the Obama administration may be more receptive to some constraints in the interest of moving toward a global environment it considers healthier. It has taken a stronger position on climate change, may need to take a new look at nonproliferation, as we saw in an earlier chapter, and will probably need to work toward new financial architecture. As India's power grows, avoiding constraints will compete with the desire to expand its voice in the world's policymaking councils.

The United States has encouraged greater Indian participation in the international economic institutions, but has been cool toward a permanent seat for it on the United Nations Security Council or Indian membership in East Asia-based regional organizations. This reflects the difficult U.S.-India relationship in the United Nations and perhaps also the relatively recent expansion in close ties between India and its East Asian neighbors.

The argument for bringing India into positions of Asia-wide and global leadership is compelling, however. India is too big a player to be left out of the issues the United States wants to tackle globally or regionally. In that sense, it already is a global player. Today's challenge is to learn how to build a global consensus with both India and the United States as active participants. Serious global engagement is not just inevitable: it is the only way for the United States and India to address global issues important to both. The smaller and more discreet the forum, the easier it will be for the United States and India to work in reasonable harmony. India's international goals will evolve as its economy becomes more entwined with the world and as its regional leadership role grows. It is time, in short, to start actively adapting the network of international institutions to the broader and messier power structure of today's world.

NOTES

1. Bureau of International Organization Affairs, U.S. Department of State, "Voting Practices in the United Nations, 2007," May 5, 2007, 89–98, 224, http://www.state.gov/p/io/rls/rpt/c25867.htm.

2. United Nations Department of Peacekeeping Operations, "United Nations Peacekeeping, Monthly Summary of Contributors of Military and Civilian Police Personnel," http://www.un.org/Depts/dpko/dpko/contributors/, accessed September 25, 2008; Ministry of External Affairs, Government of India, "India and the United Nations: UN Peacekeeping," http://www.un.int/india/india_and_the_un_pkeeping.html; author's interviews with Indian officials, February and September 2008.

3. Center for UN Reform Education, "The United Nations Security Council: Reforms Concerning its Membership—An Overview," www.centerforunreform .org.

4. See, for example, the statement submitted by India's finance minister, P. Chidambaram, at the annual meeting of the World Bank's Development Committee, October 12, 2008. Chidambaram was not present owing to the financial crisis and its impact on India, but the statement was circulated and clearly reflects official policy.

5. David H. McCormick, Under Secretary of the Treasury for International Affairs, "IMF Reform: Meeting the Challenges of Today's Global Economy," remarks at the Peterson Institute for International Economics, February 25, 2008. http://www.treas.gov/press/releases/hp838.htm.

6. P. Chidambaram, statement to annual meeting of the International Monetary and Financial Committee, International Monetary Fund, October 11, 2008.

7. Andrew F. Cooper and Ramesh Thakur, "Wishing on a Star for the G8 Summit," *The Hindu* (Madras), July 7, 2008, http://www.hindu.com/2008/07/07/stories/2008070755351000.htm; Katharina Gnath, "Beyond Heiligendamm: The G-8 and Its Dialogue with Emerging Countries," *Internationale Politik* (Autumn 2007), http://en.dgap.org/midcom-serveattachmentguid-1dc82d48117db8882d411dc9999d3793ee2a818a818/ipge_3_gnath.pdf.

8. Richard N. Haass, "Leaders Have a Flawed Gleneagles Agenda," Council on Foreign Relations, July 1, 2005, http://www.cfr.org/publication/8238/; Bruce Jones, Carlos Pascual, and Stephen John Stedman, *A Plan for Action: A New Era of International Cooperation for a Changed World—2009, 2010, and Beyond*, Managing Global Insecurity, September 2008; U.S. and Indian officials, interviews with author.

9. Manmohan Singh, Statement at the Summit of the Heads of State or Governments of the G-20 countries on Financial Markets and the World Economy, Washington, D.C., November 15, 2008, http://www.indianembassy.org/newsite/press_release/2008/Nov/7.asp.

10. Prime Minister's Council on Climate Change, *National Action Plan on Climate Change* (New Delhi: Government of India, June 30, 2008), 13–15, http://www.pmindia.nic.in/Pg01-52.pdf.

11. R. K. Pachauri, et al., eds., *Climate Change 2007: Synthesis Report* (Geneva: Intergovernmental Panel on Climate Change, 2008), http://www.ipcc.ch/ipccreports/ar4-syr.htm?wa=EPIRSS0825.

12. Jyoti K. Parikh and Kirit Parikh, *Climate Change: India's Perceptions, Positions, Policies and Possibilities*, Organization for Economic Cooperation and Development (OECD), 2002, p. 6, http://www.oecd.org/dataoecd/22/16/1934784.pdf; N. Gopal Raj, "The Great Himalayan Meltdown," *The Hindu*, October 4, 2007; see also Prime Minister's Council on Climate Change, *National Action Plan on Climate Change*.

13. Parikh and Parikh, *Climate Change: India's Perceptions, Positions, Policies and Possibilities*, 7.

14. Energy Information Administration, "India Profile: Official Energy Statistics from the U.S. Government," http://www.eia.doe.gov/cabs/India/Profile.html, accessed September 10, 2008.

15. Subodh Sharma, Sumana Bhattacharya, and Amit Garg, "Greenhouse Gas Emissions from India: A Perspective." *Current Science* 90, no. 3 (February 10, 2006): 329, available at http://www.ias.ac.in/currsci/feb102006/326.pdf.

16. Prime Minister Manmohan Singh, "Intervention on Climate Change at the Heiligendamm Meeting of the G-8," June 8, 2007, http://meaindia.nic.in/climatehome.htm.

17. Kapil Sibal, Minister of Science and Technology and Earth Sciences, statement to 13th Conference of Parties of the United Nations Framework Convention on Climate Change, Bali, December 12, 2007,http://www.meaindia.nic.in/speech/2007/12/12/12ss01.htm.

18. UN Framework Convention on Climate Change, *Report of the Conference of the Parties on Its Thirteenth Session*, Bali, December 3–15, 2007, 3-8, http://unfccc.int/resource/docs/2007/cop13/eng/06a01.pdf#page=3.

19. Emissions of CO_2 are growing by 1.1 percent per year in the United States; the annual growth rate in China is projected at 3.3 percent, and in India at 2.6 percent. China's emissions of CO_2 are expected to exceed those of the United States by 15 percent in 2010 and by 75 percent in 2030. Energy Information Administration, *International Energy Outlook 2008* (Washington, D.C.: U.S. Department of Energy, September 2008), 93–94, http://www.eia.doe.gov/oiaf/ieo/pdf/0484(2008).pdf.

20. See, for example, the statement by the heads of government of the G-8 plus Australia, Brazil, China, EU, India, Indonesia, Korea, Mexico, and South Africa, "Declaration of Leaders at the Meeting of Major Economies on Energy Security and Climate Change," Hokkaido, Japan, July 9, 2008, http://meaindia.nic.in/declarestatement/2008/07/09jd01.htm.

21. Asia Pacific Partnership for Clean Development and Climate, http://www.asiapacificpartnership.org/.

22. *Energy Insights,* September 2008, The Energy and Resources Institute, 4; author's interview with David Pumphrey, former U.S. Department of Energy official, August 2008.

23. World Public Opinion.org, "Most Indians Say India Should Limited Its Greenhouse Gases," March 1, 2006, http://www.worldpublicopinion.org/pipa/articles/brasiapacificra/169.php?nid=&id=&pnt=169&lb=bras.

24. World Public Opinion.org, "McCain and Obama Supporters Largely Agree on Approaches to Energy, Climate Change," September 23, 2008, http://www.worldpublicopinion.org/pipa/articles/home_page/542.php?nid=&id=&pnt=542&lb.

25. Bob Davis, "India Ready to Buy IMF Bonds," *Wall Street Journal Online*, April 26, 2009, http://online.wsj.com/article/SB124067299074156277.html.

11

A NEW PARTNERSHIP, A CHANGING WORLD

The ten years between India's nuclear tests and the approval of the U.S.-India civil nuclear cooperation agreement have seen remarkable changes in the way the United States and India deal with one another. A much expanded bilateral relationship and a dense web of private ties point toward increasing interaction on the global scene. Still, India's international ambitions send an ambivalent message. India sees the United States as a means of fulfilling its goals, but sometimes as a potential obstacle to them. The uneven record of U.S.-India consultations about the world beyond the subcontinent suggests that the two countries have only begun to understand where their regional and global hopes do and do not coincide.

Policymakers in both countries speak routinely of a "strategic partnership." But the scope and dynamics of that partnership are still being developed. The bilateral ties described in the preceding chapters certainly are a good start. Common international interests create the potential for a strategic connection. This final chapter will consider what kind of partnership would suit India and the United States, what it will take for it to be "strategic," and how it will be affected by changes in India, in the United States, and in the international environment.

SHIFTING POWER PATTERNS

The previous chapters have analyzed the emerging U.S.-India relationship against the background of the "unipolar moment" the United States now enjoys on the global scene and of India's emergence into a position of greater but still circumscribed power. The United States accounts for close to half of global military expenses, and has unquestioned military superiority. It produces about 25 percent of world output and is likely to remain the world's largest economy at least until mid-century. It has had the predominant voice in shaping global institutions. The rules established at the end of World War II created economic and legal systems that are familiar and for the most part congenial to the United States. India is a "revisionist state" in the sense of wanting to change the way the world looks at it, but not in the sense of wanting to overturn the system. It wants to join the system, but in a more powerful position. As one Indian observer put it, it wants to be "a member of the board of the world."

At the same time, the United States' current unipolar status is fragile. Being the world's most powerful nation is not the same as being able to work one's will unilaterally. The most recent published long-term global forecast prepared by the U.S. National Intelligence Council (NIC) predicts that the United States will remain the world's "preeminent power" through 2025 and beyond, but with diminished dominance. The study argues that U.S. military preponderance will become less important, and the relative increase in economic strength by China, India, and others more important, in the overall distribution of global power. It anticipates that the existing formal international institutions—the United Nations, the international financial institutions—will increasingly be dwarfed by private economic activity. New problems, including climate change, shortages of food and energy, and movements of people, will intensify and will bring forth new mechanisms to address them.[1]

Foreign affairs and security analysts in the United States generally agree that the country should protect its primacy. Many observers, however, also concur with the NIC forecast that relative U.S. power will decline, and that this change must be carefully managed to avoid the shocks that have historically accompanied the rise of new powers. They disagree over the nature of the main threats to U.S. national security. Some share the NIC report's emphasis on the challenge from major economic movements, climate change, and other manifestations of global disorder. Others consider great power competition the principal threat, with China as an especially important factor. The NIC study argues that China will wield "more influence than any other country" by the end of its forecast period.[2] Many observers consider radical Islam an additional danger and see U.S. military and economic dominance as the most important means to defend against them. Still others consider the primary danger to be internal state weakness in strategically important countries and the breakdown of a rule-based international order. They argue for rebuilding fragile countries and international institutions, with a larger place in this exercise for strong "emerging countries," including India. Some argue for a "concert" of great powers; others advocate a "concert" of democracies.[3] The NIC study forecasts a "global multipolar system" by 2025, in which the predominant voice in global decisionmaking comes not just from a handful of countries (including India) but also from a variety of non-state actors.[4]

The power of the United States and others is determined not just by military strength but also by economic vigor and political attraction— what some call "soft power." Global problems that have emerged in the past decade become more important, though there are different views about how much more important. These factors all demand a collective response from the United States and the other major global players. India is the principal large country with which the United States has had neither an alliance nor serious hostility in the past. As one of the major powers in Asia, it has a strong interest, as the United States does, in ensuring that China's rise takes place in a way that strengthens international cooperation rather than generating conflict, and that the world's non-military problems are dealt with effectively.

The predominance of the United States in this first decade of the twenty-first century is an attraction for Indian policymakers. It makes an understanding with the United States essential for India's global ambitions, and in that sense it is one of the foundations of the new U.S.-India relationship. But U.S. preponderance also has drawbacks for a country whose preferred future world has power distributed among a larger number of nation-states, with India as one of the major actors. India's political and policy leadership is ambivalent about how India's commitment to strategic autonomy and taste for global balancing fit in with its ties with the United States. Indian strategists and policymakers want to keep their country's options open. The common interests sketched out in the preceding chapters push India toward working with the United States on the broad outlines of security in the Indian Ocean and Asia, on maintaining the viability of a global economic system from which India is beginning to benefit, and on enhancing India's voice and presence in global councils. India's national security interests, on the other hand, will lead it to follow an independent course with regard to Pakistan. Its commitment to strategic autonomy will incline India to look for opportunities to balance the world power structure even as it works closely with the United States.

A NEW KIND OF PARTNERSHIP

The United States and India have been building a partnership since the 1990s. They bring different experience to the table. Since World War II, most partners of the United States have been treaty allies whose ties with Washington started from a common view of strategic threats. Most have been democracies, though there are some exceptions, including countries that had nondemocratic periods, such as Greece, Spain, Korea, and the Philippines, and partners with no democratic claims, such as Iran under the Shah. The NATO alliance consists overwhelmingly of countries that share common cultural roots with the United States. U.S. alliances in Asia have had to overcome much greater differences in culture. All the partners have been, at least at the outset, much less powerful than the United States, and those that achieved rough economic parity (the combined countries of the European Union, for example, or Japan) were still protected by U.S. security commitments. Based on this experience, the United States has come to expect that its partnerships would operate not just bilaterally but globally, and that its partners would work with the United States on a wide range of international issues. Where this has not been the case—as sometimes happened, for example, with France—the result has been significant tensions both in public and in bilateral relations.

The United States has also cultivated partners outside the alliance framework. Its partnership with Egypt, for example, revolved around the role past U.S. administrations played in brokering Middle East peace negotiations. Other examples have been driven overwhelmingly by economic ties, such as the one with the ASEAN countries after the end of the Vietnam War. These partners have not had global ambitions, however. The partnership with Israel is sui generis, and involves a U.S. willingness to accept Israeli priorities that goes beyond any other relationship. Like the treaty allies, the non-treaty partners were, almost by definition, considerably less powerful than the United States.

India's tradition of nonalignment, on the other hand, did not rely on partners. Solidarity with other nonaligned countries and with the major developing country forums (such as the Group of 77) was always important, but made relatively few demands on the participants' foreign policies other than routinely voting with the group in international organizations. India's concept of a multipolar world rested on the notion that India would be one of the poles, and its strict concept of sovereignty and commitment to strategic autonomy left relatively little scope for special relationships. Prime Minister Jawaharlal Nehru had a strong personal bond with leaders in Egypt, Indonesia, and Yugoslavia, and the personal bonds carried over into the leadership role the countries played in the Non-Aligned Movement. The NAM as a whole, and India's relations with those countries, decreased in importance after the Cold War.

India's other experience of partnership was its Cold War-era relationship with the Soviet Union. Moscow gave Delhi strong diplomatic support on issues on which Washington was unsympathetic. Perhaps the clearest example was Kashmir, where the United States adopted a position that the Indians regarded as hostile whereas the Soviet Union accepted India's sovereignty in the disputed area. As we have seen, the Soviet Union provided generous economic aid and military supply. However, it made relatively few foreign policy demands on India. Some issues on which it might otherwise have lobbied the Indian government were already on the agenda of the NAM. In a few cases, deference to Moscow's sensitivities clearly influenced India's policy. For example, the official Indian response to the 1979 Soviet invasion of Afghanistan was far more sympathetic to Moscow than the views privately expressed by Indian officials and foreign policy analysts would have suggested. But in the main, as India saw it, the Soviet-Indian model of partnership was beneficial and not too demanding.

The Indo-Soviet relationship has some important contrasts with the ties between India and the United States. The Soviet Union was not a member of the major international economic organizations, so it did not deal with the kinds of issues that India and the United States will face in the future: global macroeconomic management, mobilizing global aid resources, trade negotiations, or dealing with global threats like climate change or epidemics. In addition, the Indo-Soviet relationship was almost entirely government-to-government. Private relationships—trade, investment, education, scientific research, and the larger social ties that go with significant Indian migration to the United States—are a major driver of the Indian-U.S. relationship and will remain so.

Their different historical experience and different expectations from foreign policy also give India and the United States different priorities for their emerging partnership. India's priority is bilateral: removal of trade sanctions, expanded U.S. support for its defense needs, and greater access to U.S. trade and technology. Ideally, India would also like to have U.S. support for an expanded Indian role in global management. For the United States, on the other hand, improving the bilateral relationship is desirable, but it is also an investment in the kind of international cooperation that the United States sees as the strategic benefit from partnership with India.

None of these models for partnership fit the needs of India and the United States. If they wish to take their expanded but still ad hoc relationship further—if they want to make the "strategic partnership" that both governments speak about a reality—they need to develop a new model. The present pattern, with highly developed bilateral relations and close consultations on the immediate region (other than Pakistan) but relatively little reach into the wider world, is a good base to build on but insufficient to sustain a strategic partnership. The standard model for an alliance involves mutual acceptance of certain basic and quite specific commitments and obligations, especially in defense. A model suited to India and the United States would be not an alliance, but a looser arrangement, built on a shared understanding of each other's strategic importance and a core of shared interests, and providing for comprehensive consultations and selective cooperation, hopefully on an expanding agenda.[5] It would operate at each of four levels: bilaterally; regionally, in India's expanded neighborhood; globally; and at the level of values. The intensity, style of interaction, and principal participants would be different at each level. Besides the work of governments and official institutions, the partnership would be energized by the private sector and both countries' legislators. It will be a long-term work in progress, as changing international circumstances, India's expanding international role, and the experience of working together open up new areas for cooperation.

The bilateral foundation, India's priority and an essential starting point for the United States, already exists. Economic linkages will remain primarily private. Economic growth will generate increased opportunities for trade and investment. Both business and academic ties will expand scientific exchanges, especially if restrictions on the presence of foreign universities in India are loosened. The governments' role will be to set the policy environment in which growth can take place and to remove roadblocks to economic and scientific exchanges. In the security area, for three years the Indian government and nuclear establishment saw the civil nuclear agreement as the test of whether the United States was serious about relations with India. Now the agreement is in place, but it needs to be fully implemented, a process that promises a succession of difficult negotiations on such issues as the Indian liability regime and the conditions for the sale of reprocessing and enrichment technology. Beyond the nuclear deal, Americans both in business and in government will be looking on military procurement as an indicator of whether India wants a significant security relationship with the United States. From India's perspective, smooth implementation of liberalized high-tech trade is seen as the key indicator of where the United States wants to take the relationship. In a nutshell, there will be ample challenges in strengthening this bilateral core, but the structure is solidly in place.

The next level to develop is global. This may seem like an odd place to start. At this writing, India and the United States do not share a common vision of how they and the world should address global mega-problems. They approach such discussions as national negotiators, often taking defensive positions, with quite different interests in play, and their dealings in several global organizations have been difficult. However, several of the issues that will preoccupy both countries in the next decade, including climate change, epidemic disease, refugee flows, the global financial meltdown, and the spread of nuclear weapons, cannot be seriously addressed without India's participation. Where India has been included in a small, select forum, as in the G-20, the results have been positive. This argues for a partnership model that focuses on global cooperation despite the challenges it poses.

The heart of the global approach proposed here would be a U.S. initiative to draw India into a leadership role in global institutions, emphasizing the institutions that have a tradition of working discreetly with a small group of countries. The United States should declare its interest in encouraging an Indian role as a "member of the board," including membership in an expanded G-8 (or its replacement by something like the G-20), finding a formula for membership in the IEA, affiliation with the OECD, and membership in the United Nations Security Council. This would create both the appearance and the institutional structure for the genuine relationship between equals that Indians consider their due and believe the United States is unwilling to accept.

Inclusion would not resolve the underlying policy differences between India and the United States on global issues. On climate change, they start from very different positions. In the United Nations, some of India's political equities are problematic for the United States, and vice versa. India's perception of the value of trade negotiations is still dramatically different from that of the United States. Most difficult, as we have seen, is creating a new international consensus on nuclear nonproliferation. But both countries share a commitment to evolutionary change. On financial change, both approach the process with considerable caution. The United States should not extract a direct policy quid pro quo for this inclusion initiative, but should instead engage India in a candid and quiet discussion of the issues that will come up in global leadership councils. The objective would be to find common ground where possible and to create a "no surprises" rule where differences are unavoidable. Starting with inclusion and equality would improve the odds of finding common ground. The same "inclusion plus candid consultations" formula should apply to East Asia-centered forums like APEC.

The United States and India should also start thinking beyond the international institutions they inherited from the post-World War II era. These legacy institutions, valuable as they are, reflected the ideas and vision of the political architects of the 1940s. The political and economic ferment that is shaking the world at the dawn of the twenty-first century calls for a searching reexamination not so much of the institutions as of the ways they galvanize global cooperation. This is a challenge worthy of the talents of Indian and American leaders. An approach that works through institutions, but takes a pragmatic view of which institutions and how they should operate, has the added advantage that it would provide a framework within which a more diverse power structure could evolve without disrupting global systems on which both the United States and India depend.

The regional dimension of a U.S.-India partnership is in its infancy and presents the most complex challenge. India and the United States have to deal with five distinct sets of regional problems: Pakistan and Afghanistan; India's other South Asian neighbors; East Asian regionalism; Persian Gulf and Indian Ocean security; and Iran. The selective character of the U.S.-India partnership will be most strongly felt at the regional level. Once again, running through each of the subregions is a requirement for candid consultations and mutual understanding of the two countries' assessments and their strategic goals.

India and the United States have already held serious discussions about India's immediate neighbors, and Indian Ocean security is one of the established foundations of their security relationship. That leaves two areas, East Asian regionalism and Persian Gulf security, where Indian and U.S. interests are quite similar but where serious consultations are needed to turn this general convergence into parallel or coordinated policies. In principle, this should not be difficult to do. The main obstacle to such a dialogue is India's unwillingness to be associated publicly with U.S. policies in Iraq and toward China. The Obama administration should make another attempt to set up this kind of dialogue once the 2009 Indian elections are over and a new government is in place.

The Obama administration has been quick to include India in its intense consultations on Afghanistan and Pakistan. This is a useful move, but should not be interpreted as a signal that India and the United States will be moving in step in their approach to these problems. India's security interests are too intensely engaged in Pakistan to allow its policy to be constrained by a third party, however friendly toward India, especially one with a historic role in Pakistan that Indians resent. Both Pakistan's deep-seated suspicions about India and the United States' dependence on transit through Pakistan for its operations in Afghanistan will make it impossible for the United States to override Pakistani sensitivities about an Indian role in Afghan security. However, the United States and India can work together on other aspects of Afghan reconstruction. In these areas where parallel policies are out of reach, candid consultations become all the more important. Given India's stake in the viability of the Pakistani state, Indian and U.S. interests are less divergent than one might think, and a clear understanding of one another's policies will benefit both.

Similarly, the U.S.-India partnership is not likely to extend to Iran, which is likely to be the most difficult sticking point, because of its emotional and symbolic significance to both countries. Here, neither side should expect much help or sympathy from the other. The scope of parallel policies is severely limited. Once again, communication is more rather than less important as a result.

The regional and global dimensions of a U.S.-India partnership would be primarily government-oriented. However, the private sector can add value here, as it does in the bilateral relationship. Private discussions by university, think tank, and perhaps business people on the neuralgic issues of Iran and Afghanistan could help create the strategic communication that is hard to establish between the two governments. Private consultations could also lay the foundation for eventual parallel policies on Africa, where India has a substantial commercial presence and has participated in discussions with the United States and others at the G-8 and related forums. Regional trade and investment forums that include both government and private representation would strengthen the private side of the U.S.-India partnership.

The fourth level of partnership is common values, in particular democracy. As we have seen, shared democratic ideals by themselves are not an effective foreign policy bond. The two countries have quite different ideas of how democracy and foreign policy intersect. The United States wants to promote democracy outside its borders, and a vigorous debate has taken place for decades over the most effective way to do this. For India, democracy is not an export product. India has been wary of international associations of democracies. It was one of the conveners of the Community of Democracies founded under the leadership of the Clinton administration in 2000. However, it was an ambivalent participant, and when promoting democracy conflicts with more tangible interests, as in the case of Burma, the latter take priority almost without exception.[6]

The way to make democracy a force multiplier for the U.S.-India partnership is not through international organizations that divide the world into democracies and non-democracies. What is needed instead is to engage the elected politicians of both countries, and especially the legislatures, in the enterprise. Interaction between parliamentarians is relatively modest but almost always revealing for both sides. Parliamentarians speaking to one another in a collegial setting are less likely to adopt the hectoring tone one so often hears in their formal pronouncements to domestic audiences. Both Indian and U.S. parliamentarians are jealous of their prerogatives, and hence in a position to sensitize one another to the different requirements of two different democratic systems.

India and the United States both participate in the International Parliamentary Union. The Confederation of Indian Industry regularly brings groups of U.S. members of Congress to visit India. Another of India's major business organizations, the Federation of Indian Chambers of Commerce and Industry (FICCI), sponsors the India-U.S. Parliamentary Forum, a parliamentary dialogue that takes place once or twice a year, generally in Washington. This forum is the most successful recurring dialogue of this sort. On the Indian side, many of the participants have been opposition parliamentarians, perhaps an inevitable byproduct of a parliamentary system in which senior legislators from the government side become cabinet ministers and are therefore more heavily scheduled and less able to participate in parliamentary activities. To get more mileage out of these channels, it would be useful to regularize participation on the U.S. side, bring in younger Indian parliamentarians from the government side, and supplement these general contacts with committee-to-committee meetings, focusing especially on the U.S. committees with major responsibilities for the most sensitive areas in Indo-U.S. relations—Iran, for example, and nuclear issues.

To sum up, this reinvented partnership would strengthen the existing bilateral base; begin creating global collaboration by bringing India into the small, select leadership groups where global consensus is shaped; enable the two countries to work together on selected regional problems where U.S. and Indian interests coincide while not expecting parallel policies on the difficult issues like Pakistan and Iran; and use private ties and intensified connections between elected politicians to energize the partnership. The whole enterprise would be fueled by a quantum increase in the intensity and candor of consultations about world problems beyond South Asia.

This approach provides a flexible and resilient structure to work with. By working simultaneously on multiple problems, the partners could take advantage of unexpected opportunities and steer around unanticipated roadblocks. Success could be measured in several different ways: by continuing progress toward some of the complex goals that have been on the bilateral agenda for decades, by a gradual expansion of the subjects on which India and the United States are able to formulate policies that parallel one another, and by an intensification of parliamentary contacts to parallel what has already happened between the two countries' executive branch officials. Speed bumps in sensitive areas would represent a setback, but need not doom the partnership, because the structure proposed here relies on working at multiple levels simultaneously.

The strength of this approach is that it builds on durable common interests between India and the United States. It is vulnerable to some of the familiar challenges and irritants that India and the United States have dealt with over the years. Both countries are ambivalent about the value of global cooperation. From the U.S. perspective, the "inclusion first" approach proposed here assumes that if India has a seat at the high table, it will pursue its interests pragmatically, in the manner of its participation in the G-8 and G-20, rather than more confrontationally, as at the WTO. This is a reasonable guess, but still a bit of a gamble. U.S.-India partnership is also vulnerable to the emotional pull of some issues that will gain prominence in the Obama administration. Chief among these is shaping a new nonproliferation system. It is possible to find common ground on this question, as was argued in chapter 5, but that will require restraint and some policy adjustment in both countries. Iran will remain a bone of contention.

Perhaps the most fundamental challenge is the "expectations gap" between India and the United States. Chapter 5 examined the difficulty of living up to expectations in the area of nuclear and high-tech trade. But the same problem runs through most aspects of the U.S.-India relationship, starting with the two countries' different experiences of partnership. India expects to be dealt with in a way that reflects its unique status in history—a giant, diverse country, which has maintained democracy despite daunting problems of poverty, whose ancient civilization and emerging power entitle it to a relationship of equals with the world's most powerful nations. This gives added strength to India's commitment to strategic autonomy. Americans have their own exceptionalism, which has inspired them since the beginning of the republic. Paradoxically, that may make it more difficult to relate to India's. The approach spelled out in these pages deals with issues of both status and policy. It provides a structure for managing the relationship over the long term, but certainly does not eliminate the gaps in perceptions and hopes.

GLOBAL CONTINGENCIES

The dynamics of the U.S.-India partnership will also reflect changes on the world stage during the second decade of the twenty-first century.

Four drivers will be particularly important. The first is U.S. power, both actual and perceived. The benefits to India of working with the world's strongest country outweigh the drive to balance the global center of power. From the U.S. perspective, a global position of strength expands the tools available to cultivate an effective partnership. The second driver is economic "connectivity" between the two economies. In both countries, a dynamic and linked corporate sector will strengthen the political and security ties between the governments. Third comes economic success in both countries. Economic growth will expand trade and investment, creating opportunities in India and the United States and creating a greater Indian stake in an interconnected world. This is especially true if India extends the benefits of growth to the populations and regions that have been left out of the last decade's prosperity.

Finally, India's more general engagement with the world will be a critical driver. India has experienced a long run of democratic government and unprecedented economic success while the country was opening to the world, albeit much more slowly than some of its East Asian neighbors. Its founding political leaders were global personalities. The current generation of leaders includes some people comfortable on the world stage, and others more inwardly oriented. The character of India's leadership will shape how it operates internationally, including in its relations with the United States.

In the coming decade, which contingencies could strengthen the forces that are pushing India and the United States together, and which ones could push the two partners apart? Three are particularly important: the character and stability of future governments; possible international crises involving Pakistan, Iran, and China; and significant changes in the world power structure.

In India and in the United States, both major political parties helped create today's partnership. None of the major Indian parties seems disposed to discard the partnership with the United States, nor is either of the major U.S. parties likely to make sharp changes in policy toward India. Nonetheless, in both countries, there are more subtle differences of substance and style between the major parties that will affect their willingness to take risks on behalf of this emerging partnership.

In the United States, the new relationship with India began under the Clinton administration, and it took off when the Bush administration decided to depart from the previous consensus on how the global nonproliferation regime should operate. As a result, the Bush administration was seen in India as a stronger champion of the bilateral relationship, the aspect to which India is most committed. The more collegial international style the Obama administration is likely to adopt will be welcome, but may be manifested most clearly on two issues that any Indian government will have trouble dealing with: nonproliferation and climate change. A more multilateral Democratic administration may turn out to be more demanding in its expectations of how India will operate in the global dialogue on these issues.

In India, both the strongly nationalist BJP and the Congress Party are committed to building up the bilateral relationship, and support cooperation with the United States throughout the Indian Ocean area. Both share a strong commitment to strategic autonomy, though this has a more militarily assertive flavor for the BJP and a stronger orientation toward India's third-world role for the Congress. The BJP's intemperate objection to the U.S.-India nuclear deal may have represented the classic response of an opposition party, but it appeared in Washington as the rejection of a difficult and complex decision that the U.S. government had made for India's benefit. However, if the BJP returned to head a government, its leadership would probably find it easier than a Congress-led government to make the occasional gestures of public support that are so greatly valued in Washington, like the Indian government's 2001 statement supporting the Bush administration's missile defense initiative.

The bigger problem is the possibility of a fragile and inward-looking government in India. Most observers expect India to have coalition governments for some years into the future, but a coalition does not necessary imply fragility. India has had several governments headed by neither of the major parties in the past two decades. None lasted its full term, and all built their governments around a relatively small core of their own followers. Mayawati, the fiery chief minister of India's largest province, is preparing for a possible run at national office and could emerge as leader or as king-maker. Her interest in politics is resolutely domestic, indeed local. Should she head a future government, the risk to U.S.-India relations is not that she is hostile to the United States—her opposition to the nuclear deal can be explained entirely in terms of tactical politics—but that India's international posture matters less to her than to the Congress and BJP leaders. A successful India-U.S. partnership will require a political investment by both sides. Nothing in Mayawati's previous history suggests that she will be interested in taking risks on behalf of India's relations with the United States.

A second scenario that could challenge the U.S.-India partnership would be a crisis involving one of the hot-button issues in U.S.-India relations. The three most plausible candidates would involve Pakistan, Iran, or China.

The events following the November 2008 terror attacks in Mumbai provide a foretaste of a fresh India-Pakistan crisis. Secretary of State Condoleezza Rice promptly took off for India and Pakistan in a bid to discourage any military confrontation between the two. She also pushed Pakistan to take decisive action against the organization apparently responsible for the attacks, Lashkar-e-Taiba, a group banned but still active in Pakistan and with extensive past ties to Pakistan's army and intelligence service. As in the past, both India and Pakistan were receptive to this crisis management effort. India's reaction was probably colored by the fact that its military options were unattractive. But if Pakistan's actions against Lashkar are ineffective, if it appears that the Pakistani army is once again trying to manage rather than disable the organization, and if more conclusive evidence materializes of the Pakistan government's involvement in the operation, the United States could easily find itself once again caught between two important associates, blamed by both for their worsening security situation, and the object of popular demonstrations in both. The result would be at best a chill in U.S.-India relations. The Pakistan factor has been an inhibition for the U.S.-India partnership from the start, however, so this would not fundamentally change the picture.

A crisis involving Iran, by contrast, could unleash forces that would overwhelm the convergence of interests on which the U.S.-India partnership is based. Iranian nuclear weapons are a nightmare scenario for Washington and a distasteful one for Delhi. India has not wanted to get involved in multilateral efforts to prevent this from happening, based in part on its other equities in Iran and in part on a feeling that India is poorly placed to argue against another country acquiring nuclear weapons. A U.S. military intervention aimed at preempting Iran from going nuclear would spark a violent reaction in the region, among the other major global powers, and possibly in the Indian Muslim community. It could polarize international opinion, with Russia and perhaps China positioning themselves as the benefactors of the Muslim world (and, in China's case, its preferred energy customers). Faced with the prospect of domestic unrest and upheaval in its major energy suppliers, India would probably gravitate to the side of Russia and/or China, keeping the United States at a distance and protecting its other strategic equities in the Persian Gulf.

A crisis involving China, perhaps over Taiwan, would not directly engage India, which has steered clear of the cross-strait issue for years. It would, however, create uncertainty throughout East Asia over the future of the region. As countries throughout the region assessed the shifting regional power structure, India would do the same. An outcome in which China succeeded in changing Taiwan's status by military means would leave China looking like the power best able to shape the East Asian environment and the United States looking ineffective. This would influence India's hedging policy and could reduce the importance it attaches to the United States as a balancing factor in Asia.

The final contingency is the most fundamental potential challenge to the U.S.-India partnership: a major perceived change in the global power structure. A slow decline in the relative power of the United States is almost inevitable, given the vigor of China's economic expansion and the drive toward trade diversification sparked by the opening of global markets. If the U.S. government manages this with skill and sophistication, it will remain both the single most powerful country and an effective force in shaping world events. Its relationships around the world, including those in which the other partner is at least partly attracted to the power of the United States, would continue to flourish. Continued unipolarity is not a prerequisite for a healthy network of U.S. international relationships or for effective exercise of U.S. power.

The challenge for the U.S.-India partnership would come from a decline in relative U.S. power that was steeper or less well managed. The financial crisis that began in mid-2008 in the United States is affecting the whole world. If the U.S. response is slow to restore economic equilibrium to the American market, and especially if other countries are quicker to resume growth; if China navigates the crisis without too much domestic political turbulence, and uses its substantial foreign exchange reserves to position itself as a major financial decisionmaker; if China and India continue their military buildup despite the financial storms; if the U.S. presence in Iraq ends in turmoil, and the deterioration in Afghanistan gets worse; and especially if the United States turns inward under the combined pressure of the economic storms and the bad results of its two military interventions—such a situation could

lead India and others to reassess their ties to Washington. This transformation would not take place all at once, and might well take place
after the ten-year framework this analysis envisages. A country that is
seen as effective and respectful of its partners' sensitivities increases its
magnetic attraction for others. The same logic holds in reverse as well.
Some doubters on the Indian side undoubtedly question the durability
of U.S. power. Theirs is not the dominant policy voice in India today,
but it would become more prominent if the United States appeared to
be slipping more rapidly from its position of global prominence.

To mitigate this danger, the United States needs to give persistent
attention to the large global problems that could undercut its interaction with the world. Restoring a sound financial system, expanding
trade, slowing climate change, dealing with energy, and shaping a new
nonproliferation system top the list. For all of these issues, effective action requires the cooperation of the eight or ten biggest players in the
world. Despite India's relatively small economic heft compared with
the United States or China, it is one of the countries without which
these globe-shaping issues cannot be addressed. The fact that it is a
neighbor to China makes the regional balance in Asia a critical ingredient in the world's future power structure.

The same logic argues for the importance of good old-fashioned
foreign policy management by the United States. Tending the U.S.-In-
dia relationship will involve a lot of work and will require each country
to tread carefully around its partner's many sensitivities. At another
time in world history, audiences in both countries might have asked
if the goal was worth the effort. Success will not bring routine Indian
acquiescence in some of the most important priorities of the United
States, nor will it bring consistent U.S. acceptance of India's drive for
strategic autonomy.

The big reward, however, lies in positioning the United States and
the other global powers to deal with issues that have the potential to
destroy them. The chances of creating a selective but growing agenda
of issues on which the United States and India can cooperate with reasonable comfort are good. With the United States and India working
together and bringing their respective visions of the future closer together, the chances also improve that China's and India's rise will coincide with the creation of a constructive network of Asia's major players.
Common interests will push the United States and India together.
Linkages outside the government—business, science, education, and a

mobile population—and democratic politicians who understand what it means to face a feisty electorate can help this sometimes prickly partnership find its sweet spot.

NOTES

1. Thomas Fingar, "Remarks and Q&A by the Deputy Director of National Intelligence for Analysis & Chairman, National Intelligence Council," 2008 INSA Analytic Transformation Conference, Orlando, Florida, September 4, 2008, http://www.dni.gov/speeches/20080904_speech.pdf. For the full text of the study, see National Intelligence Council, *Global Trends 2025: A Transformed World*, November 2008, www.dni.gov/NIC_2025_project.html.

2. National Intelligence Council, *Global Trends 2025: A Transformed World*, vi.

3. For a good selection of different perspectives on U.S. national security threats and policies, see Melvyn P. Leffler and Jeffrey W. Legro, eds., *To Lead the World: American Strategy after the Bush Doctrine* (New York: Oxford University Press, 2008).

4. National Intelligence Council, *Global Trends 2025: A Transformed World*, vi.

5. Devin Hagerty uses the term *entente*. Devin T. Hagerty, "Are We Present at the Creation? Alliance Theory and the Indo-U.S. Strategic Convergence," in Sumit Ganguly, Brian Shoup, and Andrew Scobell, eds., *U.S.-Indian Strategic Cooperation Into the 21st Century: More than Words* (New York: Routledge, 2006), 11–37.

6. Theodore J. Piccone, *Democracies: In a League of their Own? Lessons Learned from the Community of Democracies*, Policy Paper, Brookings Institution, October, 2008, http://www.brookings.edu/~/media/Files/rc/papers/2008/10_democracy_piccone/10_democracy_piccone.pdf

INDEX

Page numbers followed by the letters f *and* n *refer to figures and notes, respectively.*

Abdullah, King, 160
Abu Dhabi: international energy strategy, 55; Middle East policy, 160
Administered Pricing Mechanism, 49
Admiral Gorshkov aircraft carrier, 174
Afghanistan: global contingencies, 223; international energy strategy, 53, 56; Middle East policy, 155, 163, 165, 167, 169; new kind of partnership, 212, 215–217; regional architecture, 134; security policy of U.S., 71; South and Central Asia policy, 118–121, 126, 127, 129–135; Southeast Asia policy, 148; space program and, 102
Afghanistan conflict: changes in U.S. outlook, 9, 10; global contingencies, 223; new kind of partnership, 216; new security relationship, 75, 78, 84; South and Central Asia policy, 130–131, 133, 135
Africa: global governance issues, 190, 194; global status and bilateral relationships, 172, 180–184; international energy strategy, 50, 54, 57; new kind of partnership, 217. *See also specific entities*
Africa Summit, 183
Agreed Minutes on defense cooperation, 74–75

Agreement on an International Energy Program, 59
agricultural sector: climate change effects, 198–199; energy policy and Indian economy, 47; energy policy background, 45; global status and bilateral relationships, 182, 183; new economy of India, 20–21, 25–26; structure of Indian economy, 21f; U.S.-Indian economic ties, 28–29, 31–33. *See also* food *headings*
Ahluwalia, Montek Singh, 192, 204
air forces. *See headings by specific country, e.g.,* Indian military
Air India bombing, 83
air pollution standards, 199. *See also* greenhouse gas emissions
air transport sector: energy policy and Indian economy, 48; new economy of India, 22, 23; U.S.-Indian economic ties, 35
Airborne Warning and Control System (AWACS), 77
aircraft carriers: global status and bilateral relationships, 174; new security relationship, 76, 80
aircraft sales. *See* defense trade
al-Qaeda, 120
American International Group, 34

American Jewish Committee, 158

Andaman and Nicobar Command, 69

Andhra Pradesh refinery plans, 55

Angola, international energy strategy, 57

Anti-Ballistic Missile treaty, 9

apparel industry. *See* garment industry

Arab countries. *See* Middle East; *specific entities*

Arab-Israeli conflict, 10–11

Arabian Sea: Middle East policy, 159; new security relationship, 78; security policy of India, 70

Argentina, space program and, 100

Ariane rocket launches, 101

armed forces. *See headings by specific country, e.g.,* Indian military

Armitage, Richard, 65, 123

arms control. *See* nuclear cooperation

arms trade. *See* defense trade

ASEAN countries: East Asia policy, 147, 148–150; new kind of partnership, 211. *See also specific entities*

ASEAN Energy Group, 60

ASEAN Plus 3, 60

ASEAN Regional Forum (ARF), 137, 149–150

ASEAN Summits, 138

Asia: changes in U.S. outlook, 11–12; drivers of policy, 16; energy policy and Indian economy, 49; global contingencies, 223–225; global governance issues, 205; Indian-Americans and IT connection, 37; international energy forums, 59–61; international energy strategy, 50; new foreign policy of India, 1, 7; new kind of partnership, 211; policy outlook, 16; public attitudes, 12, 14; security policy of India, 87*n*; security policy of U.S., 71, 73; shifting power patterns, 210. *See also specific entities and regions*

Asia Pacific Economic Cooperation (APEC) forum, 150, 215

Asia Pacific Partnership on Clean Development and Climate, 60, 202

Asian Development Bank, 188, 191–192

Asian tsunami. *See* tsunami, Asian

Association of Southeast Asian Nations (ASEAN), 59–60

Australia, East Asia policy, 146, 150

Australia Group, 91

auto parts industry, U.S.-Indian economic ties, 29, 34

automobile manufacturing: fuel economy standards, 201; new economy of India, 23, 25

Ayni airfield, 132

Azadegan field development, 55

Bab el Mandeb Strait, 159

Babbar Khalsa, 82

Bahrain, Middle East policy, 160

balance of power issues: changes in U.S. outlook, 11; drivers of policy, 16; East Asia policy, 139, 151. *See also* global power structure; multipolar world vision

Bali Conference of Parties, 197, 201

Balochistan, Middle East policy, 163

Bangalore meeting bombing, 125

Bangladesh: climate change issues, 198–199; East Asia policy, 142; global governance issues, 189; global status and bilateral relationships, 181; international energy strategy, 53, 54; new security relationship, 84; public attitudes, 15; regional architecture, 134; security policy of India, 67, 68, 70; South and Central Asia policy, 120, 127, 128–129, 135; U.S.-Indian economic ties, 29

Bangladesh, India, Myanmar, Sri Lanka, Thailand–Economic Cooperation (BIMST-EC), 148

Bangladesh liberation war (1971): security policy of India, 68; South and Central Asia policy, 120; U.S.-Indian economic ties, 29

banking sector: global governance issues, 197; global status and bilateral relationships, 175; Indian-Americans and IT connection, 39;

banking sector *(continued)*
U.S.-Indian economic ties, 33. *See also* financial institutions; *specific entities*
Barak surface-to-air missile, 156
Baru, Sanjaya, 18
Barve, Kumar, 36
Basel Committee on Banking Supervision, 196
best practices: climate change issues, 202; energy relations, 60
Bharat Petroleum Corporation (BPCL), 158
Bharatiya Janata Party (BJP): energy policy and Indian economy, 48; global contingencies, 221; nuclear cooperation, 98
Bharti Airtel, 183
Bhutan: international energy strategy, 56; regional architecture, 134; South and Central Asia policy, 128
big neighbor–small neighbor problem: new foreign policy of India, 6; South and Central Asia policy, 119
Bihar, new economy of India, 26
Bilateral Export Promotion Agreement, 141
bilateral treaties. *See* treaties
Bina refinery, 158
"blue water" fleet aims of China, 142
Borlaug, Norman, 28
Brazil: global governance issues, 190, 194; global status and bilateral relationships, 172, 180–184; U.S.-Indian economic ties, 32
Bretton Woods, 196
Britain. *See* United Kingdom
British Steel/Corus, 178
budget issues, Indian, 47. *See also* economy, Indian; *specific aspects*
Burma: East Asia policy, 142; international energy strategy, 53, 56; new kind of partnership, 217; security policy of India, 70; Southeast Asia policy, 147–148
Burns, Nicholas, 98
bus and taxi fleets, compressed natural gas use, 46, 199

Bush (George H.W.) administration, 9, 123
Bush (George W.) administration: changes in U.S. outlook, 8–12; climate change issues, 201; global contingencies, 220–221; global governance, 195; Middle East policy, 162, 164, 167; new security relationship, 75; nuclear cooperation, 89–90, 94–99, 104–106, 108–111; policy background, 2; public attitudes, 12–14; security policy, 65; security policy of U.S., 71; South and Central Asia policy, 121, 123, 127; U.S.-Indian economic ties, 32
business process outsourcing (BPO), 37–38. *See also* outsourcing

C-130J transport aircraft, 80–81
California: emissions standards, 201; Indian-American population in, 36
Canada: East Asia policy, 150; global governance issues, 189, 195; new security relationship, 83
Cancun ministerial meeting, 32
Cape of Good Hope, international energy strategy, 50. *See also* Indian Ocean sea-lanes
capital formation. *See* investment
carbon emissions. *See* greenhouse gas emissions
CARTOSAT series, 100
Caspian countries, Middle East policy, 163
Central Asia: Central Asia policy, 118–120, 131–133, 136*n*; global status and bilateral relationships, 176–178; international energy strategy, 52, 57; Middle East policy, 155, 161, 163; regional architecture, 134. *See also specific entities*
CEO Forum, 35
Ceyhan pipeline, 132
Chahbahar port, 163
Chandrayaan moon mission, 100, 102
Chechnya, global status and bilateral relationships, 176

Chellaney, Brahma, 151
chemical industry, U.S.-Indian economic ties, 30
Chemical Weapons Convention, 105
Chennai, Middle East policy, 159
Chicago Council on Global Affairs polls, 12–14
Chidambaram, P., 205n
China: changes in U.S. outlook, 8, 9, 10, 11; climate change, 200–201, 207n; East Asia policy, 137–151; economic outlook, 40; global contingencies, 220, 222–224; global governance issues, 190–191, 193–195; global status and bilateral relationships, 174, 176–177, 181, 183, 184n; Goldman-Sachs study, 181; Indian-Americans and IT connection, 39; international energy forums, 59–61; international energy strategy, 50, 53–54, 56–57; joint-venture companies, 56; Middle East policy, 156, 165, 168; new economy of India, 24, 25; new foreign policy of India, 4–6; new kind of partnership, 216; new security relationship, 73; nuclear cooperation and, 92, 109; as nuclear weapons state, 113; policy background, 2, 3; public attitudes, 13, 14; regional architecture, 134, 148–150; security policy background, 65; security policy of India, 66, 69–70, 87n; security policy of U.S., 71, 73; shifting power patterns, 209–210; South and Central Asia policy, 119, 128, 131–135; Southeast Asia policy, 147–148; U.S.-India energy relations, 58; U.S.-Indian economic ties, 29, 35; World Energy Outlook report, 44
Chinese military: East Asia policy, 142–143; global contingencies, 223; policy background, 2
Chinese navy, 142–143
cities. *See* urban areas
Citigroup, 39
civil nuclear cooperation. *See* nuclear cooperation
clean energy: East Asia policy, 146; energy relations, 58, 60; global governance issues, 192
climate change: drivers of policy, 16; energy policy and Indian economy, 48; global contingencies, 221, 224; global governance issues, 187, 192, 195, 197–203, 207n; new kind of partnership, 214, 215; shifting power patterns, 209
Clinton administration: global contingencies, 220; new kind of partnership, 217; nuclear cooperation, 90, 106; policy background, 2; public attitudes, 14; security policy of U.S., 71; South and Central Asia policy, 123, 127
coal power: energy policy and Indian economy, 46, 48; U.S.-India energy relations, 58. *See also* energy *headings*
Cold Start approach, 68
Cold War: changes in U.S. outlook, 8, 9, 11; East Asia policy, 145; economic transformation of India, 19; global governance issues, 186; global status and bilateral relationships, 172, 177; Middle East policy, 166; new foreign policy of India, 7; new kind of partnership, 212; new security relationship, 73–74, 79; nuclear cooperation, 89; policy background, 1, 3; security policy background, 65–66; South and Central Asia policy, 118, 130
Collective Security Treaty (CST), 131
Colombia, international energy strategy, 56
Combined Task Force 150, 78
Commercial Space Launch Agreement, 103
commercial space program, 100–101. *See also* space cooperation
Commonwealth of Independent States, security treaty, 131
Communists: new security relationship, 73; nuclear cooperation, 98;

Communists *(continued)*
   South and Central Asia policy, 120,
   122
Community of Democracies, 217
Comprehensive Economic Partnership
   Agreement, 145
Comprehensive Test Ban Treaty
   (CTBT): nuclear agreement and
   high-tech trade, 93, 114*n*; nuclear
   cooperation future, 106–107
compressed natural gas (CNG), 46. *See
   also* petroleum and natural gas
"concert" of great powers or democracies, 210
Confederation of Indian Industry,
   217–218
Congress Party, 221
constitutional amendment process in
   Nepal, 129
contracting: nuclear business, 110;
   outsourcing legislation, 38–39. *See
   also* defense trade
Cope 26 exercise, 77
cotton, U.S.-Indian economic ties, 32
counterproliferation efforts. *See* nuclear cooperation
counterterrorism efforts. *See* terrorism
crop production. *See* agricultural
   sector
cryogenic engines, space program and,
   102, 103
Cuba: global governance issues, 189;
   international energy strategy, 54
cyber security, 81

da Silva, Inacio Lula, 181
Dalai Lama, 140
dams. *See* hydropower
"de-hyphenation" efforts: new foreign
   policy of India, 6; South and Central Asia policy, 121
Declaration of Cooperation, 59
defense agreements: East Asia policy,
   146; new foreign policy of India, 4;
   new security relationship, 74–76,
   80. *See also* nuclear cooperation;
   treaties; *specific agreements*
defense budget, U.S., changes in U.S.

   outlook, 9
defense policy. *See* security policy,
   Indian; security policy, U.S.
Defense Policy Group, 76
Defense Policy Guidance draft, 9
Defense Research and Development
   Organization (DRDO), 102, 174
defense trade: East Asia policy, 142;
   global status and bilateral relationships, 172–176, 178–180; Middle
   East policy, 155–157, 164; new
   kind of partnership, 212, 214; new
   security relationship, 73–74, 76,
   79–82, 87*n*; nuclear agreement
   and, 91–99, 113–114*n*; nuclear
   cooperation background, 89–90;
   nuclear cooperation future, 106–
   108; security policy of India, 70;
   security policy outlook, 85; South
   and Central Asia policy, 121–122,
   127, 135; Southeast Asia policy,
   147. *See also specific aspects*
Deloitte and Touche survey, 39
democracies, international associations of, 217
democratic link: changes in U.S. outlook, 11–12; global contingencies,
   220, 225; new kind of partnership,
   211, 217–219; nuclear cooperation,
   96; policy background, 1, 3; public
   attitudes and, 15
Democrats: global contingencies, 221;
   public attitudes, 13
demographics: Indian-American community statistics, 36; new economy
   of India, 21, 25; public attitudes
   and, 14, 15
dependency ratio, new economy of
   India, 21
developing countries: climate change
   issues, 198, 200–202; global governance issues, 188, 192–196; global
   status and bilateral relationships,
   172, 180–184; new foreign policy
   of India, 6; new kind of partnership, 211–212; U.S.-Indian economic ties, 31–32. *See also specific
   countries*

development assistance: East Asia policy, 144; global governance issues, 187, 191–197, 205*n*; global status and bilateral relationships, 179, 183; U.S.-Indian economic ties, 28–29. *See also* economic aid; *specific entities*

diaspora, Indian: new kind of partnership, 212; nongovernment science cooperation, 112; policy background, 3–4; security policy of India, 70. *See also* expatriates, Indian; Indian-American community

diplomacy, Indian: East Asia policy, 137, 139, 143; global governance issues, 186, 188–190; global status and bilateral relationships, 180; Middle East policy, 154–157, 168; new foreign policy of India, 5; South and Central Asia policy, 131. *See also* foreign policy, Indian

diplomacy, U.S.: East Asia policy, 139, 143, 151; South and Central Asia policy, 121–124, 127, 136. *See also* foreign policy, U.S.

Doha Round: East Asia policy, 150; global status and bilateral relationships, 182; U.S.-Indian economic ties, 30–33

doing business abroad survey, 24

dot-com boom and bust, 36, 38

"downstream" investments: international energy forums, 60; international energy strategy, 54–55; Middle East policy, 158. *See also* oil trade; refineries; *specific entities*

drug control, Southeast Asia policy, 148, 149

"dual use" items: nuclear agreement and high-tech trade, 91, 94–95; nuclear cooperation and, 90, 104–105. *See also* high-tech trade

Dubai, 160

earth observation, 100. *See also* space cooperation

East Asia: changes in U.S. outlook, 11; East Asia policy, 137–151; global contingencies, 220, 223; global governance issues, 205; global status and bilateral relationships, 178; Middle East policy, 169; new foreign policy of India, 5; new kind of partnership, 215–216; policy background, 1; regional architecture, 148–150. *See also* Southeast Asia; *specific entities*

East Asian Summit (EAS), 149–150, 200

Eastern Europe, global status and bilateral relationships, 177. *See also specific entities*

economic aid: East Asia policy, 144; global status and bilateral relationships, 183; international energy strategy, 57; Middle East policy, 161; new foreign policy of India, 6; new kind of partnership, 212; nongovernment science cooperation, 112; policy background, 3; South and Central Asia policy, 121–122; U.S.-Indian economic ties, 28–29

economic growth, Indian: background, 18–19; changes in U.S. outlook, 12; climate change issues, 199; drivers of policy, 16; East Asia policy, 151; energy policy and, 44, 46–49; global contingencies, 220; global governance issues, 188, 190; growth record, 20*f*; new economy, 20–21, 26–27; new foreign policy, 7; new kind of partnership, 213; outlook, 40; policy background, 2–4

economic growth, U.S., 45

economic institutions. *See* banking sector; financial institutions

economic policy, Indian: background, 1–2; East Asia policy, 137–138, 140–146, 149–150; energy policy background, 44; global contingencies, 220; global governance issues, 191–197, 205*n*; global status and bilateral relationships, 176, 178–183; Indian-Americans and IT connection, 39; international

economic policy, Indian *(continued)*
energy strategy, 57; Middle East
policy, 155, 158–161, 166–168;
new economy of India, 19, 22; new
foreign policy, 4–5, 7; new kind of
partnership, 213–214; outlook, 16;
regional architecture, 148; security policy background, 66; South
and Central Asia policy, 133–134;
Southeast Asia policy, 147; U.S.-In-
dian economic ties, 29–30, 34–35.
See also specific aspects
economic policy, U.S.: background,
2, 8–12; changes in U.S. outlook,
8, 11; East Asia policy, 150; global
contingencies, 220, 223–224;
global status and bilateral relationships, 178; Indian-Americans and
IT connection, 39; new kind of
partnership, 211, 213–214; outlook, 16; public attitudes, 13–14;
security policy background, 66;
shifting power patterns, 209–210;
South and Central Asia policy, 127;
Southeast Asia policy, 148; U.S.-
Indian economic ties, 29. *See also
specific aspects*
economic slowdown of 2000-2001, 36
economy, Indian: background, 1,
18–19; climate change issues, 199;
energy policy and, 46–50, 61; global contingencies, 220; global governance issues, 192, 194, 204–205;
global status and bilateral relationships, 173, 175; Indian-Americans
and IT connection, 35–40; new
economy, 19–27, 42*n*; new foreign
policy, 4–5; outlook, 40; structure
of, 21*f*; U.S.-Indian economic ties,
27–35. *See also* economic growth,
Indian; *specific aspects*
Ecuador, international energy strategy,
57
education: global status and bilateral
relationships, 179; Indian-American community statistics, 36; new
economy of India, 25; new foreign
policy of India, 4; new kind of

partnership, 213, 217; nongovernment science cooperation, 112;
public attitudes and, 14; Southeast
Asia policy, 147; space program
history, 100, 102; U.S.-Indian economic ties, 28
eFunds, 39
Egypt: global governance issues, 188;
new kind of partnership, 211–212
elections, Bangladeshi, 129
elections, Indian, 47, 216
elections, Pakistani, 126
electric power: energy policy and Indian economy, 46–48; international
energy strategy, 56; new economy
of India, 25–26; nuclear cooperation, 96, 110; South and Central
Asia policy, 133. *See also* energy
headings
elites, Indian: new foreign policy and,
4; nuclear cooperation and, 98;
public attitudes and, 14–15
emerging countries, shifting power
patterns, 210. *See also* developing
countries; *specific countries*
eminent domain, new economy of
India, 25
emissions control. *See* greenhouse gas
emissions
employment issues: Indian-Americans
and IT connection, 36–39; Middle
East policy, 155, 159–161, 167; new
economy of India, 25–26; public
attitudes, 12; security policy of India, 70; U.S.-Indian economic ties,
34, 40. *See also* labor force
"encirclement" as concern: East Asia
policy, 139; security policy of U.S.,
71; South and Central Asia policy,
133
The Energy and Resources Institute
(TERI), 47–48
Energy Dialogue, 57–59
energy efficiency policy: East Asia
policy, 146; Indian economy and,
47–48; U.S.-India energy relations,
57
energy forums, international, 59–61.

See also specific entities

Energy Information Agency. *See* U.S. Energy Information Agency

energy policy, Indian: background, 44–46; climate change issues, 199–201; economy and, 46–50; international forum participation, 59–61; international strategy, 50–57; new foreign policy, 5; outlook, 16, 61; South and Central Asia policy, 132–133; U.S.-India energy relations, 57–59, 61. *See also specific aspects*

energy policy, U.S.: public attitudes, 12; U.S.-India energy relations, 57–59, 61. *See also specific aspects*

energy prices: energy policy and Indian economy, 46–47, 49–50; energy prospects analysis, 44–45; energy relations and, 57–60; global governance and, 193; international energy strategy, 52–53, 55; new economy of India, 23

energy sector: East Asia policy, 142–143, 145–146; energy policy and Indian economy, 48; global contingencies, 223, 224; global governance issues, 187, 193–194; global status and bilateral relationships, 173–177, 181, 183; Middle East policy, 154–155, 160–168, 170*n*; new economy of India, 23, 25–26; security policy of India, 68; shifting power patterns, 209; South and Central Asia policy, 132–133; Southeast Asia policy, 148. *See also* oil trade; *specific aspects*

energy security: drivers of policy, 16; energy policy background, 44–45; global status and bilateral relationships, 174, 181, 183; international energy forums, 59–61; international energy strategy, 50–57; new foreign policy of India, 5, 7; public attitudes, 12; security policy of India, 70; U.S.-India energy relations, 57–58. *See also* Indian Ocean sea-lanes; *specific aspects*

Energy Working Group of Asia Pacific Economic Cooperation (APEC), 60

"enhanced engagement" process of OECD, 193

entente model, 225*n*

entities list: nuclear agreement and high-tech trade, 93–94; space program and, 102

environmental issues: pollution standards, 199; public attitudes, 13; space program and, 103. *See also* climate change

Essar: energy policy and Indian economy, 49; international energy strategy, 55; Middle East policy, 162

ethnic troubles: new security relationship, 82; security policy of India, 67; South and Central Asia policy, 128–129. *See also specific groups and locations*

Europe: changes in U.S. outlook, 10, 11; global governance issues, 189, 193, 204; global status and bilateral relationships, 172–174, 178–180, 183; Indian-Americans and IT connection, 37; public attitudes, 12; space program and, 101–103. *See also specific entities*

European Space Agency, 102

European Union (EU): global status and bilateral relationships, 178–180; new kind of partnership, 211; space program and, 101, 103; U.S.-Indian economic ties, 31–32. *See also specific entities*

exceptionalism, concept of: new foreign policy of India, 7; new kind of partnership, 219

Exclusive Economic Zone, 69

expatriates, Indian, 155, 159–161, 167. *See also* diaspora, Indian; Indian-American community

Expert Committee on Integrated Energy Policy, 44–45

exports. *See* trade

F-16 fighter aircraft, 122, 135

famine. *See* food aid; food shortages

farming. *See* agricultural sector

Federation of Indian Chambers of Commerce and Industry (FICCI), 218

Feith, Douglas, 76

fiftieth anniversary of independence, media coverage of, 1

financial crisis, global. *See* global financial crisis

financial crisis of 1991, 19

financial institutions: global governance issues, 187, 191–197, 203–205, 205*n*; new kind of partnership, 212; shifting power patterns, 209. *See also* banking sector; *specific entities*

financial markets: new economy of India, 19; U.S.-Indian economic ties, 33. *See also* investment

Financial Stability Forum (FSF), 196

Fissile Material Cutoff Treaty (FMCT), 93, 96, 106–107

"flags of convenience," 108

Fogarty International Center, 112

food aid: Food for Peace Program, 28; nongovernment science cooperation, 112; oil-for-food program, 56, 166; U.S.-Indian economic ties, 28, 31

food prices: energy policy and Indian economy, 47; global governance and, 193; new economy of India, 26

food production. *See* agricultural sector

food security: global status and bilateral relationships, 181; U.S.-Indian economic ties, 32

food shortages: shifting power patterns, 209; U.S.-Indian economic ties, 28. *See also* food aid

foreign aid. *See* economic aid

foreign direct investment (FDI): new economy of India, 24; U.S.-Indian economic ties, 33–34. *See also* investment

foreign exchange earnings, Indian: Indian-Americans and IT connection, 37–38; U.S.-Indian economic ties, 29–30. *See also specific aspects*

foreign exchange rate surveillance, 192

foreign exchange regulations, Indian, 23

foreign exchange reserves, Chinese, 223

foreign investment. *See* investment

foreign policy, Indian: background, 1–8; East Asia overview, 137–151; economic transformation and, 18–19; energy policy background, 44–45; global contingencies, 219–225; global status and bilateral relationships, 172–184, 184*n*; Middle East overview, 154–169, 170*n*; new kind of partnership, 208, 211–219, 225*n*; outlook, 15–16; shifting power patterns, 208–211; South and Central Asia overview, 118–136, 136*n*; U.S.-Indian economic ties, 29. *See also specific aspects and entities*

foreign policy, U.S.: allies and alliances as emphasis, 9; background, 1–3; changes in U.S. outlook, 8–12; East Asia overview, 137–151; global contingencies, 219–225; global governance issues, 205; global status and bilateral relationships, 172–184, 184*n*; Middle East overview, 154–169, 170*n*; new kind of partnership, 208, 211–219, 225*n*; outlook, 16; public attitudes, 12–15; shifting power patterns, 208–211; South and Central Asia overview, 118–136, 136*n*. *See also specific aspects and entities*

foreign trade. *See* trade

forest cover increase, 200

Framework Agreement on Comprehensive Economic Cooperation, 149

Framework Agreement on Economic Cooperation, 159

France: East Asia policy, 150; export license processing, 95; global governance issues, 190, 195; global status and bilateral relationships, 179–180; new kind of partnership, 211; nuclear agreement and, 99, 113–114*n*; as nuclear weapons state, 113; public attitudes, 14; space program and, 101, 103; U.S. and Indian expectations for trade, 110

free trade. *See* trade

French Guyana, space program and, 101

fuel banks, nuclear, 108

fuel economy standards, 201

fuel prices. *See* energy prices

fusion energy, U.S.-India energy relations, 58. *See also* nuclear power

FutureGen project, 58

G-4, global governance issues, 190

Galileo global navigation system, 103

Gandhi, Indira, 3

Gandhi, Mahatma, 182

Gandhi, Rajiv: global governance issues, 187; new security relationship, 82; security policy of India, 67; South and Central Asia policy, 128

garment industry: new economy of India, 22; U.S.-Indian economic ties, 29

Gas Authority of India Ltd. (GAIL): energy policy and Indian economy, 48; international energy strategy, 54; Middle East policy, 162

Gates, Robert, 123

GCC–India Industrial Conference, 159

GDP, Indian: climate change issues, 199; defense budget as percent of, 66; East Asia policy, 151; energy policy and economy, 47–48; global governance issues, 192; growth rates by state, 27*f*; growth record, 20*f*; Indian-Americans and IT connection, 37; new economy, 20–27; U.S.-Indian economic ties, 29. *See also* economic growth, Indian

gems, market for, 145

General Electric engines, 81

General Security of Military Information Agreement (GSOMIA), 80

Georgia, global status and bilateral relationships, 176

Geosynchronous Satellite Launch Vehicle (GSLV), 100

Germany: global governance issues, 190; global status and bilateral relationships, 179; public attitudes, 13, 14

Glavkosmos, space program and, 102

global cooperation issues: background, 2–3, 16; global contingencies, 224; international energy forums, 59–61; new foreign policy of India, 7; new kind of partnership, 208, 211, 213–215, 217–219; nonproliferation policy of India, 105; nuclear cooperation, 98, 109; shifting power patterns, 208–211. *See also* global governance; global institutions; *specific entities and issues*

global economy: drivers of policy, 16; East Asia policy, 151; global governance issues, 194–197; new economy of India, 27; new kind of partnership, 215; shifting power patterns, 210. *See also specific aspects*

global financial crisis: East Asia policy, 151; global contingencies, 223; global governance issues, 187, 193, 195–197, 204, 205*n*; Indian-Americans and IT connection, 37; new economy of India, 19–21, 26; new kind of partnership, 214; outlook, 40

Global Fund for AIDS, Tuberculosis and Malaria, 203

global governance: background, 186–187; climate change and, 187, 192, 195, 197–203, 207*n*; global institutions overview, 187–197, 205*n*; global south relationships and, 181–184; new foreign policy of India, 6–7; outlook, 203–205.

global governance *(continued)*
See also global cooperation issues; *specific entities and issues*
global institutions: changes in U.S. outlook, 9, 10; climate change issues, 201–202; East Asia policy, 144, 150; global governance issues, 187–197, 205n; new kind of partnership, 212, 214–215, 217; policy background, 3; public attitudes and, 12, 15; shifting power patterns, 209–210. *See also specific entities*
Global Maritime Partnership, 72
Global Navigational Satellite System, 103
global power structure: bilateral relationships and, 172–184, 184n; global contingencies, 219–225; shifting power patterns, 208–211. *See also* balance of power issues; multipolar world vision; *specific entities*
"global sourcing" market, 37. *See also* outsourcing
global south, bilateral relationships with, 180–184. *See also specific entities*
global warming. *See* climate change
Goldman-Sachs research, 25, 181
Gore, Al, 202
grains: high-yielding varieties, 28; production and climate change, 198; rice exports, 26
"Great Game, new," 133
Greece, new kind of partnership, 211
green policies, 199, 202. *See also* environmental issues
green revolutions, high-yielding grain varieties, 28
greenhouse gas emissions: global governance issues, 199–203, 207n; monitoring of, 103. *See also* climate change
Group of Four (G-4), U.S.-Indian economic ties, 32
Group of Eight (G-8): climate change issues, 200, 219; global governance issues, 193, 194–195; global status

and bilateral relationships, 181; international energy forums, 60; new foreign policy of India, 6; new kind of partnership, 214, 217
Group of 20 (G-20): global governance issues, 186, 195–196; new kind of partnership, 214, 219
Group of 77, 211
Gujarat: energy policy and Indian economy, 49; new economy of India, 25, 26
Gulf, Persian. *See* Persian Gulf region
Gulf Cooperation Council (GCC), 158–159, 170n
Gulf of Aden, new security relationship, 78
Gulf wars, 166–167. *See also* Iraq war
Gwadar port, 70, 142

H-3 Sea King helicopters, 80
Hamas, Middle East policy, 157
Hambantota port, 142
Hawaii, Yudh Abhyas exercise, 77
health issues: global governance and, 188, 198–199, 203; HIV/AIDS, 182–184, 203; new kind of partnership, 214; telemedicine, 100, 102. *See also* pharmaceutical industry
heroin production, 148
high-tech trade: background, 89–90; global status and bilateral relationships, 175; Middle East policy, 156; new kind of partnership, 213, 214, 219; nuclear cooperation and, 91–99, 107–108, 113–114n; space program and, 103–104; U.S. and Indian expectations, 109–111, 113. *See also* defense trade; *specific aspects*
High Technology Cooperation Group, 94
hijackings: new security relationship, 78, 82–83. *See also* piracy
Himalayas: climate change effects, 198; East Asia policy, 140; new foreign policy of India, 6; security policy of India, 69–70
Hindi language: "Hindi-Chini bhai-

bhai" slogan, 139; Iraq war resolution wording, 167; prevalence in Dubai, 160
Hindu Kush, 6
"Hindu rate of growth," 18
Hinduja Group, 55
HIV/AIDS: global governance issues, 203; global status and bilateral relationships, 182–184
howitzer sales, 74
Hu Jintao, 141
"hub and spokes" relationships pattern, 131, 176
human rights issues, global status and bilateral relationships, 176, 179
humanitarian crises: East Asia policy, 146; global governance issues, 189; new security relationship, 77; public attitudes, 13; security policy of India, 69, 71
Hussein, Abid, 186
Hussein, Saddam, 56, 84
Hyde Act, 97, 99
hydropower, 56, 133
"hyphenation" approach, 121–122. *See also* "de-hyphenation" efforts

IBSA Dialogue Forum, 182
immigration, illegal, 67. *See also* border issues; population movements
"inclusion first" approach, 219
"inclusion plus candid consultations" formula, 215
Independent Evaluation Office, IMF, 192
India-China war, 3, 73, 88*n*
India-Pakistan war (1965), 73–74
India-U.S. Parliamentary Forum, 218
Indian air force: new security relationship, 77; security policy of India, 68–69, 86*n*; Southeast Asia policy, 147
Indian-American community: IT connection and, 35–40, 43*n*; Middle East policy, 157; nongovernment science cooperation, 112; policy background, 3–4
Indian army: new security relation-

ship, 74; security policy of India, 66–68, 86*n*
Indian central government, energy policy and economy, 47–50. *See also specific entities and individuals*
Indian Coast Guard, 160
Indian consulates, 131
Indian Council of Agricultural Research, 28
Indian courts, climate change rulings, 199
Indian Department of Science and Technology, 112
Indian economy. *See* economy, Indian
Indian embassies, Middle East policy, 157. *See also* diplomacy, Indian
Indian GDP. *See* GDP, Indian
Indian Institutes of Technology (IIT), 28
Indian military: East Asia policy, 142–144; energy security issues, 50; global contingencies, 221, 222–223; global governance issues, 189–190; global status and bilateral relationships, 173–174; Middle East policy, 160, 164, 166–168; new foreign policy, 7; new security relationship, 74–82, 84; nuclear cooperation, 92, 95–96, 108; outlook, 85–86; policy background, 4; security policy of India, 86*n*; security policy of U.S., 72–73; security policy outlook, 85–86; South and Central Asia policy, 123–124, 132; Southeast Asia policy, 147; strategic goals of India, 66–71. *See also* security policy, Indian; *specific entities*
Indian National Committee for Space Research (INCOSPAR), 99
Indian navy: East Asia policy, 142–143, 146; energy security issues, 50; Middle East policy, 160, 164; new foreign policy, 5; new security relationship, 76–79; security policy of India, 68–69, 86*n*; security policy of U.S., 72–73
Indian Ocean sea-lanes: East Asia

Indian Ocean sea-lanes *(continued)*
policy, 141, 142–143, 145, 149;
global contingencies, 221; global
status and bilateral relationships,
182; international energy strategy,
50; new foreign policy of India,
1, 5, 6; new kind of partnership,
215–216; new security relationship, 76–78; policy background,
45; security policy of India, 69–70;
security policy of U.S., 72–73;
shifting power patterns, 210;
Southeast Asia policy, 147
Indian Oil Corporation (IOC): energy
policy and Indian economy, 48;
international energy strategy, 54,
55; Middle East policy, 162
Indian parliament: Middle East policy,
164, 167; new economy of In-
dia, 26; new kind of partnership,
217–219; nuclear agreement and
high-tech trade, 97; security policy
of India, 68; South and Central
Asia policy, 123, 125; U.S.-Indian
economic ties, 34
Indian Peace Keeping Force, 128. *See
also* peacekeeping forces
Indian policy. *See specific policy areas*
Indian Remote Sensing (IRS) satellite
series, 100, 101
Indian Space Research Organization
(ISRO), 94, 99–100, 102–103
Indian Special Forces, 74, 156
Indian Zone of Peace, 69
Indonesia: changes in U.S. outlook, 11;
new kind of partnership, 212; security policy of U.S., 72; Southeast
Asia policy, 147; space program
and, 100
The Indus Entrepreneurs, 36
industrial development, new economy
of India, 24–25. *See also specific
sectors*
information technology industry:
changes in, 37*f*; Indian-Americans
and IT connection, 35–40, 43*n*;
Middle East policy, 157; new economy of India, 21, 23; policy background, 3–4; U.S.-Indian economic
ties, 29–30, 33–34. *See also specific
entities*
Infosys: new economy of India, 23;
U.S.-Indian economic ties, 33
infrastructure development: East Asia
policy, 145; energy relations, 60;
global status and bilateral relationships, 174; international energy
strategy, 52–54, 56–57; Middle
East policy, 165; new economy of
India, 25–26, 42*n*; regional architecture, 148; South and Central
Asia policy, 128, 133. *See also*
pipelines; transportation sector
INS *Tabar,* 78
INSAT satellites, 101
insurance sector, 33, 34
insurgents: changes in U.S. outlook,
10; Middle East policy, 156, 163;
new security relationship, 77,
82–83; security policy of India, 67;
South and Central Asia policy, 126,
128, 130. *See also* terrorism; *specific
groups and locations*
intellectual elites, Indian. *See* elites,
Indian
intellectual property issues: new foreign policy of India, 4; U.S.-Indian
economic ties, 30–31, 34
intelligence concerns: Middle East
policy, 155–156; new security
relationship, 83, 88*n*; nuclear cooperation and, 107; security policy
of India, 67; South and Central
Asia policy, 125, 126, 128. *See also*
security policy, Indian; security
policy, U.S.
Inter-Services Intelligence (ISI), 125
Intergovernmental Panel on Climate
Change (IPCC), 198, 202
international aid. *See* economic aid
International Atomic Energy Agency
(IAEA): Middle East policy, 164–
165; nuclear cooperation, 96, 97,
99, 104, 108
International Charter for Space and
Major Disasters, 103

international economy. *See* global economy
International Energy Agency (IEA): energy projections, 44, 46–48, 168; energy relations, 59–61; global governance issues, 187, 193–194; new kind of partnership, 214
International Energy Forum (IEF), 60
international energy forums, 59–61. *See also specific entities*
international fuel banks, 108
international institutions. *See* global institutions
International Maritime Bureau, 78
International Monetary Fund (IMF), 188, 191–193, 195–196, 204
International Parliamentary Union, 217
International Telecommunications Union, 203
International Thermonuclear Experimental Reactor (ITER), 58, 112
investment: drivers of policy, 16; East Asia policy, 141, 144–145, 151; global contingencies, 220; global status and bilateral relationships, 178–179, 181–182; Middle East policy, 158–161; new economy of India, 19, 22–24, 27; new foreign policy of India, 4–5; new kind of partnership, 213, 217; policy outlook, 16; security policy of India, 68; South and Central Asia policy, 133; Southeast Asia policy, 147; U.S.-Indian economic ties, 29, 33–35, 39. *See also* "downstream" investments; "upstream" investments; *specific sectors*
Iran: changes in U.S. outlook, 11; East Asia policy, 142; global contingencies, 220, 222; global status and bilateral relationships, 177–178; hostage crisis, 162; international energy strategy, 51–56; Middle East policy, 155, 157, 161–165, 168–169; new kind of partnership, 211, 215–216, 218; new security relationship, 84; nuclear coop-

eration and, 98–99, 104–105, 107, 113; public attitudes, 13; regional architecture, 134; security policy of India, 70; security policy of U.S., 71–72; South and Central Asia policy, 131–133
Iran, Shah of, 165, 211
Iran-Pakistan-India pipeline proposal: global status and bilateral relationships, 175; international energy strategy, 52–53; Middle East policy, 154, 162–163
Iranian military, 164
Iraq: changes in U.S. outlook, 11; global contingencies, 223; international energy strategy, 54, 56; Middle East policy, 155, 165–169; new kind of partnership, 216; new security relationship, 84; security policy of U.S., 71
Iraq war: changes in U.S. outlook, 9, 10; global contingencies, 223; Middle East policy, 166–167; public attitudes, 12, 13
iron ore, 29, 141, 145
Islamic bonds, Middle East policy, 160–161. *See also* Muslim populations
Islamic extremism: global status and bilateral relationships, 176–177; Middle East policy, 156, 163, 167; shifting power patterns, 209–210; South and Central Asia policy, 123, 126, 128, 130, 132. *See also* terrorism
Israel: changes in U.S. outlook, 11; export license processing, 95; global status and bilateral relationships, 173–174; Middle East policy, 154–158, 162, 168; new kind of partnership, 211; new security relationship, 79, 82–83; nuclear cooperation and, 92, 104; space program and, 100
Israel-Lebanon war, 157
Italy, space program and, 100

Japan: changes in U.S. outlook, 11;

Japan *(continued)*
climate change issues, 202;
East Asia policy, 137–139, 143,
144–146, 151; energy relations, 58,
60; global governance issues, 190;
global status and bilateral relationships, 176; new foreign policy of
India, 5; new kind of partnership,
211; new security relationship, 77;
policy background, 1; public attitudes, 13, 14; security policy of
India, 69; Southeast Asia policy,
147; U.S.-Indian economic ties, 35
Japanese Diet, 145
jewelry, market for, 145
Jewish-American community, 157–158
Jindal, Bobby, 36
jobs as issue. *See* employment issues
Jobs for America Act, 38
Johnson, Lyndon, 28
joint military exercises: Middle East
policy, 160, 164; new security
relationship, 76–78, 81–82; nuclear
cooperation and, 108; security
policy outlook, 85. *See also specific
entities*
Joint Oil Data Initiative, 60
"Joint Statement towards India-Japan
Strategic and Global Partnership,"
145
Joint Working Group on Counterterrorism, 83–84
jungle warfare schools, 77

Kabul embassy bombing, 125
Kanpur, U.S.-Indian economic ties, 28
Kargil campaign, 68, 71, 123
Karnataka LNG terminal plans, 55
Kashmir: East Asia policy, 142; global
governance issues, 191; global
status and bilateral relationships,
173, 176; Middle East policy, 157,
162–163; new kind of partnership,
212; new security relationship,
81–84; security policy of India,
66–67; South and Central Asia
policy, 120, 123–125, 136*n*

Kazakhstan: international energy
strategy, 57; regional architecture,
134; South and Central Asia policy,
131–132
Kerala, Middle East policy, 159
Khatemi, Mohammad, 163–164
Kicklighter, Claude, 74
kidnappings: Middle East policy, 157;
new security relationship, 83
Korean peninsula, changes in U.S.
outlook, 11. *See also* North Korea;
South Korea
Korean War, 138
Kudankulum reactors, 175
Kunming initiative, 148
Kuwait, Middle East policy, 161, 166
Kyoto Protocol: climate change issues,
200–201; public attitudes, 13
Kyrgyzstan: international energy
strategy, 56; regional architecture,
134; South and Central Asia policy,
132–133

labor force: Indian-American community statistics, 36; new economy of
India, 21, 25. *See also* employment
issues
land acquisition, new economy of
India, 24–25. *See also* agricultural
sector
Landsat remote sensing program, 102
Lashkar-e-Taiba, 222
Latin America: East Asia policy, 150;
global status and bilateral relationships, 183; international energy
strategy, 50. *See also specific entities*
law and legal issues: climate change
rulings, 199; food aid, 28; Indian-
Americans and IT connection,
38–39; land transactions, 24–25;
Middle East policy, 164; new kind
of partnership, 213, 217–219; nongovernment science cooperation,
112; nuclear cooperation future,
108; shifting power patterns, 209–
210; South and Central Asia policy,
123; U.S. and Indian expectations

for trade, 110. *See also* intellectual property issues; *specific policy areas*

Lebanon, Middle East policy, 157

leftist coalition partners, 97–98. *See also specific entities*

legal issues. *See* law and legal issues

letter of intent regarding nuclear power, 110

liberalization of trade. *See* trade

Liberation Tigers of Tamil Eelam, 67, 82, 128

licensing and process requirements: energy policy and Indian economy, 49; "license-permit raj," 22; Middle East policy, 156; new security relationship, 74, 79–81; nuclear agreement and high-tech trade, 94–95; U.S.-Indian economic ties, 30

life insurance sector, 34

Light Combat Aircraft (LCA), 74, 81, 87*n*

Line of Actual Control, 140

Line of Control, 80

liquid natural gas (LNG): international energy strategy, 50–53, 55; Middle East policy, 158, 162. *See also* petroleum and natural gas

"Look East" policy, 5, 138

Louisiana, first Indian-American governor in, 36

lunar mission, 100, 102

machinery industry, 29

Madhya Pradesh, 158

"Malabar" series of exercises, 76

malaria and global governance, 198, 203

Malaysia: global status and bilateral relationships, 181; international energy strategy, 50, 54; security policy of U.S., 72; Southeast Asia policy, 147

Maldives, regional architecture, 134

Manas air base closure, 132

manufacturing sector: East Asia policy, 141, 145; fuel economy standards, 201; new economy

of India, 21, 23, 25; structure of Indian economy, 21*f*; U.S.-Indian economic ties, 29–30, 33. *See also specific entities*

Maoists, 67, 128–129

maritime security. *See* Indian Ocean sea-lanes; security policy, Indian; security policy, U.S.

Maryland, first Indian-American legislator in, 36

Mauritius, investment treaty, 33

Mayawati, 221–222

media coverage, 1, 49

"medium control," zone of, 69

medium-sized enterprises. *See* small and medium-sized enterprises

Mehta, Sureesh, 160

Mekong-Ganga Corporation Plan, 148

Mellor, John, 28

Memorandums of Understanding: on gas imports, 162; on joint ventures, 56; on technology transfers, 74

merchandise trade. *See* trade

Mexico: East Asia policy, 150; global governance issues, 193–194; public attitudes, 13

Middle East: changes in U.S. outlook, 10–11; global status and bilateral relationships, 178; international energy strategy, 50; Middle East policy, 154–169, 170*n*; new kind of partnership, 211; new security relationship, 83; nuclear cooperation, 109; security policy of India, 68, 70; security policy of U.S., 71–72; South and Central Asia policy, 120. *See also specific entities*

Middle East peace process: Middle East policy, 157; new kind of partnership, 211

MiG-21 aircraft, 74

migration of population. *See* population movements

military equipment supply. *See* defense trade

military forces. *See headings by specific country, e.g.,* Indian military "minimum credible deterrence" benchmark, 93

Ministry of Commerce, 170n

Ministry of External Affairs (MEA): global status and bilateral relationships, 181; nuclear agreement and high-tech trade, 114n; security policy background, 65; security policy outlook, 86

Mischief Reef, East Asia policy, 142

missile defense: global contingencies, 221; global status and bilateral relationships, 178; new security relationship, 75, 81–82; security policy background, 65

missile programs: global status and bilateral relationships, 174; Middle East policy, 156; nuclear cooperation background, 90; space program history, 101–102

Missile Technology Control Regime (MCTR): nuclear agreement and high-tech trade, 91, 96; space program history, 101–102

Mizoram, Southeast Asia policy, 147

Mobile Telephone Networks, 183

Mongolia, regional architecture, 134

monsoons: climate change effects, 198; monitoring of, 103

moon mission, 100, 102. *See also* space cooperation

mountain warfare schools, 77

Mukherjee, Pranab, 146

Multi-Role Combat Aircraft (MRCA), 81

multilateral institutions. *See* global institutions

multilateral treaties. *See* treaties

multipolar world vision: global status and bilateral relationships, 173, 176, 178, 180, 184n; new foreign policy of India, 7–8; new kind of partnership, 212; shifting power patterns, 210. *See also* global power structure

Mumbai: call center outsourcing, 39; global contingencies, 222; Middle East policy, 159; new security

relationship, 83; security policy of India, 67; South and Central Asia policy, 124–125

Musharraf, Pervez, 121, 126, 136n

Muslim populations: global contingencies, 222; global governance issues, 195; Middle East policy, 154–155, 166; South and Central Asia policy, 119–120, 125, 135. *See also* Islamic *headings*

Mutual Assured Destruction, 65

Mutual Legal Assistance Treaty, 84

Myanmar, international energy strategy, 52–54, 56

Nagaland, Southeast Asia policy, 147

Nair, G. Madhavan, 100

Nano car, 25

Narayanan, M. K., 125

narcotics control, Southeast Asia policy, 148, 149

NASSCOM, 36

Nasser, Gamal Abdel, 154

Nath, Kamal, 32

National Action Plan on Climate Change, 198–199

National Aeronautics and Space Administration (NASA), 102–103

National Institutes of Health, 112

National Iranian Gas Export Corporation, 162

National Oceanic and Atmospheric Administration (NOAA), 103

national security policy. *See* security policy, Indian; security policy, U.S.

National Security Strategy, 8–9, 10, 12

nationalists: East Asia policy, 151; nuclear cooperation and, 105; security policy of India, 70

NATO: changes in U.S. outlook, 10; global status and bilateral relationships, 180; new kind of partnership, 211; new security relationship, 76; South and Central Asia policy, 130, 132, 135

natural gas. *See* petroleum and natural gas

naval forces. *See headings by specific*

country, e.g., Indian military

Naxalite disturbances, 67, 82, 128

Nehru, Jawaharlal: global status and bilateral relationships, 172–173; Middle East policy, 154; new foreign policy, 4, 6; new kind of partnership, 212; policy background, 3

"neighbor's neighbor" approach, 119

Nepal: East Asia policy, 142; international energy strategy, 56; new security relationship, 84; regional architecture, 134; security policy of India, 67; South and Central Asia policy, 127, 128–129, 135

New Delhi market bombing, 125

New Exploration Licensing Policy (NELP), 49

"New Framework for the U.S.-Indian Defense Relationship," 75–76

"new Great Game," 133

New Jersey: Indian-American population in, 36; outsourcing legislation, 39

New York Life, 34

New Zealand, East Asia policy, 150

Next Steps in Strategic Partnership (NSSP): new security relationship, 80; nuclear agreement and high-tech trade, 94–95; space program and, 102

Nigeria, international energy strategy, 52, 54, 57

Nike-Apache rocket launches, 101

"no surprises" rule, 215

Non-Aligned Movement (NAM): global governance issues, 189; global status and bilateral relationships, 180; Middle East policy, 154; new foreign policy of India, 7; new kind of partnership, 211–212

Non-Proliferation Treaty (NPT): background, 89; East Asia policy, 138; future of nonproliferation, 104–109, 111; high-tech trade and, 91–99, 113–114*n*; Middle East policy, 164–165; U.S. and Indian expectations, 113

nonaligned countries: global governance issues, 186; Middle East policy, 166; new kind of partnership, 211–212; policy background, 3. *See also* Non-Aligned Movement (NAM); *specific entities*

nongovernment science cooperation: climate change issues, 202–203; overview, 90, 111–113. *See also* research and development

nonproliferation. *See* nuclear cooperation

North Korea: new kind of partnership, 211; nuclear cooperation and, 98, 104–105, 107, 108; policy background, 1

Northeast Asia, regional architecture, 149. *See also specific entities*

nuclear cooperation: background, 2, 89–90, 113; changes in U.S. outlook, 9; East Asia policy, 141–143; expectations for future trade, 109–111, 113; future shape of, 104–109; global contingencies, 221, 224; global governance issues, 187, 189, 204–205; global status and bilateral relationships, 175–176, 180; high-tech trade and, 91–99, 113–114*n*; Middle East policy, 164–165; new foreign policy of India, 5; new kind of partnership, 208, 214–215, 218–219; new security relationship, 85; public attitudes, 15; South and Central Asia policy, 127; U.S. and Indian expectations for trade, 109–111, 113

nuclear establishment, cooperation agreement and, 98

nuclear fuel banks, 108

nuclear fuel reprocessing: Middle East policy, 164; U.S. and Indian expectations for trade, 110–111

Nuclear Non-Proliferation Act, 91

nuclear power: global status and bilateral relationships, 175–176; growth of, 96–97; Middle East policy, 164–165, 168; "proliferation-proof" fuel production, 108; Tarapur plant, 80, 89; U.S. and Indian expectations

nuclear power *(continued)*
for trade, 110–111. *See also* nuclear cooperation
Nuclear Suppliers' Group (NSG): East Asia policy, 141; global status and bilateral relationships, 175–176; high-tech trade and nuclear agreement, 91–92, 94, 96–97, 99, 113–114*n*; nuclear cooperation future, 106, 108, 111
nuclear tests, Indian: East Asia policy, 137, 145; high-tech trade and nuclear agreement, 91–93, 96–99, 114*n*; new foreign policy of India, 4–5; new kind of partnership, 208; new security relationship, 75, 80; nuclear cooperation background, 89–90; nuclear cooperation future, 107, 109; space program history, 102
nuclear weapons: changes in U.S. outlook, 11; drivers of policy, 16; East Asia policy, 138; global contingencies, 222; global status and bilateral relationships, 177; Middle East policy, 155, 161, 164, 169; new foreign policy, 6; new security relationship, 81–82, 88*n*; policy background, 1; policy outlook, 16; public attitudes, 12–13; security policy background, 65; security policy of India, 67–70; security policy of U.S., 72; South and Central Asia policy, 119–120, 122, 126. *See also* nuclear cooperation; weapons of mass destruction (WMD)
"nuclear weapons states," as defined by NPT, 91–92, 96, 107, 113

Obama administration: changes in U.S. outlook, 11, 12; climate change issues, 201, 204, 219; East Asia policy, 150; global contingencies, 221; global governance, 195; Middle East policy, 162, 169; new kind of partnership, 216; nuclear cooperation, 106–107, 109, 111,
204–205; policy background, 2; public attitudes, 12; security policy of U.S., 71
ocean exploration, space program history, 100
OECD. *See* Organization for Economic Cooperation and Development
offshore outsourcing. *See* outsourcing
Oil and National Gas Corporation (ONGC): energy policy and Indian economy, 48; international energy strategy, 53–57; Middle East policy, 158, 162, 166–167; South and Central Asia policy, 132
oil-for-food program, 56, 166
oil trade: energy policy and Indian economy, 46–50; energy policy background, 45; global status and bilateral relationships, 174, 176, 181–183; import sources, 51*f*; international energy forums, 59–60; international energy strategy, 50–57; major suppliers, 51*f*; Middle East policy, 155, 158–167; new foreign policy of India, 5; security policy of India, 70; South and Central Asia policy, 132. *See also* energy *headings;* petroleum and natural gas
Olympic Torch protests, 141
Oman: international energy strategy, 54; Middle East policy, 158
Oman Oil Company, 158
"one-stop shopping" for investors, 22
123 agreement, 97
ONGC Videsh Ltd. (OVL), 53–54, 132, 174
Operation Enduring Freedom, 78. *See also* Afghanistan conflict
Organization for Economic Cooperation and Development (OECD): energy relations, 59; global governance issues, 193–194, 196; new kind of partnership, 214
Organization of the Islamic Conference (OIC), 157
Organization of the Petroleum Exporting Countries (OPEC), 59

"outreach countries," 195. *See also specific entities*
outsourcing: Indian-Americans and IT connection, 37–39, 43*n*; new economy of India, 23; public attitudes, 14
overseas investment. *See* investment

Pachauri, R. K., 202
Pakistan: Bangladesh liberation war, 29, 68, 120; changes in U.S. outlook, 8; democratic link and, 15; drivers of policy, 16; East Asia policy, 140, 142; global contingencies, 220, 222; global governance issues, 188–191; global status and bilateral relationships, 173, 176–177; international energy strategy, 51–53, 56; Middle East policy, 154, 157, 160–165, 167, 169; new foreign policy of India, 4–5, 6; new kind of partnership, 213, 215–216, 218; new security relationship, 73–75, 78, 80, 82–84; nuclear cooperation and, 90, 92–94, 104–105, 108–109; policy background, 3; policy outlook, 16; public attitudes, 15; regional architecture, 134; security policy of India, 66–68, 70; security policy of U.S., 71; security policy outlook, 85; shifting power patterns, 211; South and Central Asia policy, 118–136, 136*n*; Southeast Asia policy, 147
Pakistani army, 222
Pakistani military, 126
Palestine: changes in U.S. outlook, 11; Middle East policy, 155, 157, 168
parliament, Indian. *See* Indian parliament
patents, 30. *See also* intellectual property issues
"peace dividend," 8
peacekeeping forces: East Asia policy, 149; global governance issues, 189–191; security policy of India, 67–68; security policy of U.S., 73; South and Central Asia policy, 128.

See also military *headings*
pearls, market for, 29
Pentagon, transformation of, 75
Persian Gulf region: global contingencies, 223; Middle East policy, 155, 158–161, 168–169; new kind of partnership, 215–216; remittances from, 159–161; security policy of India, 70; security policy of U.S., 71–72. *See also* Middle East; *specific entities*
Petro Canada, 56
petroleum and natural gas: climate change issues, 199; energy policy and Indian economy, 46, 48, 49; global status and bilateral relationships, 174–176, 183; international energy strategy, 50–56; Middle East policy, 154, 158, 162–163, 168; South and Central Asia policy, 132–133; Southeast Asia policy, 148; strategic petroleum reserves, 60–61; U.S.-Indian economic ties, 33. *See also* oil trade
Petropars, 162
Phalcon radar system, 156
pharmaceutical industry: global status and bilateral relationships, 181, 182; U.S.-Indian economic ties, 29, 30, 34, 39–40
Philippines: East Asia policy, 138; new kind of partnership, 211
phone services. *See* telecommunications sector
pipelines: global status and bilateral relationships, 175; international energy strategy, 52–54, 56–57; Middle East policy, 154, 162–163; South and Central Asia policy, 132; U.S.-India energy relations, 57. *See also* oil trade
piracy: East Asia policy, 149; new security relationship, 78; security policy of India, 68; security policy of U.S., 72; security policy outlook, 85
Planning Commission: energy policy and Indian economy, 47; energy

Planning Commission *(continued)*
policy background, 44–45; global
governance issues, 204; U.S.-India
energy relations, 58
Polar Satellite Launch Vehicle (PSLV),
100
political action committees (PACs), 36
political campaigns, U.S., 36, 38
political issues: climate change, 199–
200; East Asia policy, 140–141,
144–145; energy policy and Indian
economy, 47–50; energy policy
background, 45; global contingencies, 220–223, 225; global governance and, 187, 191, 194; global
status and bilateral relationships,
175, 178–182; Indian-Americans
and IT connection, 38–39; international energy strategy, 53, 56;
Middle East policy, 159, 161, 163–
166; new economy of India, 25–26;
new foreign policy of India, 5; new
kind of partnership, 213, 215–219;
new security relationship, 81,
83–85; nuclear cooperation, 98,
105, 107, 113; policy background,
2; security policy of India, 68–70;
shifting power patterns, 210; South
and Central Asia policy, 128, 130,
132; Southeast Asia policy, 147;
U.S.-India energy relations, 57–59;
U.S.-Indian economic ties, 32–33.
*See also specific entities and policy
areas*
political parties: climate change issues, 202–203; global contingencies, 220; new economy of India,
26; new kind of partnership, 218;
policy background, 2; public attitudes and, 12, 13, 15; South and
Central Asia policy, 126, 129. *See
also specific entities*
poor. *See* poverty and poor
population growth, new economy of
India, 21, 25
population movements: climate
change effects, 198; new foreign
policy of India, 6; new kind of

partnership, 214; security policy of
India, 67–68; shifting power patterns, 209. *See also* diaspora, Indian
"positive control," zone of, 69
poverty and poor: energy policy
and Indian economy, 46; global
governance issues, 199, 203; new
economy of India, 20, 26; policy
background, 1
Pradesh, Uttar, 26
preemption doctrine, changes in U.S.
outlook, 9–10
private-sector–public sector focus,
U.S.-Indian economic ties, 34–35
privatization: energy policy and Indian economy, 48–49; new economy
of India, 22–23. *See also specific
sectors*
process and licensing requirements.
See licensing and process requirements
procurement. *See* defense trade
productivity growth, new economy of
India, 21, 25. *See also* GDP, Indian
Proliferation Security Initiative (PSI),
9, 105, 108
protectionism, economic outlook, 40
public opinion, Indian: climate change
issues, 202; Middle East policy,
166; policy background, 14–15
public opinion, U.S.: climate change issues, 202–203; policy background,
12–14
Puri, Hardeep, 181
Putin, Vladimir, 173

Qatar: international energy strategy,
50, 52–53; Middle East policy, 160

radar technology: Middle East policy,
156; new security relationship, 77,
80–81; space cooperation, 102
radical Islam. *See* Islamic extremism
Raha, Subir, 55
rail transport sector, 23. *See also* transportation sector
Reagan administration, 74
recession, outlook, 40

refineries: energy policy and Indian economy, 48–49; international energy strategy, 50–51, 54–55; Middle East policy, 158, 162. *See also* oil trade

"reform by stealth," 22

refugee flows: new kind of partnership, 214; security policy of India, 67–68. *See also* population movements

regional cooperation issues: global contingencies, 223–225; international energy forums, 59–61; new kind of partnership, 208, 213, 215–217; policy background, 2–3; security policy of India, 69; U.S.-Indian economic ties, 32. *See also specific policy areas, regions, and entities*

regional institutions: East Asia policy, 139, 148–150; global governance issues, 205; South and Central Asia policy, 134. *See also specific entities*

Reliance Industries Ltd.: energy policy and Indian economy, 48–49; international energy strategy, 54–55; Middle East policy, 158, 162, 167; new economy of India, 23

Republic Day celebrations, 160, 164, 181

Republicans, public attitudes, 13

research and development: Middle East policy, 156–157; new economy of India, 25; new kind of partnership, 213–214; new security relationship, 76, 79–82; nongovernment science cooperation, 111–113; nuclear cooperation future, 111; U.S.-India energy relations, 58; U.S.-Indian economic ties, 28, 30, 39–40. *See also* intellectual property issues; *specific sectors*

Resolution 1540 (U.N.), 92, 114n

retail sector, U.S.-Indian economic ties, 34–35

"revisionist state," India as, 209

rice: exports, 26; production and climate change, 198

Rice, Condoleezza, 222

roads. *See* infrastructure development; transportation sector

rocket launches. *See* space cooperation

Rodman, Peter, 166

Rosneft, 55

Royal/Dutch Shell, 57

rupee-ruble debt, 175

rural areas: energy policy and Indian economy, 46; new economy of India, 25–26; public attitudes, 14. *See also* agricultural sector; *specific locations*

Russia: changes in U.S. outlook, 9, 10; global contingencies, 222–223; global governance issues, 190–191, 194; global status and bilateral relationships, 172–178, 184n; Goldman-Sachs study, 181; international energy forums, 59; international energy strategy, 50, 54, 55; Middle East policy, 156, 165; new foreign policy of India, 4; new security relationship, 79; nuclear agreement and, 99; as nuclear weapons state, 113; public attitudes, 14; regional architecture, 134; security policy of India, 70; South and Central Asia policy, 119, 131–134; space program and, 100–103; U.S. and Indian expectations for trade, 110

Sakhalin fields, 54, 55, 174

Salyut 7 space station, 101

sanctions, U.S.: new foreign policy of India, 4; new kind of partnership, 213; new security relationship, 75, 82; nuclear agreement and high-tech trade, 93, 95, 98; South and Central Asia policy, 125; space cooperation and, 103; U.S.-Indian economic ties, 30

Sarabhai, Vikram, 99

Saran, Shyam, 200

Satellite Instructional Television Experiment (SITE), 101

satellites: Middle East policy, 154,

satellites *(continued)*
157; space program current state,
102–103; space program history,
99–102
Saudi Arabia: international energy
strategy, 50; Middle East policy,
160–161, 165
savings, new economy of India, 22
scientific research. *See* research and
development; *specific sectors*
Sea Tigers, 67
"second India," new economy of India,
26
Secretary-General of the Commonwealth, 190
security policy, Indian: background,
65–66; climate change issues, 198;
drivers of policy, 16; East Asia
policy, 142–143, 145–146, 149,
151; economic transformation and,
18–19; energy policy background,
44–45; global contingencies, 220,
222–223; global status and bilateral
relationships, 178–180, 182; India
strategic goals, 66–71, 86*n*, 87*n*;
international energy strategy, 50;
Middle East policy, 155–161, 164–
165, 167–169; new foreign policy,
1, 3–5, 7; new kind of partnership,
213, 214, 216; new security relationship, 73–84, 88*n*; outlook, 16,
84–86; shifting power patterns,
210–211; South and Central Asia
policy, 128, 130–132; U.S. strategic
goals, 71–73, 87*n*. *See also* foreign
policy; Indian military; *specific
aspects*
security policy, U.S.: changes in U.S.
outlook, 8–12; East Asia policy,
144, 146, 150; global contingencies, 220, 222–224; Middle East
policy, 166–169; new kind of
partnership, 211, 214, 216; new
security relationship, 73–84, 88*n*;
public attitudes, 12–14; shifting
power patterns, 208–211; South
and Central Asia policy, 122, 132;
Southeast Asia policy, 148. *See also*

foreign policy; U.S. military; *specific aspects*
September 11 attacks: changes in U.S.
outlook, 8–11; Middle East policy,
156; new security relationship, 75,
82, 84; South and Central Asia
policy, 120–122, 125, 127, 129
services sector: Indian-Americans and
IT connection, 38; new economy
of India, 21, 23, 25; structure of
Indian economy, 21*f*; U.S.-Indian
economic ties, 33, 39. *See also*
information technology industry;
specific aspects
Shanghai Cooperation Organization
(SCO), 131, 134
"ship to mouth policy," 28
shipping security. *See* Indian Ocean
sea-lanes; security policy, Indian;
security policy, U.S.
Shwe field, 54
Sibal, Kapil, 200
Siberia, international energy strategy,
55
Sikh separatists, 82–83, 125
Sikkim border trade point, 140
Simons, Paul, 45
Singapore: new economy of India, 25;
security policy of U.S., 72; Southeast Asia policy, 147, 151
Singh, Jaswant: East Asia policy, 137;
new security relationship, 75;
nuclear cooperation, 93, 107; security policy background, 65
Singh, Manmohan: climate change
issues, 200; East Asia policy, 138,
145, 146, 149; economic perfor-
mance, 18; global governance
issues, 186, 196; global status and
bilateral relationships, 175; Middle
East policy, 164; new economy of
India, 19–20; new foreign policy of
India, 4; nuclear cooperation, 95;
policy background, 2
Sinopec, 56
Sittwe port, 147
skills development, new economy of
India, 25. *See also* education

small and medium-sized enterprises: Middle East policy, 159; new economy of India, 22

"soft control," zone of, 69

"soft power," shifting power patterns, 210

Solarz, Stephen, 36

South Africa: global governance issues, 194; global status and bilateral relationships, 172, 180–184; public attitudes, 13

South Asia: changes in U.S. outlook, 11; drivers of policy, 16; East Asia policy, 141, 145; global status and bilateral relationships, 178–180; Middle East policy, 168; new foreign policy of India, 5–6; new kind of partnership, 215, 218; policy outlook, 16; regional architecture, 134, 148–149; security policy of India, 66, 69–70; South and Central Asia policy, 118–119, 127–129, 134–136, 136*n*; U.S.-Indian economic ties, 36. *See also specific entities*

South Asian Association for Regional Cooperation (SAARC), 134, 200

South China Sea, East Asia policy, 142

South Korea: energy relations, 60; global governance issues, 193; new economy of India, 25; public attitudes, 13, 14

South Pars field, 55, 162

Southeast Asia: changes in U.S. outlook, 11; East Asia policy, 137–139, 146–149, 151; international energy forums, 59–60; international energy strategy, 50; new foreign policy of India, 5; regional architecture, 148–150. *See also specific entities*

sovereignty concept: East Asia policy, 144; global governance issues, 187; global status and bilateral relationships, 176; new kind of partnership, 212

Soviet Union: changes in U.S. outlook, 8, 10; democratic link and, 15; global governance issues, 186,

194; global status and bilateral relationships, 173–175, 177–178; international energy strategy, 54; new kind of partnership, 212; new security relationship, 73–74, 79; nuclear cooperation and, 107; policy background, 3, 4; South and Central Asia policy, 118, 120–121, 130, 131; space program and, 102

space cooperation: background, 90, 94; current state, 102–104; expectations for future trade, 109–111, 113; global status and bilateral relationships, 175; history, 99–102; Middle East policy, 157; U.S. and Indian expectations, 109, 111, 113

Spain, new kind of partnership, 211

Special Economic Zones, 24–25, 147

special envoys, South and Central Asia policy, 124. *See also diplomacy headings*

Spratly Islands, East Asia policy, 142

Sri Lanka: East Asia policy, 142; new security relationship, 82, 84; regional architecture, 134; security policy of India, 67–68; security policy of U.S., 72; South and Central Asia policy, 127, 128–129, 135

standard of living, Indian, 20

State Electricity Boards (SEBs), 47

state sponsors of terrorism list, 82, 125

states, Indian: energy policy and economy, 47–49; growth rates of, 26, 27*f*; international energy strategy, 57; land transactions and, 24–25. *See also specific entities*

states, U.S.: emissions standards, 201; Indian-American community statistics, 36; outsourcing legislation, 39; Yudh Abhyas exercise, 77

"status quo power," 187

steel industry, 23

stock markets. *See* financial markets

Strait of Hormuz: international energy strategy, 50; Middle East policy, 159

Strait of Malacca: East Asia policy, 146; new security relationship, 77;

Strait of Malacca *(continued)*
  security policy of India, 68
strategic autonomy goal: drivers of
  policy, 16; East Asia policy, 146;
  global contingencies, 221, 224;
  global status and bilateral relationships, 177–178; Middle East
  policy, 154, 163–165, 169; new
  foreign policy of India, 7; new kind
  of partnership, 212, 219; nuclear
  cooperation and, 98, 109, 113;
  policy outlook, 16; public attitudes
  and, 15; shifting power patterns,
  210–211; U.S.-Indian economic
  ties, 32
"strategic dialogue" with Iran, 164
strategic petroleum reserves, 60–61
"strategic restraint" benchmark, 93
students from India: global status and
  bilateral relationships, 179; new
  foreign policy of India, 4; nongovernment science cooperation, 112.
  See also education
submarines, 69, 76
Sudan: global governance issues, 189;
  international energy strategy, 50,
  52, 54, 56, 57
Sukhoi Su-30 aircraft, 174
Summit on Financial Markets and the
  World Economy, 186
Sunni population, 165
Swaminathan, M. S., 28
Syria: international energy strategy,
  54, 56; Middle East policy, 157

T-90 tanks, 174
Taiwan: East Asia policy, 138, 143;
  global contingencies, 223
Tajikistan: international energy strategy, 56; regional architecture, 134;
  South and Central Asia policy,
  131–133
Talbott, Strobe: new security relationship, 75; nuclear cooperation,
  93–94, 107
Taliban government: new security
  relationship, 75; South and Central
  Asia policy, 119, 129–131

Tamil Eelam: security policy of India,
  67, 82; South and Central Asia
  policy, 128
Tarapur power plant, 80, 89
Tariff Trade Restrictiveness Index, 23
tariffs: new economy of India, 23; U.S.-
  Indian economic ties, 31
Tata: global status and bilateral relationships, 178; new economy
  of India, 23, 25; U.S.-Indian economic ties, 33
Tata Consultancy Services, 23
Tata Motors, 33
tax code, U.S., 39
taxi and bus fleets, compressed natural
  gas use, 46, 199
technical assistance: Southeast Asia
  policy, 147; U.S.-Indian economic
  ties, 29. *See also* economic aid
technical research. *See* research and
  development
Technology Safeguards Agreement,
  103
technology transfers, 74. *See also* defense trade; high-tech trade
telecommunications sector: energy
  policy and Indian economy, 48;
  global status and bilateral relationships, 182–183; new economy of
  India, 22, 23, 25; space program
  history, 100; U.S.-Indian economic
  ties, 33, 35
telemedicine, space program and, 100,
  102
television, space program and, 102
terrorism: changes in U.S. outlook,
  8–10, 11; East Asia policy, 149;
  Middle East policy, 156, 161–162;
  new foreign policy of India, 6; new
  security relationship, 75, 82–84;
  public attitudes, 12–13; regional
  architecture, 134; security policy
  of India, 67, 68; security policy of
  U.S., 72; South and Central Asia
  policy, 121, 124–126. *See also*
  insurgents; *specific groups and
  locations*
textiles, U.S.-Indian economic ties, 31.

See also garment industry
Thailand, new security relationship, 78
thermonuclear weapons. *See* nuclear
   weapons
"thousand-ship navy," 72
Tibet: East Asia policy, 140; new security relationship, 88*n*
Tibet Autonomous Region, 140
Tiruvananthapuram launch site, 101
TOW anti-tank missiles, 74
trade: drivers of policy, 16; East Asia
   policy, 137–138, 140–146, 149–
   151; "export pessimism," 33; global
   contingencies, 220, 223–224;
   global governance issues, 187, 188,
   191–192; global status and bilateral relationships, 173, 175–176,
   178–183; Indian-Americans and
   IT connection, 36–40; Middle East
   policy, 157–164, 166, 170*n*; new
   economy of India, 19, 22–24, 26,
   27; new foreign policy of India,
   4–5; new kind of partnership,
   213–215, 217, 219; outlook, 40;
   as percentage of GDP, 24*f*; policy
   outlook, 16; public attitudes, 14;
   security policy of India, 68; South
   and Central Asia policy, 131–135;
   Southeast Asia policy, 147–148;
   space program and, 101–104;
   U.S.-Indian economic ties, 29–33,
   35, 39–40. *See also* defense trade;
   high-tech trade; oil trade
Trade Adjustment Assistance (TAA),
   39
Trade Restricting Intellectual Property
   (TRIPS) agreement, 30
transportation sector: energy policy
   and Indian economy, 46, 48; energy relations, 60; global status and
   bilateral relationships, 174, 181;
   metro system funding, 145; new
   economy of India, 22, 23, 25–26;
   South and Central Asia policy, 133;
   U.S.-Indian economic ties, 35. *See
   also* infrastructure; pipelines
treaties: changes in U.S. outlook, 9;
   energy relations, 59; investment

treaty, 33; new kind of partnership,
   211; new security relationship, 84;
   South and Central Asia policy, 128,
   131. *See also* defense agreements;
   nuclear cooperation; *specific agreements*
Treaty of Amity and Cooperation in
   Southeast Asia, 150
triangulation: global status and bilateral relationships, 176; Middle East
   policy, 166
Trusted Customer Program, 95
tsunami, Asian: East Asia policy, 146;
   global governance issues, 189; new
   foreign policy of India, 6; new
   security relationship, 77; security
   policy of India, 69, 71
tuberculosis and global governance,
   203
Turkey, South and Central Asia policy,
   131
Turkmenistan: international energy
   strategy, 53, 56; South and Central
   Asia policy, 132

UN Standby Arrangement, 190
unilateral action, U.S.: changes in U.S.
   outlook, 9–11; public attitudes, 12;
   shifting power patterns, 209
unipolar movement: global contingencies, 223; new foreign policy of
   India, 7; shifting power patterns,
   208–211. *See also* balance of power
   issues; global power structure
United Arab Emirates (UAE): Middle
   East policy, 158–161; UAE army,
   161
United Kingdom: East Asia policy,
   150; export license processing,
   95; global governance issues, 190;
   global status and bilateral relationships, 178–180; as nuclear weapons
   state, 113; South and Central Asia
   policy, 129
United Nations: climate change, 197,
   200–201; East Asia policy, 149;
   global governance issues, 186–191,
   194, 196–197, 200–201, 203, 205;

United Nations *(continued)*
global status and bilateral relationships, 176–177; Middle East policy, 157, 167; new foreign policy of India, 6; new kind of partnership, 215; new security relationship, 78; nuclear agreement and high-tech trade, 92, 114*n*; public attitudes, 13; shifting power patterns, 209

United Nations Framework Convention on Climate Change (UNFCCC), 197, 200–201

United Nations General Assembly: global governance issues, 188–191; global status and bilateral relationships, 183; Middle East policy, 155; nuclear agreement and high-tech trade, 93

United Nations Security Council: East Asia policy, 144; global governance issues, 186, 188–191, 205; global status and bilateral relationships, 172, 177, 179–182; Middle East policy, 164, 166; new foreign policy of India, 6; new kind of partnership, 214; nuclear cooperation and, 92, 104, 114*n*; public attitudes, 13; Resolution 1540, 92, 114*n*; South and Central Asia policy, 135

"upstream" investments: energy policy and Indian economy, 49; international energy forums, 60; international energy strategy, 53–55. *See also* oil trade; *specific entities*

urban areas: new economy of India, 25–26; public attitudes, 14. *See also* specific locations

Urdu language, prevalence in Dubai, 160

Uruguay Round, 30

U.S. African Command, 78, 85–86

U.S. Agency for International Development (USAID), 112

U.S. Air Force, 77

U.S. Army, 74

U.S. Census, 36

U.S. Central Command: Middle East policy, 169; new security relationship, 78; security policy outlook, 85–86

U.S. Chief of Naval Operations, 72

U.S. Coast Guard, 72

U.S. Commerce Department, 95

U.S. Congress: climate change issues, 200–202; Indian-American community and, 36, 38; Middle East policy, 158, 162; new kind of partnership, 218; new security relationship, 80; nuclear agreement and high-tech trade, 93, 97, 99; nuclear cooperation background, 89; nuclear cooperation future, 106; South and Central Asia policy, 121, 126

U.S. courts, U.S. and Indian expectations for trade, 110

U.S. Department of Agriculture, 112

U.S. Department of Energy, 58

U.S. Energy Information Agency, 47, 53

U.S. executive branch: new kind of partnership, 218; South and Central Asia policy, 126. *See also specific administrations*

U.S. House of Representatives: Caucus on India and Indian-Americans, 36; outsourcing as issue, 38

U.S.-India Business Council, 36

U.S. Marine Corps, 72

U.S. Maritime Strategy, 72

U.S. military: changes in U.S. outlook, 9–10; East Asia policy, 138; global contingencies, 222–224; Middle East policy, 166–167, 169; nuclear cooperation, 108; policy background, 3; public attitudes, 13; security policy outlook, 85–86; shifting power patterns, 209–210; South and Central Asia policy, 130, 132, 134, 135; strategic goals of U.S., 72–73. *See also* security policy, U.S.; *specific entities*

U.S. National Intelligence Council, global forecast, 209–210

U.S. Navy: new security relationship, 76–79; security policy of U.S.,

72–73; security policy outlook, 85
U.S. Pacific Command (CINCPAC): East Asia policy, 138; Middle East policy, 169; new security relationship, 74, 78; security policy outlook, 85–86
U.S. policy. *See specific policy areas*
U.S. Senate: India Caucus, 36; nuclear agreement and high-tech trade, 93; nuclear cooperation background, 89; nuclear cooperation future, 106; outsourcing as issue, 38
U.S. Special Forces, 74
U.S. State Department, 45
USNS *Mercy,* deployment of, 77
USS *Trenton,* 80
Uzbekistan: regional architecture, 134; South and Central Asia policy, 132

Vajpayee, Atal Behari: Middle East policy, 167; new foreign policy, 4; nuclear agreement and high-tech trade, 93; policy background, 2
"value-added" services, new economy of India, 22
Varanasi bombing, 125
Videsh Ltd. *See* ONGC Videsh Ltd.
Vietnam War, 211
Viking liquid propulsion engine, 101

Wal-Mart, 34–35
war on terror, 8–10, 121. *See also* terrorism
Wassenaar Arrangement, 91
water resources: climate change effects, 198–199; new foreign policy of India, 6; space program history, 100
weapons of mass destruction (WMD): new security relationship, 84; nuclear agreement and high-tech trade, 94, 114*n*; nuclear cooperation future, 108; security policy of U.S., 72; space program history, 102. *See also* nuclear weapons
Weapons of Mass Destruction and their Delivery Systems (Prohibition of Unlawful Activities) Bill,

94, 114*n*
weapons trade. *See* defense trade
West Bengal, new economy of India, 25
wheat production, climate change issues, 198
White House briefing (March 25, 2005), 12
Wipro, 23, 33
Wisconsin, outsourcing, 39
working groups, U.S.-India energy relations, 58
World Bank: development assistance formula, 28; global governance issues, 188, 191–193, 204, 205*n*; Middle East policy, 167; Nepal electricity generation, 56; survey of doing business abroad, 24; Tariff Trade Restrictiveness Index, 23
World Energy Outlook report, 44
World Health Organization, 188
World Intellectual Property Organization, 203
World Meteorological Organization, 203
World Postal Union, 203
World Trade Organization (WTO): climate change issues, 219; global governance issues, 187, 188, 191–192, 196; U.S.-Indian economic ties, 30, 32
World War II: changes in U.S. outlook, 10; new kind of partnership, 211, 215; shifting power patterns, 209

Y2K computer bug, 36
Yemen, international energy strategy, 54, 55
Yudh Abhyas exercise, 77
Yugoslavia, new kind of partnership, 212

Zangger Committee, 91, 114*n*
Zionism, resolution condemning as racism, 155
Zoellick, Robert, 143

ABOUT THE AUTHOR

Teresita C. Schaffer is director of the CSIS South Asia Program. She joined CSIS in 1998 after a 30-year career in the U.S. Foreign Service. She devoted most of her Foreign Service career to international economic issues and to South Asia, on which she was one of the State Department's principal experts. From 1989 to 1992, she served as deputy assistant secretary of state for South Asia, at that time the senior South Asia position in the department; from 1992 to 1995, she was the U.S. ambassador to Sri Lanka; and from 1995 to 1997, she served as director of the Foreign Service Institute. Her earlier posts included Tel Aviv, Islamabad, New Delhi, and Dhaka, as well as a tour as director of the Office of International Trade in the State Department. She spent a year as a consultant on business issues relating to South Asia after retiring from the Foreign Service.

Ambassador Schaffer's publications include *Kashmir:The Economics of Peace Building* (CSIS, 2005); *Engaging India: The U.S. Role in India's Fight against AIDS* (CSIS, 2005); *Pakistan's Future and U.S. Policy Options* (CSIS, 2004); "Kashmir: Fifty Years of Running in Place," in *Grasping the Nettle* (USIP, 2004); *India at the Crossroads: Confronting the HIV/AID Challenge* (CSIS, 2004); *Rising India and U.S. Policy Options in Asia* (CSIS, 2002); and "Sri Lanka: Lessons from the 1995 Negotiations," in *Creating Peace in Sri Lanka* (Brookings, 1998). She has taught at Georgetown University and American University, and she speaks French, Swedish, German, Italian, Hebrew, Hindi, and Urdu, and has studied Bangla and Sinhala.